Originalism in Theology and Law

Originalism in Theology and Law

Comparing Perspectives on the Bible and the Constitution

Edited by Mark J. Boone and Mark D. Eckel

LEXINGTON BOOKS

Lanham • Boulder • New York • London

Published by Lexington Books
An imprint of The Rowman & Littlefield Publishing Group, Inc.
4501 Forbes Boulevard, Suite 200, Lanham, Maryland 20706
www.rowman.com

86-90 Paul Street, London EC2A 4NE

British Library Cataloguing in Publication Information Available

Library of Congress Cataloging-in-Publication Data

Names: Boone, Mark J., editor. | Eckel, Mark, editor.
Title: Originalism in theology and law : comparing perspectives on the Bible and the Constitution / edited by Mark J. Boone and Mark D. Eckel.
Description: Lanham : Lexington Books, 2024. | Includes bibliographical references and index.
Identifiers: LCCN 2023051781 (print) | LCCN 2023051782 (ebook) | ISBN 9781666932126 (cloth) | ISBN 9781666932133 (ebook)
Subjects: LCSH: Religion and law—United States. | Constitutional law—United States—Religious aspects. | Constitutional law—Religious aspects—Christianity. | Originalism (Law)—United States. | Law (Theology)—Biblical teaching. | Christianity and law.
Classification: LCC KF4551 .O75 2024 (print) | LCC KF4551 (ebook) | DDC 220.6—dc23/eng/20231106
LC record available at https://lccn.loc.gov/2023051781
LC ebook record available at https://lccn.loc.gov/2023051782

Contents

Introduction

Two Originalisms

Mark J. Boone

Shortly after Harriet Miers was nominated by George W. Bush to the US Supreme Court, an interesting clue to her legal philosophy was revealed by Marvin Olasky:

> Texas Supreme Court Justice Nathan Hecht says she has a philosophy that grows out of evangelical exegesis and carries over into legal issues: "She's an originalist—that's the way she takes the Bible," and that's her approach to the Constitution as well: "Originalist—it means what it says."[1]

Although the Miers nomination was short-lived, the ideas suggested by Olasky's report are timeless. What a remarkable convergence of topics took place here—the Bible, the law, hermeneutics, authority! We have written this book to explore the interconnections among these topics. Our book's thesis is simple: there *are* connections; originalism as a theory of biblical interpretation has some important links to originalism as a theory of Constitutional interpretation, and these connections are worth exploring.

We are not saying that there are no differences between originalism in theology and originalism in law. Indeed, this volume was not written to tout either version of originalism, nor any particular theory regarding their connections. Although individual essays may tout one view or another, as far as the thesis of this book is concerned, any of the following positions, and more, are possible.

- Originalism in theology and law are both correct and are much the same; believers should approach the Bible, and American government the Constitution, in submission to its authority and seeking to understand its requirements according to the original meaning of the text.

- Perhaps both are correct but significantly different; the legal authority of the Constitution and the authority of the Bible both have some close connection to original meaning, but there are contrasts pertaining to the evidence for or the application of the two originalisms.
- Perhaps originalism in law is correct but not originalism in biblical theology (or vice versa), certain subtle theoretical connections notwithstanding.
- Perhaps originalism in theology and law are largely the same, and in fact both are *in*correct.

Once again, the goal is merely to *explore* the connections between two theories of originalism. More precise claims are the purview of the authors of individual chapters.

But let us first take a closer look at our thesis. Afterwards, we will review the preexisting literature on the subject and preview the rest of this book.

ORIGINALISMS

We say that there are some interesting connections between two theories—originalism in biblical theology and originalism in American law. Let's first clarify what the scope of this book is and just what these originalisms are, and then take a closer look at that thesis and why it matters.

The Scope of This Book

We are talking about originalism in American law and in biblical theology. In other words, we are concerned with the theory of originalism in the interpretation of the Bible and in the interpretation of the American Constitution. These are the primary authoritative texts for major religions and for American law and governance, although a theory of originalism may find an application or extension to other texts. Interpretation of statutory law, laws passed by a legislative body under the Constitution, is also an important matter in American law, and in biblical theology we sometimes have occasion to consider the right way of interpreting a creed, a church council, a great theologian, a rabbinic or patristic tradition, and so on.

Why are we considering these particular originalisms? One reason is because they are important; for example, originalist-leaning hermeneutics motivate rather a lot of Christian theology and, in law and at the time of the writing of this introduction, the US Supreme Court has a strong originalist wing of five originalist Justices (out of a total of nine Justices).[2] But why not consider originalism in interpretation of the Quran or the Hindu Vedas and Upanishads? Why not consider originalism in interpretations of the

Constitutions of Zimbabwe and Pakistan, or the Basic Law of Hong Kong? To be sure, originalisms in other theologies or with respect to other laws are important, and so are their connections to each other and to originalism in biblical theology and American law. However, originalism in these areas seems to capture at least as much attention as in other areas; people are always talking about how to interpret the Bible and the Constitution in academia, in the news, and on the internet. Moreover, originalism in biblical theology and American law are topics that happen to interest me, my coeditor, and the authors, and, of course, one has to start *somewhere*.

Which Originalist Theories Are We Dealing With?

In very broad terms, originalism might be defined as the theory that the meaning of a text is its original meaning. This is just a bit ambiguous: Are we talking about *all* meaning *or* just *some*? We could define originalism a bit more precisely as the theory that the meaning of a text only changes when the words of that text change. In this book we are considering the theory in American law that precisely this is the case with the meaning of the Constitution as well as some traditions in biblical theology that adhere to looser definitions of originalism, some of which come close to this stricter definition.

In American law, originalism is nicely defined in these terms. Originalism means that we can only get a new meaning for the Constitution by amending it through the formal amendment process. We may have questions or disagreements concerning what the original meaning *is*, but, whatever it is, it only *changes* in this way. Our understanding or application of it may change, but *it* does not change. The original meaning, by the way, is, because of that amendment process, not limited to the generation of the American founders; the original meaning of *most* of the Constitution is still tied to that earlier time, but the original meaning of an amendment may date back to that time or to the late 1800s, the early 1900s, the 1970s, and so on.

Originalism in biblical theology is a bit more complicated. In the discussion below I will focus on what I know best, Christian theology. This is also a topic for Jewish theology, however, as some essays in this book demonstrate. In the broadest and simplest terms, we could consider as an originalism the theory that everything meant by the authors of the Bible is a part of its meaning; we could stipulate a name for this view, calling it *weak biblical originalism*. We might add to this the theory that *all* biblical meaning is in the category of that intended by its authors; we could call this view *strong biblical originalism*. Technically, only strong biblical originalism fits the more precise definition of originalism; both strong and weak biblical originalism fit the looser definition.

And this gets to the heart of one of the puzzles involved with considering Christian theology in originalist terms. Orthodox Christianity from the church fathers to the present day has recognized the authority of the Bible and paid close attention to the intention of the biblical authors as a locus of that authoritative meaning. That places Christian theology squarely in the realm of weak biblical originalism. Strong biblical originalism—not so much. It is often thought that the Bible means more than was or even could have been intended by its human authors. For example, any number of Old Testament prophecies which Christian theologians regularly take as pointing to Jesus the Messiah would not likely have been understood by the same prophets in quite so detailed a manner as these interpretations require. So, on the one hand, orthodox Christian theology is deeply committed to weak biblical originalism; but, on the other hand, it leans away from strong biblical originalism. But (and back to the first hand) evangelical inerrancy tends to resist allegory, focusing on original meaning. And (to return yet again to the other hand) even this strain of Christianity recognizes the importance of those prophecies.

So how we categorize biblical theology with respect to originalism depends on how we define the categories. Using our terms, Christian theology is committed to weak but not strong biblical originalism and can only loosely be said to be an originalism proper.

Another complication arises when we consider the doctrine of the inspiration of scripture, according to which the Bible is written not by human beings alone but is the Word of God. So we might stipulate some new terms. We could define *human originalism* as originalism with respect to human authors and *divine originalism* as originalism with respect to God. Thus Christian theology, precisely when it tends to resist strong *human* originalism, tends to adhere to strong *divine* originalism: if some things the Bible means were not intended by its human authors, it remains the case that *all* things the Bible means were intended by *God.*

This leads to another question. Strong divine originalism is originalism according to our more strict definition. It treats the meaning of the text as not changing when the words of the text do not change, since any meanings understood much later by us were *always* intended by *God.* Yet we might wonder what is the point of calling it an "originalism" when a good bit of the meaning of a text can only be understood long after the writing. Originalism references originality in time, and strong divine originalism is not an exception inasmuch as God intended that meaning from the beginning. But shouldn't originalism pertain to some textual meaning that is accessible *to the original readers*? If we were to stipulate that this is a requirement for originalism strictly defined, then it would seem that Christian theology does not count as an originalism, although some strains come close.

I will consider these matters again in chapter 7. There are subtleties and tensions and questions, but at the least we can say that Christian theology has a close relationship to originalism and incorporates its central claim that textual meaning, in the case of the Bible, includes its original meaning; moreover, at least one tradition in Christian theology leans heavily toward the additional claim that the meaning of the Bible should be sought in its original meaning and not in ideas learned later.

With this background firmly in place, it would be well to distinguish the originalisms in question from some related views with which they may be confused.

Originalism in *biblical theology* is not the same thing as *biblical literalism*. Originalism is the view that the Bible's meaning is its original meaning, and literalism is the view that its meaning is literal. Perhaps nearly all biblical literalists are originalists, but not vice versa. Originalism itself requires that we interpret the original meaning of a text according to the literary conventions of the time of its writing. This, of course, calls for a literal, or at least a historical, reading of various biblical passages, but it leads away from a literal reading of the Bible when the original meaning appears to be imprecise, metaphorical, analogical, or otherwise non-literal.

Originalism in biblical theology is not the same thing as *biblical inerrancy*. The former is the theory that the Bible's meaning is its original meaning, and the latter is the theory that the Bible's meaning is never wrong. An originalist might reject inerrancy, and many do. Indeed, one common form of objection to the Bible is this: *The Bible's original meaning is such-and-such, which we now know to be an error, and therefore the Bible is wrong*. This kind of argument intentionally relies on an originalist hermeneutic in order to *reject* the Bible's accuracy. One could possibly also be an inerrantist who rejects originalism, as is the case with those who take the Bible to be the inerrant Word of God but consider its meaning not to be identical to its original meaning. (However, to my knowledge more or less all inerrantists are at least weak originalists, thinking the meaning of the Bible *includes* its original meaning.)

Originalism in biblical theology is not the same thing as *sola scriptura*, although this doctrine is more closely related than others (and is rightly associated, if incorrectly identified, with originalism by, for example, Jeroslav Pelikan[3]). The Reformation doctrine of *sola scriptura* is the doctrine that the Bible and only the Bible has infallible authority—authority such that all of its claims are true. No doubt many originalists are *sola scriptura* Christians, and vice versa. However, a person could believe that only the Bible is an infallible authority and still suppose that the meaning of some part of it was unknown to its author—perhaps an Old Testament prophecy about Jesus or about the Second Coming, for example, was given by God to the prophet, who had no idea what it meant. And it is possible to be an originalist who accepts some other authority as infallible; one could believe that the Bible's meaning is its original meaning and still recognize Creeds, Councils, bishops, Popes, or a Magisterium as infallible interpreters of it. (It seems to me that this is, or is at least rather similar to, the thinking of Catholic theologian John Henry Newman; the Roman Catholic Magisterium can give no new information; it can only infallibly interpret, clarify, and elaborate on the original meaning of the Bible.[4]) Moreover, it is possible to be an originalist who accepts *no* authority as infallible for, as noted, someone who does *not* accept the Bible's authority might be an originalist.

Originalism in *law* is not the same thing as *the theory that the meaning of the Constitution is that intended by its founders.* Although some originalists are intentionalists, originalism in law has recently developed (with, in fact, some influence from at least one founder, James Madison) in the direction of textualism rather than intentionalism; in other words, the meaning of the text is not thought to be determined by its authors, but by what a well-informed and rational reader would have read at the time of the adoption of the text.[5] (On this difference from originalism in theology, see my chapter 7 below.)

Moreover, originalism in law is not the same thing as *the theory that the meaning of the Constitution is the meaning it had at the time of the founding.* Originalism stipulates that a text's meaning is its original meaning—the meaning it had at the time of its writing (or, in the case of the Constitution, its being adopted as law[6]). This principle applies to *portions* of a text; so the meaning of a later amendment to the Constitution is, according to originalism, that which it meant when it was adopted. For the meaning of most of the Constitution, an originalist indeed looks to the time of the founding. For the meaning of the fourteenth amendment, an originalist looks to the Reconstruction era; for later amendments, she looks later.

In other words, originalism teaches that the meaning of any part of the Constitution is the meaning that part has at the time of its becoming law; originality in time refers to different times stretching from the 1780s to the 1990s and, probably, well into the future. This is not, by the way, a difference between originalism in theology and law, since the Bible was also written over a very long period of time—much longer, in fact! On this point, the two originalisms, as far as I can see, are the same; the difference is only where *we* stand in relation to the texts; for us, the Bible was completed long ago, but the Constitution as it now stands was completed in living memory, and probably has not yet reached its final form.

Originalism in law is not the same thing as *the theory that the meaning of the Constitution does not change,* nor is it the same as *the theory that the meaning of the Constitution* should *not change.* An originalist thinks the meaning of the Constitution is what it means *at the time it is written.* But the writing of the Constitution can be changed, and so can the meaning, and no doubt one can make a reasonable case that it *should* change in one way or another.

The Thesis of This Book and Why It Matters

Our thesis is that these originalisms have something to do with each other. Originalism in theology and in law are connected both theoretically, inasmuch as both look to the origin of a text for access to its meaning, and practically, for they entail similar hermeneutics focused on historical factors such as grammar and historical context. Moreover, these connections are worthy of careful study.

Both originalisms state that the meaning of an authoritative text is to be sought in its original meaning—that, as far as interpreting the meaning of the text goes, we are under certain restrictions. This is not, of course, an absolute denial of the possibility of the meaning in the text changing in some sense or by some means. Even Christian theology tends to recognize that there is some biblical meaning which was not available to the original writers and readers. The Constitution can be changed by an amendment. (As noted, this is not an exception to originalism; the meaning of the amendment would be *its* original meaning; originalists understand that the Constitution can change.) Still, there are significant restrictions on finding new meaning in the text. We do not get to make up new meanings as we go, and the meaning does not change just because the meaning of a word changes in the surrounding culture. We are bound to seek textual meaning only within certain parameters. The Constitution is a "living document" only in the sense that we can replace, cut, or add to the words of the text; the meaning of each clause is the same now as it was when it became law.

For a text bearing authority, this idea matters a great deal. Biblical theology and biblical religious practice are under the authority of the Bible. American law and government are under the authority of the Constitution. Our take on originalism is our take on the meaning of the texts that shape our lives. Religion, law, culture, nations, and the future course of civilization are determined in large part by what we make of originalism.

WHY THIS BOOK?

If this is so important, why hasn't it already been studied? In fact, it has, or very nearly so. Of course, a topic which has been studied can be studied some more. New books about the Bible and the Constitution are being written all the time. Why not more books about prominent ways of interpreting both of them?

In fact, much has been written in that very field. However, it seems that something is still lacking.

For example, Cass Sunstein has called originalism the "fundamentalist" position in law, and has compared it to "religious fundamentalism" on the grounds that the latter "usually represents an effort to restore the original meaning of a sacred text."[7] However, he characterizes fundamentalism as the view that "it is illegitimate to understand the words of those texts in a way that departs from the original meaning or that allows changes over time," further connects fundamentalism with "literal interpretation," and plainly is thinking of those who venerate "the Koran or the Bible" as holy.[8] This is a bit off the mark, inasmuch as these ideas may be separated: an atheist critic may object to the Bible on the grounds of what he takes to be its original meaning, one who recognizes the Bible as the Word of God may for that very reason depart from its original meaning, and allegorical interpretation has a long tradition even among conservative believers. In any case, Sunstein does not wish "to say anything about religious fundamentalism,"[9] so the comparison is left undeveloped.

Similarly, Peter Smith and Robert Tuttle's "Biblical Literalism and Constitutional Originalism" compares legal originalism and biblical *literalism*—not quite the same thing as biblical originalism.[10] This article is a helpful introduction to the literature in the area, and it correctly points out that originalism in law is not itself committed to the notion that the Constitution contains correct moral teachings, unlike biblical literalism with its commitment to biblical authority and the truthfulness of biblical teachings. However, the article does not compare two originalist theories; the biblical literalism in question is characterized in the first sentence: "Many conservative Protestants contend that every word of the Bible must be taken literally."[11] But biblical originalism is the theory that the Bible's meaning is its original meaning—a theory which can be held by anyone. Besides Protestants and Catholics, atheists regularly employ originalism when they *disagree* with the Bible's original meaning. Moreover, even a Protestant who believes the Bible to be the Word of God need not always interpret it literally. (In fact, I've never even met a Protestant who takes *every* word literally. I have *heard* of one who took "a land flowing with milk and honey" to describe the chemical makeup of the rivers in the Holy Land.)

Theologian Jeroslav Pelikan has written the book that perhaps comes closest to ours. His *Interpreting the Bible and the Constitution* considers the similarities of the hermeneutical issues surrounding both documents.[12] This volume is an interesting set of reflections on such ideas as the Constitution as "American Scripture" the Bible and Constitution as "Great Codes" governing their respective communities, the church and America; and their having hierarchies of interpreters. Although not focused directly on originalism in theology and law, there are some interesting objections to originalism in both spheres. One disadvantage of the text is that it does not develop a proper understanding of originalism and, in my view, errs in tying originalism too closely to the Reformation doctrine of *sola scriptura*.

Gregory A. Kalscheur responds to Pelikan in a thoughtful article.[13] Kalscheur builds on Pelikan's account of an analogy between the Bible and the Constitution, drawing from sources such as theologian John Henry Newman and law scholar Michael J. Perry to help us understand how we might apply Pelikan's insight in interpretation. Kalscheur suggests that "Pelikan helps us to see more clearly that the process of interpreting texts which give rise to living communities might best be understood as a sort of developmental originalism that ought to manifest creative fidelity."[14] This *developmental originalism* is key: Kalscheur argues that for the Bible and the Constitution the interpreter must attend to the original meaning but also be "open to allowing the lived experience of the community to shed new light on the text."[15]

Sanford Levinson's *Constitutional Faith*[16] is a reflection on the idea that the American community and its commitment to the Constitution are analogous to religious faith and covenant. Levinson compares the divisions in Abrahamic religion over sources of authority and over authority in interpretation to their analogues in American law.[17] On his analysis originalism and its rejection would fall, respectively, on the "Protestant" and "Catholic" sides of theology and law.[18] (However, he distinguishes between two different ways of making this very distinction.) Levinson endorses Constitutional faith in his last chapter (while recanting it in a later edition's afterword and calling for a new Constitution in a later book[19]). Though not focused on originalism directly—or on theology—Levinson articulates some of the reasons for our own book:

> It should be clear by now that the ability of 'the Constitution' to provide the unity so desperately sought as a preventative against disorder depends on the resolution of the same issues that split Judaism, Christianity, Islam, and, indeed, all other religions that have text as a central part of their structure.[20]

In his article "Comparative Normative Hermeneutics: Scripture, Literature, Constitution,"[21] Ronald R. Garet explains "normative hermeneutics," that "species of moral reflection" in which we seek moral guidance by interpreting a text.[22] Biblical and constitutional interpretation are two examples of normative hermeneutics, along with literature. The interpretation of Scripture and Constitution should avoid the opposite errors of *literalism* and *scientific policymaking*. *Literalism* is simple submission to the interpreted text without reflective application—all explication and no application. *Scientific policymaking* is all application without explication—a mere effort to apply the text without caring to get the interpretation right.[23] In normative hermeneutics both textual interpretation and moral guidance are necessary and inseparable. Although he finds originalism in law incomplete in that it lacks an account of the source of constitutional authority,[24] Garet is constructive, aiming to help theories like originalism by developing the resources needed to complete them.[25] Though I can find no reference to originalism as a theory in theology, there are closely related discussions, for example on *sola scriptura* (a doctrine he apparently disfavors).[26] Garet's article is a careful study of normative hermeneutics in theology and law, but unfortunately for our purposes it doesn't zoom in much on originalism.

In short, although many have noted correspondences between, on the one hand, originalism in law and, on the other hand, originalism in biblical theology or corresponding theories, it seems that there is little direct focus on these two theories.

AND WHAT CAN WE LEARN?

Our book begins with a series of essays exploring the threads tying together biblical and constitutional originalism.

Mark Eckel's contributions to this volume (its first and last chapters) are more like two parts of an extended reflection on how the concepts of biblical theology tend to correlate with originalist perspectives in law. The first part, chapter 1, argues that originalism makes sense based on a Hebraic-Christian worldview. An understanding of origins points to originalism. All reality has for its foundations a personal Creator, whose self-revelation according to his own character and intentions is the paradigm for all discovery. When we learn anything, we can expect it to depend, ultimately, on God, its ultimate origin. When we learn anything from a text, we can likewise expect it to be shaped by the character and intentions of its proximate origin, the author or authors. The biblical worldview, Eckel says, is what makes the most sense of everything, and it also justifies originalism in law.

Jonathan Johnson (chapter 2) makes a general case for originalism from his own expertise in aesthetics, an unusual and interesting connection of different fields of study. He explains that there are rigorous defenses of the importance of the creator's intentions in the visual arts. But the creator's intentions are less likely to matter here than in written texts and, therefore, originalism in such fields as theology and law is on solid ground. Johnson's article is interesting in that it confronts head-on the phenomenon of subjectivity in interpretation, not only arguing that it does not overrule or replace the intent of an author or of an artistic creator, but also arguing that the study of artistic experience can inform the interpretation of legal and religious texts. A word of advice to any reader who may not wish to spend much time in the world of aesthetics and philosophy of art: the main import of Johnson's contribution is the novel argument from aesthetics for the importance of original intent in legal and religious texts. If he succeeds in establishing the argument's premises that originalism in theology and law is on ground at least as solid as artistic intention in artwork, and that the latter *is* on solid ground, then his hermeneutical conclusions should be well worth the effort.

Daniel Weissglass (chapter 3) argues for "a modest originalism" that includes more than just the authorial intent for the meaning of a particular law, but also the intent behind the legal systems designed for the interpretation, modification, and application of the law. Weissglass's explanation of this idea draws from Jewish interpretation of the Torah. He begins with the intriguing Talmudic story of the Oven of Akhnai, in which the voice of God himself is apparently *rejected* as an interpreter of the law on the grounds that the law is not in heaven—it was, as the Torah itself testifies (in Deuteronomy 30), given to the Jews and is now in *their* mouths, in *their* hands, *their* responsibility to interpret. This corresponds to a doctrine called *living* originalism (articulated by Jack Balkin), according to which the Constitution is interpreted not according to its original meaning in all cases, but always according to the original fundamental principles which the Constitution establishes. Weissglass describes the Torah as a constitution for the Jewish people, develops the connection of the Talmud to living originalism, and elaborates on what this would mean for the practice of interpreting the American Constitution, focusing in both cases on the importance of interpretive practices that maintain the integrity of the community.

Nicholas Higgins and Micah Allred (chapter 4) link religious and legal hermeneutics in an analysis arguing that originalist methods of reading sacred religious texts correspond to originalist methods of interpreting the Constitution in the minds of American voters. Those accustomed to reading sacred religious texts in this way tend to read the Constitution the same way, independently of policy preferences. And those who tend *not* to read sacred texts the same way tend also to *not* read the Constitution the same way, independently of policy preferences. It's not just the policy that motivates citizens' views on how to interpret the Constitution; it's the hermeneutics. And voters' legal hermeneutics are influenced by their religious hermeneutics.

John Ehrett (chapter 5) offers some interesting reconsiderations of originalist theory in law—considering natural law principles as a complement to written law, and shifting back towards intentionalism and away from textualism. Drawing on the Lutheran tradition of philosophy of law, Ehrett considers how in both theology and law Lutheran thought has honored the authority of a written text while recognizing the importance of applying its original meaning to new circumstances. This application must be guided by the principle of equity, which applies the principles of natural law to whatever varying circumstances may arise. Ehrett explains how in Lutheran theology the Bible itself has a purpose fixed by its divine author, a purpose that guides the application of the Bible's original meaning. Analogous to this is the application of the Constitution guided by equity in accordance with its authors' intentions to establish equity by rightly arranging the nation's governing institutions.

Our book continues with a series of essays exploring some differences between originalism in theology and in law.

Mark A. Snoeberger (chapter 6) draws from the study of originalism in law to cast some light on a question prominent in some regions of evangelical theology: What is the best way of describing a dispensationalist hermeneutic? Although evangelicals in the dispensationalist tradition have often described their reading of the Bible as a literal one, this is not quite right, and it has not proven easy to find the best description. Snoeberger proposes that the term "originalism" and its key concepts can get the job done, while also clarifying how the same originalist hermeneutical method can look different when applied to different texts. For example, the doctrine of the divine inspiration of the Bible entails that a specifically *biblical* originalism makes sense as an intentionalism, not just as a textualism. With the Constitution, it is possible that authorial error resulted in some difference in meaning between what the authors were thinking and what came to be written in the text; but, according to the doctrine of divine inspiration of scripture, this is just what cannot happen with the Bible.

I (in chapter 7) explore a key difference in biblical and legal originalism. The source of the Constitution's authority is the people of the United States, but the Bible's authority comes from God and is channeled through the prophetic and apostolic sources of its various books. This tells us something about where the meaning of the text is located. The Bible's meaning is closely tied to the intent of its authors, but the meaning of the Constitution must be where the people who are the source of its authority have access to it, rather than in the mind of its authors. Accordingly, biblical originalism is better understood as a form of intentionalism, whereas constitutional originalism is better understood as a form of textualism, and this is just what we find in some major originalist sources in both legal and biblical hermeneutics. (I hasten to add that the reader would do well to consider the arguments in John Ehrett's chapter against a simple textualism for the Constitution. If I am wrong, Ehrett's argument might be one good reason why.)

Menashe C. Roberts (chapter 8) explains an important difference between American legal originalism and an originalism for the Hebrew Torah. The Torah was originally written without vowels, making for significant ambiguities in its meaning. We have to rely on some information not included in the text in order to know what many words in the Torah actually are. Therefore, unlike originalist interpretation of the Constitution, originalist interpretation of the Torah must use a different methodology. Roberts also distinguishes vagueness from ambiguity, discusses cases of vagueness in the Torah, and explains the importance of the Rabbinical tradition which uses diacritical characters to convey the vocalization of the Torah, thereby disambiguating its meaning.

Finally, Eckel's closing chapter (chapter 9) looks toward last things in the sequel to his introductory essay. A thing's beginning, he explains, determines both its ultimate goal and the means by which it gets there. Eckel contrasts two worldviews and their relevance to authority. On a biblical worldview, God is our origin and sets our purpose and the parameters within which we strive toward it. On a biblical worldview, God and His laws are the ultimate source of all authority, and all of us are under that authority. By contrast, on a worldview in which there is no higher authority than humanity, nothing is fixed, and there is neither a standard nor a judge to mediate between competing personal preferences. Both worldviews may share some common goals, such as peace and justice; but their different views of origins result in very different ways of achieving those goals. Overlapping with Eckel's first essay, one of his themes here is that originalism works well with a biblical worldview and its attending natural law perspective. But Eckel is also arguing that originalism doesn't work well otherwise and, moreover, that without that biblical worldview and its attending natural law perspective, little in addition to the rule of the strongest human preference *does* work. Eckel's concluding reflections on the importance of originalism serve to remind us that we are not the final authority. We are responsible, first but not exclusively, to the authority of the author of our world. Thus, he argues, originalism reminds us to be humble.

Our studies of originalism in theology and law reveal the following insights.

First and most importantly, originalism is a theory to be reckoned with in more than one field. No doubt the authors of this book lean more towards originalism than the current academic mainstream, but that is neither here nor there. Originalism, and the ideas that motivate it, are relevant to many fields including (at least) all the ones that closely involve interpretation of texts. Originalism matters to theology and law, and, beyond them, to philosophy, literature, history, political science, and so on.[27] Originalism's detractors are welcome to disagree with the theory, but the point here is only that they would do well not to simply ignore it.

Second, there is the central thesis of this book: that there are significant connections between originalism in theology and originalism in law.

However, third—and a crucial theme in some essays in this book—originalism in biblical theology and originalism in American law must be applied with attention to differences between the texts involved. Differences in the type of text, in the purpose and function of a text, or in the origins or sources of a text's authority may all affect which nuanced version of originalism best fits a particular text, or may affect the best method of applying originalism when interpreting the text.

While we believe we have made a good beginning here of exploring the theoretical and practical connections between originalism in theology and in law, we recognize that it is only a beginning. There is much else to explore in this area, and we hope that other scholars will join in further investigations of this world-shaping topic. In addition to critical responses to our own work, a broader set of perspectives would be useful on this topic. The writers of this book come from several different Jewish and Protestant perspectives. Among other things, we have studied law, theology, philosophy, and political science, but on the whole we have studied more theology and philosophy than law. Future work on this topic would be valuable from additional scholars of law; from scholars representing Catholic perspectives not to mention, casting a wider net, Eastern Orthodox, Mormon, or Islamic scholars; and from additional critics of originalism. Prospects are good for research exploring this area in greater detail. These essays are not the original work on originalism. May they not be the last work on originalism in theology and law.

NOTES

1. Marvin Olasky, "Blessed Are the Meek," *WORLD Magazine* online (October 15, 2005), https://wng.org/articles/blessed-are-the-meek-1617337715.

2. I count Justices Clarence Thomas, Samuel Alito, Neil Gorsuch, Amy Coney Barrett, and Brett Kavanaugh as originalists.

3. Jaroslav Pelikan, *Interpreting the Bible and the Constitution* (New Haven: Yale University Press, 2004), 85–93.

4. I am no Newman scholar; the interested reader may pursue this matter further in Newman's *Essay on the Development of Christian Doctrine*, for an introduction to which see Gerald McDermott, *The Great Theologians: A Brief Guide* (Downers Grove: InterVarsity, 2010), 157–158.

5. I am following a common convention in using the word "textualism" to refer to a theory on the location of the meaning of a text. The word has also been used to refer to a theory for interpreting statutory law, not the Constitution; see John Ehrett's and Mark Snoeberger's contributions to the present volume for this use of the term.

6. In the case of the twenty-seventh amendment to the US Constitution, the writing and the adopting were a long time apart.

7. Cass Sunstein, *Radicals in Robes: Why Extreme Right-–Wing Courts Are Wrong for America* (New York: Basic Books, 2005), xiii.

8. Sunstein, *Radicals in Robes*, xiii–xiv.

9. Sunstein, *Radicals in Robes*, xiv.

10. Peter Smith and Robert Tuttle, "Biblical Literalism and Constitutional Originalism," *Notre Dame Law Review* 86, no. 2 (2011): 693–764.

11. Smith and Tuttle, "Biblical Literalism and Constitutional Originalism," 694.

12. Pelikan, *Interpreting the Bible and the Constitution.*

13. Gregory A. Kalscheur, "Christian Scripture and American Scripture: An Instructive Analogy?" *Journal of Law and Religion* 21, no. 1 (2005/2006): 101–142.

14. Kalscheur, "Christian Scripture and American Scripture," 141.

15. Kalscheur, "Christian Scripture and American Scripture," 141.

16. Sanford Levinson, *Constitutional Faith* (Princeton: Princeton University Press, 1988).

17. Levinson, *Constitutional Faith*, chapter 1.

18. A connection also made in Thomas Grey, "The Constitution as Scripture," *Stanford Law Review* 37, no. 1 (November 1984): 1–25.

19. Sanford Levinson, *Our Undemocratic Constitution* (New York: Oxford University Press, 2008).

20. Levinson, *Our Undemocratic Constitution*, 51.

21. Ronald R. Garet, "Comparative Normative Hermeneutics: Scripture, Literature, Constitution," *Southern California Law Review* 58, no. 35 (1985): 35–134.

22. Garet, "Comparative Normative Hermeneutics," 37–38.

23. Garet, "Comparative Normative Hermeneutics," 42–43.

24. Garet, "Comparative Normative Hermeneutics," 117–119.

25. Garet, "Comparative Normative Hermeneutics," 43–44.

26. Garet, "Comparative Normative Hermeneutics," 70–77.

27. A claim I explore in Mark J. Boone, "Is There Life in This Author? The Living Author and the Business and Importance of the Humanities in South Asia," in *Transcultural Humanities in South Asia: Critical Essays on Literature and Culture*, ed. Waseem Anwar and Nosheen Yousaf: 83–94 (London: Taylor & Francis, 2022).

WORKS CITED

Boone, Mark J. "Is There Life in This Author? The Living Author and the Business and Importance of the Humanities in South Asia." In *Transcultural Humanities in South Asia: Critical Essays on Literature and Culture*, edited by Waseem Anwar and Nosheen Yousaf: 83–94. London: Taylor & Francis, 2022.

Garet, Ronald R. "Comparative Normative Hermeneutics: Scripture, Literature, Constitution." *Southern California Law Review* 35 (1985): 35–34.

Grey, Thomas. "The Constitution as Scripture." *Stanford Law Review* 37, no. 1 (November 1984): 1–25.

Kalscheur, Gregory A. "Christian Scripture and American Scripture: An Instructive Analogy?" *Journal of Law and Religion* 21, no. 1 (2005/2006): 101–142.

Levinson, Sanford. *Constitutional Faith.* Princeton: Princeton University Press, 1988.

———. *Our Undemocratic Constitution.* New York: Oxford University Press, 2008.

McDermott, Gerald. *The Great Theologians: A Brief Guide*. Downers Grove: InterVarsity, 2010.

Olasky, Marvin. "Blessed Are the Meek." *WORLD Magazine* online (October 15, 2005). https://wng.org/articles/blessed-are-the-meek-1617337715.

Pelikan, Jaroslav. *Interpreting the Bible and the Constitution*. New Haven: Yale University Press, 2004.

Smith, Peter and Robert Tuttle. "Biblical Literalism and Constitutional Originalism." *Notre Dame Law Review* 86, no. 2 (2011): 693–764.

Sunstein, Cass. *Radicals in Robes: Why Extreme Right-Wing Courts Are Wrong for America*. New York: Basic Books, 2005.

Chapter 1

Originalism

First Theology, First Things

Mark D. Eckel

I was taking a class on literary theory in public university for an MA in English. Assignments in the course included critiques of various approaches to literature. Part of my requirements included an engagement with E. D. Hirsch's *Validity in Interpretation*, an approach that confirms "authorial intent," meaning that when a writer writes she has a purpose—an objective—in her composition. I critiqued and then personally affirmed the theory. The professor, a look of consternation on his face, said to me in front of the class, "You really believe in authorial intent?!"[1] I smiled as I said, "Yes, sir, I do." For the next three weeks the professor would drop comments such as "Anyone who believes in authorial intent is naïve."

Why would a literary theory that asserts a writer's motivation for writing be so problematic? The issue comes down to a basic premise: as soon as you say "author," an assumption of "*author*ity" exists. In the main, university English departments utilize the words "writer" or "text" to sidestep any conclusion that might suggest an authoritative tone. Inconsistencies abound, however. Margaret Atwood's *The Handmaid's Tale* is given full-throated acceptance against authoritarianism. Maya Angelou's *I Know Why the Caged Bird Sings* is taken at face value, esteemed for its obvious connection to the author's experience. Why are some messages accepted and other texts seen as opportunities for revision? And if authorial intent is not accepted, why am I spending tuition dollars to hear from academics who have their own intentions to communicate their views in class?

So, what happens when we read Harriet Tubman or Frederick Douglass, the great progenitors of American civil rights? Suddenly, the academe reverses itself (some might reference the word "hypocrisy") and claims the validity (note the word!) of a certain person's argument. What about the leaders of LGBTQ+ and their written claims? My same professor, when the subject of sexualities was broached in class, would immediately demur, saying, "We will need to ask the university diversity leaders about how they would address this question." For every other question about topics outside of gender-sex-identity, he would wax eloquent, displaying his brilliant depth of knowledge and literary coverage of a vast swath of human understanding. But he would suddenly leave the academic field of play when that particular "opponent" would enter the arena. I encountered this essential principle throughout my master's work in English. If there is a cultural narrative considered to be sacrosanct, that totem will be bowed to; proper obeisance will be maintained. But if someone such as I would deign to bring forward a universal, overarching, transcendent, original concept—such as "authorial intention"—that transcendent view was rejected out of hand and attacked as outdated or wrong.

In the same vein, a friend asked me, "How does what you learned in the academy relate to Eve's reinterpretation of God's words?" My response was, "Nothing has changed." In literary theory, academics will prize one or more views of literature from the many that exist. But each theory is based on one seminal idea: a human person will interpret what they are reading in whatever way they think is necessary. The hermeneutical lens in higher education teaching about knowledge is what is commonly referred to as "Reader Response." My professor would say, "I don't care about the author's intention. All I care about are the words on the page. And I will interpret them in the way I see fit." *Someone*'s intention will be heard; *someone*'s origin story will be validated.

The source or origin of an idea is an assumption made on the part of every person, no matter their field of inquiry or vocational directions. And that preexisting "beginning" ideal immediately conveys authority. Every epistemology starts with assumed ideas. The reason for the importance of "originalism" is simply that people begin their point of view from some original foundation. Indeed, those who disagree with "originalism" have their own origin base. For the humanist, she may begin with reason alone. For the Buddhist, he may start with the original teachings of Buddha. Daoists begin with the belief that there is a force that unites all things. Everyone starts somewhere in their thinking. The Hebraic-Christian view of life is no different. The Personal Eternal Triune Creator is the starting point for those who trust in the original writings of the prophets and apostles whose words are authoritative because they come from the One and Only True God.

If there is "law," by direct implication law is premised upon a preexisting framework, before assumptions, a comprehensive understanding of existence, the very nature of where thought begins. What I know follows where my knowing originates. The Declaration of Independence begins, "We hold these truths to be self-evident." A person surmises that something must be true because there are universal affirmations which emanate from a source of being. So, our epistemology must arise out of ontology; the existence of being makes thinking possible. Any idea has an origin from which thinking about that idea begins. Choose a word like "justice," "freedom," "identity," or "empathy." Before any ethical discussion on these ideals, we must admit that the very thought of having an idea about those words has an ontology, a locus of being that made that word important or even possible to contemplate in the first place. The phrase "first things" has been used by many to unequivocally state a beginning, but the very thought of the need for "first things" precedes even that discussion. As a Hebraic-Christian thinker, my thought emanates from the Alpha and Omega, the Beginning and the End (Isaiah 44:6-8; Revelation 1:8 and 22:13). That I have any standing on any issue relies on the very existence of the issue, necessitating the Personal Eternal Triune Creator's self-existence.

To be sure, the Bible's statement, "Thus says the Lord," is a claim not only of authorship, but of original authority. We should expect YHWH's "bias" since His is the authority from which the words arise. One may agree or disagree with the words. However, a counter-perspective does not automatically suggest untruth of the original; nor does a counter-perspective suggest YHWH's original document is simply one truth among many truths, therefore discounting YHWH's perspective as untrue. His claim of authority can be accepted or rejected but it cannot be discounted simply because the origin of the claim is supernatural. Everyone, if they were honest, holds, if not always with complete consistency, to "originalism"—the idea that a document means what the authors said within the cultural context of its writing. To repeat, everyone everywhere begins somewhere in their thinking. The origins of truth claims may differ, but they are still origins.

Neutrality of human interpretation is impossible (a truth claim in itself). Calls of "fallacy" or "conspiracy" only mask the potential discovery of another point of view which may illuminate or—dare I say it?—give evidence toward a perspective rejected only because it does not agree with one's own. I, as a Hebraic-Christian thinker, readily admit that my first assumptions are that (a) a supernatural world exists; (b) the Personal Eternal Triune Creator, YHWH, is the Head over that supernatural world; (c) YHWH has supernaturally disclosed Himself through the natural words of the prophets and apostles in the First and Second Testaments; (d) my interpretation of all things is seen through the lens of YHWH's supernatural point of view; (e) any natural points of view are necessarily interpreted by me through that supernatural lens; and (f) any naturalistic, humanistic rejection of Hebraic-Christian interpretation without acknowledging the purely natural, wholly humanistic origins of bias, is its own blinding bias.

Imperative to our commitment to originalism is our commitment to YHWH revealing Himself to humans in Genesis through Revelation. We take God at His inerrant Word that Scripture exposes the lens through which we may view His world from His perspective. YHWH tells His Story and explains how we are to interpret His Story. We know, for instance, that Moses' documentation of the Spirit's revelation took place after Israel's exodus from Egypt. Not only was Moses aware of hundreds of Egyptian gods but those also from surrounding nations, having been in Egypt's highest rings of power. Further, Moses heard the origin stories of other religions. Within the mix of ancient Near-Eastern religious allegiances, God speaks the original origin Story, the one from which all errant renditions flow.

Genesis 1 and 2, properly understood in the Divine storyline, display The Godhead's original intention for creation. By "origins" we are not only, nor specifically, concerned with the beginning of time-space-matter but also with the origin of everything. "Originalism," understood within the context of God's revelatory interpretation of creation, leaves significant markers of how all things should be first understood. Additionally, theological understanding undergirds First Testament law codes, providing the basis for universal human law. Originalism in law is justified by the principles of a biblical worldview. If we assume the academe's umbrella constituents of "the sciences" and "the humanities," not as binary but as explanatory, discoverers can mine great riches from Genesis 1 and 2.[2] From these first chapters of God's Word, then, we can observe at least five baseline principles, the origin of originalism for the Hebraic-Christian thinker. The Hebraic-Christian worldview affirms that the necessary theological underpinning of original intention begins with a Person who is Eternal, working in concert with other Persons in a Trinity, a creative Creator who functions as a Revelator, setting the stage for His creatures to know purpose. In this essay I will consider these things, drawing connections both to Mosaic and American law as I go.

PERSONAL

Whenever I taught on origins in the high school classroom, I would write two equations on the whiteboard:

Impersonal force + Time + Chance = Purposelessness
Personal God + Plan + Power = Purposefulness

"You have two choices," I would explain, pointing to the comparisons. "You either begin with a naturalistic mindset, something inhospitable, cold, and aloof, or a supernatural mindset where the progenitor of life is designing, welcoming, and approving." Directing attention to the results, I would add, "You can't have it both ways. Believing in a chance universe you cannot suddenly believe in purpose. Luck has nothing to do with purpose." Then I would draw a comparative table (below).

The personableness of God leading to intentional purposefulness is unique in the ancient world. Origin understanding in Genesis 1 and 2 demonstrates a care and closeness of God to His creation; theologians refer to the doctrine of *immanence*. Although God is separate from His work (*transcendence*), He is also the attentive custodian of His Work (*immanence*). The Almighty personally designs, constructs, and superintends both the creative process and the creational outcomes. The very existence of time, space, and matter—each necessary to exist for the trio to exist—shows the worth God infuses within His world (Gen. 1:1). Creation is imbued with meaning. Value in God's creative process is shown through His skill, the finesse and craftsmanship described as God's work (2:2). God's personal purposes are a result of His design noted in phrases such as "it was so" (1:7, English Standard Version) and "the heavens and the earth were finished" (2:1). The doctrine of *providence* finds its first place in Genesis as the Creator personally plans and oversees all people and events (2:5).

Wrapped within the Personhood of God is His freedom for authorship *in* His creation yet *apart from* His creation. Other ancient origin stories made the gods *a part of* creation; YHWH is apart. There is no link between, no dependency upon the natural by the Supernatural. YHWH is not limited by the very essence of physicality—time, space, and matter—as is true for all the other rival belief systems. YHWH is not stymied by unpredictability; rather, prediction is the very nature of God's works. Mystical magic did not control Genesis as it did the *Enuma Elish*. The Psalmist exclaims in wonder about the creation but does not, as other ancient peoples did, find a god in mountains, rivers, and seas. No, YHWH's Personhood is separate, distinct from His handiwork, as His handiwork bears witness of the Author's intentions.

Table 1.1 My Own Whiteboard Chart

Designed Universe	*Chance Universe*
God is eternal.	Matter is eternal.
Reality includes the supernatural.	Reality includes only the natural world.
Truth comes from an outside source of authority.	Truth comes from inside oneself.
Work has purpose.	Work is for survival.
Sex roles allow procreation.	Sex is for self-gratification.
Ethics have a transcendent source.	Ethics are based on who is in control.
The material world is good and is a gift to benefit people.	Matter is all that matters; materialism and consumerism result.
If justice is incomplete in this life, God, the Just Judge, will have the final word in the next life.	There is no justice, and so power and revenge are our only recourse.

The Hebraic view of origins affects our view of everything, including authorial intention. If we were created by a personal God, then life has meaning and purpose. Our human identity has worth, value, and dignity. Our accountability begins with the One who has invested a desire for an objective standard in us. Our designs follow the patterns He has established, in line with the way His world works. Our temporal living is impacted by eternal anticipation. Our understanding of what we have come to expect as "ordinary" is only understood because life is first extraordinary. Our claims for diversity can only be made because of both the unity and uniqueness of the Creator's aim. The Personal God created the earth and everything in it (Ps. 24:1) for the benefit of humanity (Isa. 45:12, 18), since everything created is good (1 Tim. 4:4) and since we were created for His glory (Isa. 43:7). The demonstration of this is a testimony to everyone who observes the creation (Rom. 1:20) as a marker for everyone to ponder the awe of God (Ps. 64:9 and 65:8).

The origin of the Bible's originalism—"authorial intent"—begins with a Person, the God who is before all things (Isa. 41:4; 48:12; Heb. 13:8; James 1:17). The baseline assumption of God's personableness in eternity ("from everlasting to everlasting you are God," Ps. 90:2) is the foundation for originalism ("Forever, O LORD, your word is firmly fixed in the heavens" Ps. 119:89). So, it should come as no surprise that First Testament prophets made it clear they spoke YHWH's words, not their own (Deut. 13:1–5 and 18:15–22). When the disciples wondered after Jesus's authority, it always came back to Him, the individual who made the claims (John 5:24; 8:51).

Suffused within biblical authority was the manifesto of human rights for all people. Law codes in the ancient Near East treated slaves and women as chattel property. Hebraic law countered with law codes that assumed and gave worth, value, and dignity to all people premised in the image of God, coming from God's person (Gen. 1:26–27; James 3:9). Israel was to repulse class and caste systems; God's people were all "brothers," necessitating generous treatment (Lev. 25:39–43). Moreover, foreigners—"aliens," "strangers," or "sojourners"—were to be given respect based on the recurrent idea that Israel was to remember what it meant to be a slave in Egypt (Lev. 10:18–19; Deut. 15:12–15). Interestingly enough, the word God uses to identify His "love" for His people is the same word God uses to identify *any* Gentile (Lev. 19:33–34). The same covenantal care God had for His people was made manifest to all people (Deut. 10:15–19). Western law codes beginning with the Magna Carta and continuing through Blackstone's *Commentaries* all the way down to the United Nations Declaration of Human Rights fostered equality of all people based on the preexisting Hebrew ideal that all people deserve equal treatment no matter their socioeconomic, national, or ethnic status. The premise for modern law can be historically traced to First Testament origins.[3]

The poster hung in my classroom for years: "The authority of Words is based upon the authority of a person without which there is no authority." The original Word of God confers the inalienable rights of human persons. Another Person must first exist to impart, and then sustain, human rights. "Inalienable"—something given from outside humanity, incapable of being taken away—human rights are predicated upon inherent human worth given by the transcendent source, the Personal God. Personhood depends upon God's Person and is *not* premised upon government edict, group characteristics, or self-identity. Protection of people in God's Word (e.g., Ex. 20–25; Deut. 19–26) is premised upon YHWH's person, then YHWH's speech, which is then believed and practiced (Ex. 19:9; Deut. 26:16–19). The Authorship and authority of God's original Words is the reason why intentional authority can exist in any author's words.

ETERNAL

Blackboards, greenboards, and whiteboards were always full of diagrams in my classrooms. One such drawing on the board (below) would be two simple word-filled rectangles, one upon the other. On the top, I would write the word "ethics"; on the bottom, the word was "eternal."

My point to students was always the same: the basis for right and wrong cannot originate from a temporal, earth-bound source. Were that so, ethics could shift and change with whoever held the power. Only an everlasting basis for right and wrong could create, and then adjudicate, ethics. A simple two-block diagram shows the origin of God's intention for His Word originates in eternity. The personal nature of God must also be eternal. Only the eternal can create permanent things. And enduring ideals, including ethics, have their origin in a Person who is Eternal.

Physicists tell us that time, space, and matter must all exist at the same time or not at all. Each structure needs the other. Immediately in Genesis 1 and 2 we see the inception of God's originality, Author of the physical world in all

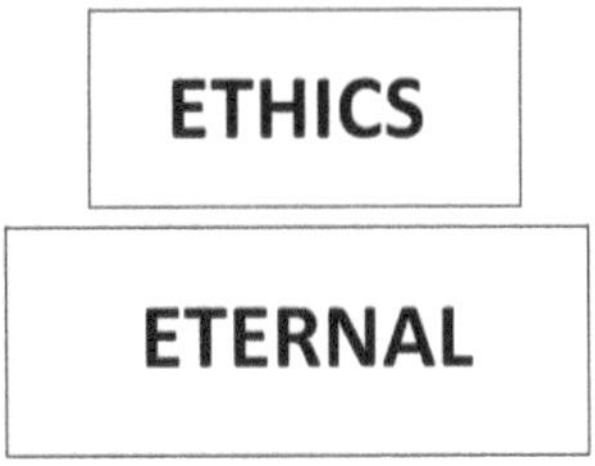

Figure 1.1 Author's Whiteboard Illustration.

its aspects; ages which could not be conceived apart from ageless beginnings. Time is marked and identified in the phrase "there was evening and there was morning" within the concept of a "day" (1:5). Space is seen in God's separating "the waters that were under . . . from the waters that were above" (1:7). Matter exists in water and ground (1:6, 9). Energy (the power, yet to be humanly, adequately defined) resides within the creation itself, a result of supernatural intentionality; when God creates "light" (1:3), the light itself is full of its own power. Only an Eternal God can deliver originality as the imbuing impulse of life, the enduring legacy of all things.

In the ancient world, "water" was considered to be primordial, the preexistent stuff in a chaotic world. But Genesis shows that water submits to and obeys the command of the Creator. The Spirit superintends the creation out of nothing (1:1) from the second verse of Genesis. Much like the action of the Hebrew word for "hover"—the term used in Deut. 32:11 for an eagle protecting its hatchlings—is God's jurisdiction over His creation in Gen. 1:2. Nothing existed before the eternal God brought it into being; the Hebrew term *bara* is used only of God's power to create. Not only does water do His will but the great "sea creatures" are brought into being by *bara* which is surely a statement to the surrounding nations that God had no equal, no cocreator in the nonhistoric mythologies of the day. And only an eternal God could create and then give the sustaining, creative power for trees to *asah*, the Hebrew word for "make," fruit (1:11). The Eternal gives the temporal authority.

Since God is independent from His creation, it is important to mention at least two other theological words which sustain the idea. *Transcendence* is coupled with *immanence* to demonstrate that YHWH both personally cares for His creation and is separate from it at the same time. No other ancient origin story attributes these symbiotic concepts to their deities. All immaterial and material entities are brought into being at the behest of YHWH. *Aseity* augments transcendence citing YHWH as self-sufficient. He needs no one and nothing to participate with Him in His creativity. David and Paul communicate YHWH's sentiment in Psalm 50 and Acts 17, declaring that God does not need sacrifices killed nor a temple built by humans. Again, the focus of Genesis 1 and 2 on God's established intention and authority creates the space in which His creatures create. If the trees can continue to produce fruit based on the creative power of reproduction, then people, even more so, can create in their temporal lives because of the Eternal God.

Law codes are just one avenue to display the Eternal Creator's mark on humanity's ability to legislate. Jurisprudence is inexorably linked to the eternality of God as the basis for all ethics. The practical application of originalism in First Testament law is the literal seriousness of God's Word to His people. By "*literal*" I mean the intentionality of Israelite law within its cultural-historical context. The *serious* reason for a parapet around the open roof of an ancient house was the protection of human life, the homeowner bearing responsibility for construction (Deut. 22:8). "Cities of refuge" (Ex. 21:12–14; Num. 35; Deut. 19; Josh. 20:1–9) existed both for manslaughter recompense as well as familial protection in the case of unintentional death. "Meaning" was not derived from some arbitrary human interdiction. Laws invoked to care for the poverty-stricken were directly tied to fearing the eternal God (Lev. 25:23–55, esp. 17, 36, 43). The eternality of God sets a universal, transcendent standard for law over the capricious nature of some autocratic sovereign whose human demeanor could shift and change "either to the right hand or to the left" (Deut. 17:18–20). In contrast, the Eternal God does not "change" (Num. 23:19; Deut. 33:27; 1 Sam. 15:29); neither does His law (Ps. 119:89; Isa. 46:9–10). The necessity of a fixed, durable, enduring basis for interpretation of law is imperative. This corresponds, in our own day, to the originalist or textualist approach to the US Constitution which depends on permanence, unlike the "Living Constitution" interpretive approach which depends on impermanence; change of meaning is constant depending on cultural shifts and popular whims.

By "serious" I mean that God's law is both crucial *and* consequential for lived life. "I am." The very idea that *words* are so important to YHWH is found in virtually every pericope of Moses' writing, which sets the standard for law codes as indicated in Deuteronomy 4:5–8. Nations would compare laws with other nations, thereby establishing the hierarchy of gods. Later in the same chapter the reader is pressed to consider the eternal basis for such a law code claim: "ask from one end of heaven to the other," declaring "YHWH is God; there is no other besides him" (4:32–35). Restitution instead of retribution, for example, is a marked distinction between cultural laws. Hammurabi's code required the death of a person who stole from the temple. Moses's code was not so materialistic. Exodus 21–22 displays multiple examples of restitution; the guilty perpetrator, no matter their socio-economic status, would be held accountable to repay what was taken, whether the acts were intentional or unintentional. Hebraic law displayed the crucial nature of objectivity together with the consequential nature of not following the laws of God.

The origin of origins and the intention of intentions is recited throughout Scripture. That names are "written before the foundation of the world in the book of life" (Rev. 13:8 and 17:8) expresses God's eternal purposes. Planned before time, the space-time event of "eternal life" was seen and testified by Jesus's followers (1 John 1:2). Restoration of all things (Acts 3:21) was promised to the prophets marked by specific fulfillments (such as the gospel going to the Gentiles) which were known by God for all ages (Acts 15:18). The "secret and hidden wisdom of God, which God decreed before the ages" (1 Cor. 2:7) is in direct contrast to the spirit of the age held by rulers during a given time (1 Cor. 2:6, 8). Revelatory truth was written down for us "on whom the end [from Greek *telos*, purpose or end or fulfillment or goal] of the ages has come" (1 Cor. 10:11).

The "eternal purpose" of Jesus's accomplishment is now made known "through the church" to "the rulers and authorities in the heavenly places" (Eph. 3:10–11). His power now works "within us," the church, for His glory (Eph. 3:20–21). So, we fix our eyes not on what is seen but what is unseen; "the things that are unseen are eternal" (2 Cor. 4:17–18, 5:1). Whoever "sows to the Spirit will from the Spirit reap eternal life" (Gal. 6:8). Jesus's sacrifice "through the eternal Spirit" moves us "to serve the living God" (Heb. 9:14) based on "the eternal covenant" which equips us with "everything good" for doing His will (Heb. 13:20–21). For in this life we have "eternal comfort and good hope" which strengthens us for every "good work and word" (2 Th. 2:16–17). We are to "take hold of the eternal life" (1 Tim. 6:12) because faith and knowledge rest on the "hope of eternal life" promised by God (Tit. 1:1–2; 3:7), prompting us toward devotion "to good works" because "these things are excellent and profitable for people" (3:8). Scripture affirms the simple diagram I drew for my students: doing what is right is based on the Eternal God whose original intention is good.

TRIUNE

Harvard's crest includes three books: the book of God's Word, the book of God's world, and the book of logic. Overlaid on these books is the word *veritas*, Latin for "truth." The search for truth was to begin through the lens of Scripture examining the whole world through God-given logic. William Ames, a forerunner of John Amos Comenius, established Harvard's early Christian view through his then-famous theses, one of which reads, in part,

> Thus, let us not become the slaves of anyone, but, . . . under the banner of free truth, let us freely and courageously follow the truth . . . . Testing all things, retaining that which is good, let Plato be a friend, let Aristotle be a friend, but even more let truth (*veritas*) be a friend. (Thesis #77, *Technometry*)[4]

Truth, The Author's intention, is our friend because The Triune God holds all things together. God made the world to resemble Himself: perfect plurality in perfect unity. All things find their connection and function within the Triune Godhead. In creation, as with The Creator, there is distinctiveness and diversity yet uniqueness and inclusiveness. Creational harmony shows earth using its creative power given by the Creator to produce all kinds of "vegetation" which produced "according to its kind" (Gen. 1:12). Form, structure, orderly arrangement, and the parts interrelated with the whole—this pattern is displayed throughout the first two chapters of Genesis. We read of light and darkness, water and sky (1:3–8), four forms. Each form then had a function and structure: each thing had a purpose (1:14, "let them be for"). And, perhaps most importantly, God is said to have "separated" (1:4, 6, 7, 14, 18) the forms. In Hebrew, this word means to assign each part a place, to see its unique qualities, giving an orderly arrangement of these elements to make a better whole. The Triune God made the world to mirror Himself in its organization and work.

Israelite law focused attention on judicial rulings which mirrored the communitarian nature of YHWH's personhood. Multiple officials were necessary to connect God's people to "righteous judgment" (Deut.16:18–20). Deuteronomy 17–18 provides an overview of leaders' regulatory responsibility for law. Direct revelation from YHWH was given to the prophets which was then adjudicated by priests and, later, judges. A king had the power of the sword but was beholden to copy revelation so that he might limit excesses and have a God-centered mindset (Deut. 17:18–20). The need for two or three witnesses confirms the need for transparency, limiting the potential abuse of the judicial process by just one person (Num. 35:30; Deut. 17:6; 19:15). Elders at the gate demonstrated a need for multiple points of view not unlike present courts which depend on three, five, or nine justices to adjudicate cases (Ruth 4:1–4; Prov. 31:23; Lam. 5:14). Human leadership with its finitude and fallenness still bore the marks of God's original intention in Genesis 1:28 to manage and conserve what God had given, including the law's original intention that God set the standards (Gen. 2:16–17).

All things fit together based on the Hebraic-Christian doctrine of *coherence*. Everything fits together or coheres because there are unity, wholeness, and consistency in reality. Creation makes sense because of the Triune Creator. Scripture regularly establishes the work of each person of the Godhead: the Father plans, the Son provides, and the Spirit protects. Ephesians 1:3–14, an early Christian hymn, celebrates the work of each eternal Person in the work of salvation accomplished pre-creation. A focus on creation shows the immediate work of the Spirit protecting God's material world (Gen. 1:2). The Father's plan and The Son's provision are clearly repeated throughout the Bible, Colossians 1:15–20 being another musical encore to God's Genesis work. Indeed, the first verse of the Bible teaches coherence. "The heavens and the earth," in the Hebrew mind, included everything from A to Z. Believers and unbelievers alike declared that the Hebrew God created and unified all things, from Rahab to Hezekiah to Hiram, king of Tyre (Josh. 2:11, 2 Kings 19:15, 2 Chron. 2:12). Prophets throughout Scripture declare the same—all things come from and are held together by YHWH (Neh. 9:6, Prov. 30:4, Isa. 44:24).

The Trinity gives the basis for the unity within the plurality of the universe. Creation, salvation, and prayer suggest the divergence and convergence of

God's person and ways. Generally, the Father plans (originator), the Son provides (agent), and the Spirit protects (sustainer). In creation, the eternal decree of the Father (1 Cor. 8:6) is carried out through the Son (John 1:3; Col. 1:16), sheltered by the Spirit (Gen. 1:2). In salvation, the Father chose before the world was (Eph. 1:3–6), the Son died for the sin of the world (Eph. 1:7–12), and the Spirit sealed believers in the world for eternity (Eph. 1:13–14). In prayer, believers pray to the Father (Luke 11:1), through the Son (1 Tim. 2:5) and aided by the Spirit (Rom. 8:26–27). Authorial intention begins with Someone who helps me understand reality because of His Trinitarian Personhood.

For educators, coherence allows study in a stable, ordered, structured universe. God alone gives

the physicist properties to obey,
the biologist observations to make,
the chemist sequences to expect,
the physician diagnoses to follow,
the geologist patterns to pursue,
the meteorologist models to predict,
and the environmentalist laws to encourage.

Scientists, grammarians, counselors, theologians, economists, historians, mathematicians, and educators in all disciplines depend on coherence to do their work. And it was the influence of Comenius whose work established the foundations of modern education. The reason I work in the university setting is the coherent, synthetic, wholistic unity of all things under the jurisdiction of the Personal Eternal Triune Creator. Comenius had a teaching called pansophy, of which he said,

> And praised be thou, O Lord, for ever, which dost likewise give us thy workes and word for a patterne . . . : that as thy word and workes are a true and lively representation of thee: so this [education], which we are about, may prove a true, and lively image of thy word and works.

Together with the original vision of Harvard's crest, as a university professor I am constantly interested in understanding how everything fits together, because He holds everything together (Col. 1.18). The Creator's Triune nature demonstrates again the Author's intention and its possibility for humanity.

CREATOR

Picture a small group of students and me sitting around a table over lunch. On the public university campus, I have had many opportunities to converse with

Christian young people who are confronted with very different worldviews for the first time in their lives. Some of the discussions come out of science classes. Someone mentions that their professor begins her lecture with a naturalistic, evolutionary view of the universe. All faces turn to me anticipating an answer to the question, "How would you respond?" Here is one of my approaches taken over one such lunch conversation.

"Does your professor ever talk about origins, where things come from in your study?" I began.

"No," she shook her head, "We don't discuss ideas such as creation or evolution. Evolution is a given."

"Let me ask a different question. Does your professor ever use the words 'awe,' 'beauty,' 'wonder,' or 'amazement' when talking about human cell structure?"

"Oh, yes! All the time! He would say things like, 'If the molecular structure changed a fraction or the cell structure shifted ever so slightly in this or that direction the immune system would not work'."

She paused. Then she said, "You know, now that I think about it, my professor assumes design all the time! He will use the word and I will think to myself, 'How can you use that word if you believe in evolution?'"

"And there it is!" I declared, looking around the table. "No one—Christian or non-Christian—can operate in their respective fields of study without depending on concepts that come from outside themselves.

"Do you see?!" I further explained, "The Christian worldview provides the presuppositions for everything! Humans assume beauty, logic, and wonder as results of any investigation without giving a thought about where those ideas originate."

The centerpiece of originalism is that an original must exist, and, hence, an originator must create the original. Embedded within this concept is intentionality. Contrary to the mythologies within the ancient Near Eastern communities, order, not chaos, directed the original creative process. Not only is there order, but the organization is also directly subordinated to God's sovereignty: He is in charge; He gives purpose to His creation. Moreover, procreation has no part in the Genesis creation. Other cultural origin stories depend on sexual liaisons between the gods for creation to come into existence. But YHWH acts alone as the Originator. There are no battles between warring gods such as Tiamet versus Marduk. The "great sea creatures" (Gen. 1:21) are given passing reference in Genesis rather than a rival role in creation. Elohim is Elohim; there is no other. God's existence is not argued in Genesis; rather His presence ahead of the physical world is implicit. Other creation accounts give the origin of the gods. Genesis says that the origin of creation is God, the Author with an intention for His cosmos.

Furthermore, and to the point of my conversation with students above, the order of origins jumps off the pages of Genesis 1 and 2. Beauty, perhaps a better Hebrew translation than "good," marks the regulation of God's creation: "And God saw that it was beautiful" (1:10, 12, 18, 21, 25). The exquisite creation is then evaluated and appreciated by the Artisan: God saw what He had made (1:4). A blossoming of variety exists "according to their kinds" (1:11–12, 21, 24–25). What is "pleasant to the sight" is also "good for food" (2:9), beauty wed with use as God gives us the plants for food (1:29). In keeping with the trajectory of the Author's intention, He transferred the same to His image bearers. Human beings have the responsibility to represent God on earth, to cultivate creation in God's name. One of my many mantras developed over decades of instruction included this phrase, "The Creator created creatures who creatively create from creation." God has given us purposeful designs, and designed us to form our own purposes in creatively developing creation.

America's founding documents were conceived, fashioned, and predicated on deep research into historic ideas. The creation of originalism is predicated on the founders' original thinking extrapolated in a document such as *The Federalist Papers*. Hamilton, Madison, and Jay among others considered classical and biblical laws and how they were created within their time and place. The ideals found in Plutarch's *Lives* or Moses's *Pentateuch* were considered not just for their verbiage and ideals but for the consequences of those laws in their time and place. America's founders were concerned not simply for the best law, as important a result as that may be, but wondered whether the origins produced the best ends. For instance, why were constitutional protections for personal creations of "science and useful arts" written into copyright law (Art. 1, Sec. 8, Clause 8)? Intellectual property which creates wealth is just as important as tangible wealth. Ancient law codes cared for physical wealth; America's founders extended the concept of wealth to the origin of the wealth itself: ideas. Embedded within copyright law is the seed, the germ of originalist thinking. The origin of a thing is just as important as its result because the idea itself is productive. The end of a matter means little if the origin of the matter is ignored. Protecting patents and copyrights was unprecedented in the origin documents of any nation up until the US Constitution. Protection of the human creator mirrors YHWH's intention to give humans authority to create, including the nomenclature of animal categories (Gen. 2:5, 15, 19).

Our knowledge of origins originates with God's intentions (Gen. 1–2; Heb. 11:3). God cares and provides for the needs of His creation. All life is dependent on God (Gen. 8:22; Ps. 147:7–9; Matt. 6:25–34). Everyone and everything is responsible to God the Creator and Lord of life (Jer. 32:27; Rom. 9:19–21; Acts 4:12). Right and wrong are established by YHWH (Ex.

20:1–17; Matt. 5–7). Ethics are transcendent, eternal (Rom. 1:18–20), and, at the same time, implanted in every person (Rom. 2:14–15). God is the source and unity of all knowledge. All truth has its root in God (Ps. 19:1–11; Col. 1:15–17; 2:2–3). Life has value, worth, and purpose because God made it possible (Ecc. 2:24–25; 3:11–13; 5:18–20). As Creator, God exists independently of His creation (Job 38–42). God made the universe and everything in it (Isa. 40:26; 42:5; 44:24; Amos 4:13; John 1:3; Rom. 1:25; 1 Cor. 8:6; Eph. 3:9; 1 Pet. 4:19). And as all of God's intentions are woven through His creation, we reflect the wonder of His words and works in our creative intentions.

REVELATOR

A chaplain in a K–12 Christian school, I was asked by the primary grades to speak at their chapel. For a high school teacher, the experience of teaching six- through nine-year-olds can be a stretch! There was always a focus on "authority" in my classes, so I decided to communicate the concept to first, second, and third graders. My brief talk was full of connections for little ones, applications they would understand. But every idea was punctuated with the Genesis phrase "And God said." I would give an example and then ask the question, "And why should I obey?" The young audience would enthusiastically respond in unison, "And God said!" God's revelatory authority, the reason for our obedience, is captured in three words.

"And God said" is the plainspoken, repetitious phrase in Genesis 1 which marks the inception of authoritative speech, Truth, material origins, and the supremacy of the Word (Gen. 1:3, 6, 9, 11, 14, 20, 24, 26, 28, 29). Genesis—unlike every other ancient Near Eastern creation story—says the physical world is a result of God's speech. Psalm 33:9 simply says, "For he spoke, and it came to be." Other worldviews in the time of Genesis also depended on *words* but only as incantations to manipulate matter, what we would call today "a magician's trick." On the contrary, YHWH's will was a decision expressed as divine fiat creatively through His creation. While the creation account begins by verifying what we see, what we see is based on what God says.

The five principles from Genesis toward authorial intention noted in this essay end where they must: a Person—Eternal, Triune, and Creator—Reveals Himself through His Words. The essence of intentional authority originates not with our words, but with His. Ultimately, the person who communicates is the one who discloses His authorship. "And God said" indicates that the Almighty took the initiative to communicate Himself to humans (Heb. 1:1). God's openness as Revelator demonstrates (a) disclosure, an uncovering of His person (Matt 11:27; Rom. 1:18; Eph. 1:17; Phil. 3:15); (b) His willingness to be Known (Jer. 9:23–24); (c) His planned communication set in eternity (Rev. 13:8; 17:8); and (d) the need for preserving the revelation (John 14:16; 16:13; 1 Cor. 2:13; 1 Thes. 4:15; 2 Thes. 2:15; 2 Pet. 3:2; Rev. 22:18–19). It is obvious in a reading of Scripture that God intended to maintain His authoritative voice.

A common question about the Bible's authority arises when someone asks, "Can we trust the second, third, fourth, or one-hundredth copy of God's Word?" Do copies of Scripture still carry with them YHWH's authorial intention? A few brief biblical examples suggest a positive answer, although the evidence is clear that biblical copies have faithfully preserved the original text to a very significant degree.[5] The king was to make a written copy in his own hand to be recounted as God's authoritative voice (Deut. 17:18–20). Moses had a copy of the law preserved (Deut. 31:24–28). The reading of God's commands to the people was authoritative (2 Chron. 34:29–31). Jeremiah rewrote the burned scroll of the law (Jer. 36:27–28). Jesus read from a copy of Isaiah saying that the words were fulfilled that day (Luke 4:16–21). The phrase "It is written" from Jesus (e.g., Matt. 4:4, 7, 10) accepts the First Testament as authoritative;[6] these words are preeminent even over visitations of the dead (Luke 16:27–31). Second Testament believers received, believed, and accepted "the Word of God" given to them (1 Thes. 2:13), comparing the verbal teaching of Paul with the written word from First Testament teaching (Acts 17:11). God's written revelation should be the final authority for evaluation of other written or spoken communication (1 Cor. 10:3–5; Heb. 5:11–14).

If there is one ongoing concern about originalism in American law, it is: By what interpretive lens will anyone evaluate the US Constitution? "The separation of powers," a unique concept within human law codes, was one of the most important boundaries created to maintain the original intention of America's founding. Lifetime judicial appointments were meant to maintain the constitutional order through disinterested interpretation. Further, the intention for Supreme Court judges was to eliminate arbitrary, personal, or political biases by basing opinions on the enduring principles of the Constitution. As Article III, Section 2, Clause 1 clearly states, "Judicial power shall extend to all cases, in Law and Equity, arising under this Constitution, the Laws of the United States." Essential to the understanding of this statement is not only the broad interpretation of case law but also, most importantly, the separation of the judicial branch from the legislative and executive branches, thereby protecting the Supreme Court's interpretive ability from outside influences. It was the intention of the law that was the primary adjudication for the famed *Lex Talionis*—"an eye for an eye" in Exodus 21:24–25. The intention of the law was not retribution—if I knock out your eye, you get to knock out mine—but restitution, which is exactly enumerated in the verses immediately following (Ex. 21:26–27). As such, particular safeguards were fixed within the fourth through eighth amendments to the Constitution. Originalism in law found both its intention and application supported by the revelatory genius of Pentateuchal law.

Yes, reader response is important for interpretation of law, but only if there is an intentional written record to respond to. "Have you not read?" is a repeated condemnation by Jesus, suggesting that people bore responsibility to know what God had said (Matt. 12:3, 5; 19:4; 21:16, 42; 22:31). Beyond the original hearers, writers of Scripture expected understanding of the text by redeemed people of all backgrounds (Rom. 4:1–25; 15:4; 1 Cor. 10:1–11). Numerous principles for personal responsibility to Scripture must then be noted: (a) The Bible is written clearly assuming people can read or listen and obey (Deut. 4:5–8; 6:7–9; 11:18–20); (b) the Bible is capable of being understood (Ps. 19:7; 119:130); (c) understanding the Bible is the reader's responsibility (Matt. 11:20–24); (d) understanding the Bible may be deterred by unbelief (2 Cor. 3:14–16), sin (James 1:19–25), lack of knowledge (Deut. 29:29), poor interpretation (Gal. 2:11–15), or honest disagreements (Acts 15:7); (e) spiritual discernment of God's Word comes through The Spirit (1 Cor. 2:14–16); and (f) spiritual discernment helps people apply the Revelator's truth to life (2 Tim. 3:16–17). Primary age children through adults bear responsibility to the Revelator's Words. "And God said" is just as much an authoritative revelation to The Church as it was to Israel.

CONCLUSION

"Authorial intent" means that a document should be interpreted as the writer—the author (assuming "authority")—meant when the writing was originally created. The words in the document should be understood within the context of their time, place, and cultural milieu. "Reader response" is the literary approach to a text that suggests that the view of the individual reading the text matters more than the original author's intention (or even that it is the only thing that matters). The words in the document are interpreted within the frame of the time, place, and cultural milieu of the reader as a "living, breathing document." Readers of the US Constitution understand their approach to law based on originalism ("authorial intent") or progressivism ("reader response"). I adhere to an "originalist" mindset in my study of written or oral works (including Genesis to Revelation), yet I know that my response as a reader is essential to understand for two reasons: I bear responsibility for what I read, and my interpretation ("response") has its own biases. Without apology I bear witness to the theological bases for authorial intention as the prejudicial lens through which I view my studies. Genesis 1 and 2 establish the necessary theological underpinnings of original intention beginning with a Person who is Eternal, working in concert with other Persons in a Trinity, a creative Creator who functions as a Revelator. Originalism in theology sets the stage for originalism in everything else.

NOTES

1. Conversations in this essay (and my next essay in this volume) are true stories from my years in academia. The quotations include the exact ideas expressed with verbiage allowing for smooth flow of thought.

2. My focus will be on what theologians refer to as "Pre-Fall" or before sin entered Eden. Even here I would emphasize God's original intention for His world.

3. A spate of journals and books have weighed in on the extraordinary influence of First Testament law in our modern world. Tom Holland's *Dominion* is an important reference since Holland has affirmed an agnostic mindset while at the same time praising Hebraic-Christian influence on legal concerns. Tom Holland, *Dominion: How the Christian Revolution Remade the World* (New York: Basic Books, 2019).

4. William Ames, *Technometry*, trans. with introduction and commentary by Lee W. Gibbs (Philadelphia: University of Pennsylvania Press, 1979), 106–107.

5. Beyond the scope of this brief essay, it is important to note scholars who have undertaken to analyze the full scope of biblical preservation. The academic discipline known as "textual criticism" is the study of how a text is transmitted through copies and of how to reconstruct the original from those copies. The interested reader might consider, as an introduction to the study of New Testament textual criticism, Bruce M. Metzger and Bart D. Ehrman, *The Text of the New Testament: Its Transmission, Corruption, and Restoration*, 4th ed. (Oxford: Oxford University Press, 2005). For an introduction to the textual criticism of the Hebrew Old Testament, see Emmanuel Tov, *Textual Criticism of the Hebrew Bible*, 4th ed. (Minneapolis: Fortress Press, 2022). For an older introduction that considers both Hebrew and the ancient Greek Old Testament tradition, the Septuagint, see Ralph W. Klein, *Textual Criticism of the Old Testament: From the Septuagint to Qumran* (Minneapolis: Fortress Press, 1974).

6. Jesus believed (a) the smallest letter and stroke of a pen to be reliable as recorded (Matt 5:17–19); (b) Jonah's experience as historical fact (Matt 12:40); (c) Genesis to be literal and Moses the author of Deuteronomy (Matt 19:3–9); (d) Elijah's experience as historical fact (Luke 4:25–26); (e) the destruction of Sodom and Gomorrah to be historical fact (Luke 17:29–32); and (f) His authority to be equal with the First Testament (John 5:39–40, 46–47).

WORKS CITED

Ames, William. *Technometry*, translated with introduction and commentary by Lee W. Gibbs. Philadelphia: University of Pennsylvania Press, 1979.

Comenius, John Amos. *A Reformation of Schooles.*

Holland, Tom. *Dominion: How the Christian Revolution Remade the World.* New York: Basic Books, 2019.

The Holy Bible. English Standard Version.

Klein, Ralph W. *Textual Criticism of the Old Testament: From the Septuagint to Qumran.* Minneapolis: Fortress Press, 1974.

Metzger, Bruce M. and Bart D. Ehrman. *The Text of the New Testament: Its Transmission, Corruption, and Restoration*, 4th ed. Oxford: Oxford University Press, 2005.

Tov, Emmanuel. *Textual Criticism of the Hebrew Bible*, 4th ed. Minneapolis: Fortress Press, 2022.

Chapter 2

Reading Pictures

Comparing Aesthetic and Hermeneutic Discussions of Intention

Jonathan Johnson

Texts communicate, and so do pictures. This truism of experience led someone to pen the idiom "a picture is worth a thousand words." The media-saturated world we inhabit is a testimony to the efficacy of visual alongside textual communication. But in the face of these facts of experience, there are philosophies which undermine the commonsense understanding of communication in both texts and visual media. Some theorists have allowed the post-Kantian recognition of subject-centric aspects of experience to undermine the object-centric grounds for experience; for some in textual and visual studies, the reader or viewer has ironically become the author and artist.

Defenses of communication from author to audience occur in discrete camps. In textual studies, there is discussion of originalism pertaining to both constitutional and scriptural studies. In visual studies, and aesthetics generally, there is discussion of such concepts as intentionalism and depiction. In this chapter, I address the former by way of the latter, introducing insights from aesthetic philosophies of interpretation to those of textual studies. This is a novel approach not only because of its transdisciplinary comparison of originalism in one field and intentionalism in another, but also because it points to a sort of *reductio ad absurdum* argument—that if rigorous cases can be made for originalism in the notoriously subjective field of art, we may readily expect to make them in historical and hermeneutical textual studies. The main aim of this chapter is to make such an argument, by introducing the several ways originalism or intentionalism are legitimate pursuits in aesthetic and art theories of interpretation. If the aims of originalism can be justified in art, they can also be justified in hermeneutics.

In the sections that follow, I will first give some simple definitions as to what I mean by certain terms like "originalism," "aesthetics," and "art." I then go on to introduce to readers in hermeneutics the discussion of intentionalism in aesthetics, as well as mentioning concerns with depiction and gestalt composition. This is followed by a swift perusal of Gordan Graham's response to those art theories which undermine confidence in original intent, before finishing with a summary of where we have been, and where future explorations might go. My conclusion is that, without denying the contributions of the reader or viewer, we can and should recognize the importance of original intentions to communications visual, legal, and religious.

DEFINING THE DOMAINS—ORIGINALISM, AESTHETICS, AND ART

The intended novelty of bringing in a third strand of discourse—aesthetics—into an already doubled discussion—of theology and law—presents some problems along with the hoped-for promise. One of these problems is being clear from the outset about the definitions and concepts I intend to compare and contrast, and another is properly addressing this collection's context (hermeneutics) while saving room for the "outside" contribution from an ostensibly disparate field (aesthetics). Like all crowded conversations, there is the risk of being unclear about terms and being limited by time. To avoid these problems as much as possible I will briefly describe what I have in view in the context of originalism in scriptural and legal contexts, and then more extensively describe what I have in view in the equally controversial realm of philosophical aesthetics.

Contextual Focus—Originalism and Hermeneutics

The easiest route to refer to this collection's context is simply to sample it. I refer the reader to the aims of Mark Boone's introduction to this book, where he provides both a weak and a strong definition of originalism, and goes on to describe the overlaps and distinctions between originalism in scriptural (here, biblical) and legal (here, American constitutional) texts. In the weaker or "broad" sense, Boone says that originalism could refer to "the theory that the meaning of a text is its original meaning." In a stronger, more specific sense, originalism could refer to "the theory that the meaning of a text only changes when the words of that text change." This gloss of the term "originalism" has an eye especially to the legal and religious domains of discourse, and especially toward the constitutional context wherein "the words of that text change" via constitutional amendment.

My own focus in reference to "originalism" as so deployed will rest largely on the connection of *a meaning's relation to a text*; more specifically, *an original meaning's relation to an original text.* This may seem much broader or more basic than Boone's broad version, but in the field which I present for comparison, this broadest of connections which I have raised is contested and sometimes denied. This contestation is the context of the minor *reductio* which I hope to put forward. Before leaving Boone's prefacing remarks, there are two caveats he gives which are altered, somewhat, in my comparison. Speaking of originalism in the legal context, he argues it is not synonymous with "intentionalism," comparing it with "textualism," and addressing the distinctions in his own chapter.[1] In his usage the latter (text shared by author and reader) is sometimes highlighted as the locus of meaning more reliably than the former (authorial intent), whereas I merely argue for the inclusion of the former in the latter. Further, "intentionalism" as I explain below, is used in my context as "aesthetic intentionalism," which is a specific position in the field of aesthetic philosophy.

The second caveat for Boone in legal, constitutional originalism is that meaning need not be fixed to the time of its initial conception. Again, this is given with an eye towards acknowledging the practice of *amendation.* In my discussion, I will address this idea of fixity somewhat figuratively and playfully, again for the ends of a *reductio* argument, as demanded by aesthetic concerns with first-person experience. For I am interested in personal present aesthetic concerns which unavoidably involve first-person experience. I had better define these concerns before going any further.[2]

Contributional Focus—Aesthetics and Art

For the reader with interest in originalism in hermeneutics—particularly biblical, constitutional, or their overlap—I have tried to be mercifully brief in my definitions of aesthetics and art. For readers in philosophical aesthetics, I must be *scandalously* brief in laying out the first two sets of definitions only assertorially, without justification. The third concept, intentionalism, which may also need definition, is taken up in the section immediately following. There I also speak of issues relating to depiction and other aspects of art theory as well. Although these are defined less idiosyncratically, and in greater length, their treatment is still painfully selective.

The term "aesthetic" in contemporary English discourse can have a range of senses, from a narrow, casual referral in conversation to the look or style of something or someone ("I like this coffeeshop's *aesthetic*") to a broad, serious referral in philosophy to the study of sensation, perception, and the forms of response, including judgment and emotion, which arise from our experience of the world. The throughline from the term's etymology to philosophy is helpful to understand both its history and how I use the term in this chapter:

> Its etymological origin lies in a Greek term αἴσθητικος which referred to perception and assessment through the exercise of the bodily senses.[3] In this usage it is akin to a type of judgment, evaluation, or discernment about our experience of the world, and whose exercise could result in a sort of being-experienced, or having discernment. It would appear that this sense of the term underlay Baumgarten's attempt to designate a distinct field of philosophical inquiry under the same name, but the term—and philosophical sphere—quickly became associated with a narrowed interest in the attractive studies of beauty or art.[4] In both its broad and narrow senses (sensory perception/evaluation and beauty), it is easy to see how the discipline also became the repository for philosophical discussions of the arts as well.[5]

I prefer the broader, etymological sense of the term "aesthetics," and use it herein to mean that philosophical field and its wide-ranging concerns. Of course, historically and currently, aesthetics is popularly associated with art and beauty.[6]

What do I mean by "art"? Avoiding the debates over what makes something a work of art, its general sense for many contemporary readers would be "an artifact or performance creatively expressing an idea for a subject's contemplation."[7] Besides having the merit of being rather noncommittal on definitional or normative theories of art, this sense is vague enough to encompass both children's drawings and the Sistine Chapel, and should serve as a placeholder for the discussion at hand. I refer curious and contentious readers to Graham's excellent gloss of popular theories of art and his normative alternative.[8] I will return to Graham's collection later for listing of opponents of normative theories, which also often oppose originalism, textualism, or, in aesthetics, intentionalism.

Before turning to a brief overview of aesthetic intentionalism, I wish to restate that the above concepts, aesthetics and art, have become—at least in western philosophical and cultural traditions—the domains of a type of subjectivity which verges on skepticism or solipsism. Beginning with the Enlightenment, the received tradition now is that art is the arena of the *genius*, working not by rule but by *intuition* and *inspiration*, and whose works interact with our own aesthetic *tastes*, in engagements where we must have aesthetic *distance* and *disinterest*.[9] From the side of the artist to the side of the audience, the apparently irrational (nonrational?) nature of the production and perception of art and aesthetic experience seems to deny description or explanation in objective terms. Besides, asking what a work of art *means* seems to some to be unachievable or less accurate, and we ought to ask only what a work *means to me*. While we must, and I will at my close, give acknowledgment to the essential role of subjective experience in aesthetics and art, we need not think that some subjectivity annuls all objectivity. Or put another way: the truth that art can have very personal meaning need not prevent us from discovering the meaning of the art itself—a meaning put there, in part, by the artist's original intentions.

INTENTIONALISM, DEPICTION, AND GESTALT

What is meant by "intentionalism" in aesthetics? Just as aesthetics is a branch of philosophy, so too intentionalism is discussed at the general philosophical level and at the specific level of aesthetics. Philosopher Kieran Setiya suggests recognizing "three forms" of intention, which could be described as: future (what we intend to do), aim (the intention of what we are doing), and act ("intentional action" of knowledgeable doing).[10] From these bare groupings it may readily be seen that intention, for philosophers, holds great interest for its connection to action, knowledge, and the relation (and responsibility) of the inner world of mind and the outer world of deed. The current discussion of intention, at least in analytic philosophy, has been greatly influenced by G. E. M. Anscombe's seminal work, *Intention*.[11] As might be expected from the latter two of Setiya's "forms," Anscombe's work is influential in the study of philosophy of action.[12]

But the concerns of this chapter, and that of aesthetic intentionalism, have a special sort of interest in action—action that is archived or demonstrated in art and aesthetic experience. Laying aside the interesting personal questions (Why did *you* do something?, What do *you* mean by doing something?), it asks equally interesting questions which are both personal and public (Why did *they* do this?, What did *they* mean by this?). Obviously, these questions also arise in hermeneutics of texts. Whether or not an author's intent is knowable, and to what degree we ought to be influenced by such intentions, if knowable, is pertinent to the theological and legal discussion in this collection. But aesthetic intentionalism must also navigate contemporary concepts associated with art and creative endeavors that threaten to further muddy the waters of interpretation. Is a work of art's meaning a matter of taste alone? Is our response to an aesthetic experience culturally dependent? Is content subservient to or subsumed by form? Does disinterestedness or aesthetic distance preclude communicability? And so on. Perhaps if these muddied waters of intention in aesthetics can be navigated, the relatively clearer waters of textual hermeneutics might appear less daunting.[13]

One writer dealing with such questions is the aesthetic philosopher Paisley Livingston. In his comprehensive work, *Art and Intention*, Livingston surveys and analyzes the relevant discussions of intention in philosophy and psychology as they relate to works of art and our experience of them.[14] Interested readers desiring a general discussion of intention in greater breadth and depth will be helped by his vast yet concise survey in his opening chapter.[15]

Guiding between the extreme poles of art either being purely works of inspired, unbidden epiphany, or calculated, purely rational methodologies, Livingston argues that whatever the complex flux of creative artistry is, it includes intention:

> Writing a literary text, fabricating a sculpture, and staging a performance of a play are intentional actions. So are finishing a given work and presenting it to the public. Such deeds are usually prompted, guided, and informed by intentions, the contents of which are the author's or artist's plans—it being understood that the latter can emerge on the spur of the moment, often quite unconsciously, in the process of the artist's active engagement with artistic media or materials.[16]

Laying aside the question of "conscious" and "unconscious" intentions, which Livingston addresses, our simple interest at the moment is whether or not intentions are imprinted into works of art, and whether or not we as audience members are able to usefully discover them, if they be discoverable at all. The question is pertinent, in passing, for at least one reason: it is not the case, Livingston argues, that just because *some* intentions are unknown to an artist, that *all* intentions must be unknown. By extension, that *some* intentions were unknown to the artist need not entail that *all* are unknown to the audience, whose possible knowledge is a separate issue. As Livingston proceeds to build a complex picture of how intentions relate to the creation of works of art, he addresses counterclaims along the way.

Among them are Michel Foucault's famous (apparent) denial of any text's author, or "author-function," in the genre of the "death of the author" era.[17] Among the claims Foucault made in this era was that the author, or our idea of the author as author, is a creation of our own, by means of various and sundry factors. Livingston's first critique of such a notion is to state that such an idea collapses when the idea of a reader—the supposedly constructing (or deconstructing) individual—is put to a similar investigation. If the author disappears, why not the reader?

In chapter 6 of Livingston's work, "Intention and the Interpretation of Art," the author returns to other objections about valuing (or even viewing) the role of intention in art. These include critics he groups under the heading of "*absolute anti-intentionalists*" in his taxonomy of various positions.[18] Although some might simply be intention-skeptic, it should also be noted that some aestheticians exclude intentions from consideration in an aesthetic experience, especially in one having to do with art, based on non-intention-denying grounds. This may include concerns to have a "pure" experience by attending to more formal concerns, unclouded by artistic intent. I mention this because it need not be mere author-skepticism or authorial dismissal that creates an anti-intentionalist stance in aesthetics.[19]

Livingston's first response to anti-intentionalists whose anti-intentionalism is born of some sort of deep metaphysical skepticism or structuralist gesturing is that they themselves are not offering a coherent and comprehensive explanation of our ordinary, intuitive, practical experience of intention and its extension in artistic practice.[20] Secondly, he responds to a claim that artistic intentions might be so successful as to be hidden, or so unsuccessful that they remain unknown. The claim, which might be given by some anti-intentionalists, is found to be challenging only for some set of what the author calls absolute intentionalists, who might despair of losing sight of the author's real intentions. Livingston suggests a "partial or moderate intentionalism" which can account for meanings which arrive via all sorts of "linguistic conventions and contextual factors."[21] That some intentions remain unknown by merit of success or failure need not mean all are never known. Here is an extended quotation from Livingston which summarizes a minimal role of intention-recognition for the moderate intentionalist. Following Carroll,[22] he says:

> Intentionalist constraints on interpretation follow directly from basic norms of conversation and communication, said to be applicable to all (or at least most) appropriate art-interpretative projects. The background premiss here ought to be fairly uncontroversial: whatever your theory of linguistic meaning may be, it is correct to assume that one key goal in conversational exchanges is that the speaker's words be interpreted along the intended lines, and this through the recognition of the speaker's intentions. The basic idea, then, is that utterance meaning in conversational contexts is a function of linguistic conventions, contextual factors, and the speaker's meaning; given that the interpretation of art falls within the framework of conversation, it follows that the meaning of a work of art will be determined by the same combination of factors, including the speaker's (or writer's or artist's) intended meaning.[23]

Livingston adds that Carroll's conversation-*esque* view of art engagement is limited, and he goes on to add other supports (e.g., desirability of genuine understanding), but I include the above as demonstrating one sort of reasonable account of at least minimal support for the reality and receivability of intentions in works of art.

Again, I anticipate the reader with interest in originalism in legal and scriptural contexts will be benefited by the concise and precise discussion of artistic intentionalism in Livingston's work. My aim in introducing it here has been simply to introduce a well-reasoned defense, in aesthetics, of the ability and advisability of referring to artists' original meaning, or intentions, when addressing their work. At the end of chapter 6 of *Art and Intention*, the author gives nine motivations for acknowledging the role of intentions in works of art. They include positive motivations, such as the salutary role intention-awareness plays, such as the "explanatory and descriptive value" of dealing with intentions; its role in "interpretation," "evaluation," and "appreciation"; the aid it lends in developing a sophisticated understanding of how artists as agents create and communicate. At the close of his work, Livingston states,

> In spite of their fallibility, intentions regularly contribute decisively to the determination of the story a fiction conveys, which makes a difference for those readers and viewers *who want to understand the story told, as opposed to undertaking a new telling of their own.*[24]

Aesthetic intentionalism reminds us that works of art retain meaning and intention from their original creators, in their original conditions, which we may be informed by if we so choose. Someone may choose to completely ignore artists' meaning and intention as originally conceived. For one thought-provoking example, consider the punning reappropriation of artworks in the Pop Art era by figures like Andy Warhol, Eduardo Paolozzi, and Jasper Johns; or more recently, the viral use of internet memes which feature recognizable images repurposed for pithy—and often absurd—purposes. Part of the force of such media, it should be noted, is that even these reappropriations make use of original intent and meaning. Pop, memes, or any other playful use of artwork are depending on the communication of original ideas that are to be inverted, ironicized, or indicted. If the original artwork was not recognized for what it was (and is), then its reappropriation would not be provocative. Its original meaning has a dual existence: what the original creator meant, and what the re-appropriator now means by its inclusion.

In making this caveat about original intent being played with, we are already in a basic, broad realm of aesthetics. "Form" and "content" remain usefully simple ways of glossing the two spheres of aesthetic communication. By "form" we mean the elements of our aesthetic experience which inform our senses—the shapes, sounds, tastes, feels, or smells which compose a composition. As noted below, these are almost always presented to us in a meaningful whole, or arrangement. By "content" we mean the ideas which are communicated by the work, or experience, mainly by means of the forms. Of course, some of what makes art so meaningful to us is that form and content are not operating in isolation upon us. Aesthetic experiences are had by *us*; according to some fields of aesthetics, they are *our* phenomena. Mightn't that alone mean that they are impenetrably idiosyncratic, produced by us, the viewing subject, and not by the object? More about this form-level aesthetic worry in a moment. Aesthetic experiences are also colored by us, freighted with significance by our own memories, education, emotions, and so on. Mightn't that also mean we see only what we want them to show, painted by our personalities? Although I will return to this, the discussion above about intentionalism has gone some distance toward clarifying that—assuming we attend to them—artists' original intentions *can* be informative and formative for our understanding of their work.

On the formal side, we are touching on issues in aesthetics relating to a host of other issues, ranging from basic perception to higher identification. We can simply note the apparently brute fact that we all do have shared basic perception, assuming our faculties are functioning and well-formed. Readers in need of rational support may consider Kant's uptake of the classic idea of *sensus communis* in consideration of how our communication and creativity is connected by our commonly shared faculties and sensibilities.[25] Less philosophically, it is obvious that basic human experience of colors[26] and shapes are shared,[27] and every instance of visual communication ranging from symbols to advertisements is predicated on this reality.

Building on this basic awareness, there are also philosophical inquiries as to how we are able to imitate or depict content and ideas in the arts. As we share basic aesthetic faculties, we are able to create and communicate imitations of things, even complex scenes or events, which others are able to receive with understanding. This is easiest to see in the visual arts, where paintings or sculptures resulting from mimesis beguile the beholder into seeing the thing the artist was portraying. More mysteriously, music too can depict, even instrumentally (listen to Ralph Vaughan Williams's "Lark Ascending" or Nikolai Rimsky-Korsakov's "Flight of the Bumblebee"), albeit rather more inexpressibly than visual arts. Theater and film seem too obvious to mention, but they too depict, often so successfully that our "suspension of disbelief" is automatic. And texts depict scenes and thoughts which we realize mentally. At play in all of these is the notion of depiction.

Although depiction has intrigued writers as old as Plato and Confucius,[28] it continues to be explored by aesthetic philosophers today. Alberto Voltolini's *A Syncretistic Theory of Depiction* is a more recent, rigorous analytical discussion of what is taking place in our ability, as humans, to depict and to understand depictions.[29] Amidst the many helpful studies taking place in this work, Voltolini clarifies that just because our aesthetic experiences are subjectively processed, and somewhat subjectively determined as they occur to us, this does not mean they are not influenced by objects, or those objects' objective properties. Regarding how visual perception works, including occlusion, skewing, and other commonalities of perspective, Voltolini calls properties of objects that are affected by our experience of them "*weakly mind-dependent* properties."[30] We could say that, just because a square table changes in its visual shape as we change our position relative to the table, appearing at times as a square, rhombus, trapezoid, or even a rectangle (depending on our elevation and angle), this does not all mean that the table's equidistant sides, with corners of 90-degree right angles, no longer exist.

> One property may be taken to be mind-dependent insofar as it depends on a perspective or a way of perceiving: it changes whenever such a perspective or a way changes. Yet insofar as that perspective or way has a geometrical or optical character, that property is no less objective than non-perspectival properties of objects. One such property is still a property of the object that is grasped under such an orientation or perception and not a property of the subject that grasps such an object.[31]

While Voltolini recognizes that our aesthetic experiences shift with our perception, the experiences are perceived in part because of underlying or preexisting properties in the objects of our experience.

> Whichever way we look at it, this property [occlusion or outline shape] is surely mind-dependent: if the observer's point of view changes, the relevant occlusion or outline shape changes as well. Yet it is a property of objects, not of perceivers, for it is one of the objects' geometrical properties.[32]

Taken as a whole, the elements of our aesthetic experiences, including those had in experiencing a work of art, are not merely products of our subjective perception. We perceive objects, and these objects themselves have properties which communicate their existence to us.

Part of Voltolini's syncretistic method echoes elements of a preceding system, which aids our understanding of aesthetic meaning. This is the notion of "gestalt"—holistic compositions which constitute most of our aesthetic experiences. The idea of gestalt, which at its simplest is giving recognition to the fact that experiences are processed as complex wholes, rather than isolated elements, was inspired in part by findings in gestalt psychology, and later adopted by aestheticians.[33] While Voltolini mentions well-known analytic aesthetic philosophers such as Frank Sibley and Kendall Walton,[34] I have great affection for the writer Rudolf Arnheim, whose works triangulate psychology, aesthetic principles, and artistic practice in writings that are just as useful to theorists as they are to art practitioners.[35] As a trained illustrator, I find his practical principles to be compellingly descriptive of the way that artists and designers actually create and design, and the way that audiences encounter and make sense of creative works. In fact, the basic formal principles which unify theories of color and shape as shared by all people, mentioned above, partake of important gestalt ideas. A perusal of the literature in those areas uncovers the central role gestalt theories play in how we make aesthetic judgments.

Among the sorts of observations these writers make are those relating to our tendency to establish understanding by groupings and relationships among lines, shapes, and colors. Sometimes these relate to ideas of "grounding," where we establish background and foreground relationships, process depth, assess height, and determine overall positioning of elements in a scene or experience. Similar observations in perspective and positioning relate to occlusion, relative size, and placement in a perceived horizon. Similarities in color, sound, shape, and line are also shown to establish perceived relationships among entities that would appear to be discrete apart from an aesthetic perceiver.

Why is this important for art, and how can we it tie back into the discussion of intentionalism and originalism? First, acknowledging that perception is not entirely subjective, but occurs in relation to objective properties, helps establish a baseline avoidance of a sort of subjective aesthetic idealism. Second, acknowledging that our aesthetic perception and judgments take place along observable, describable lines of assessment like those of gestalt observations helps to show that aesthetic experiences should not be viewed as entirely idiosyncratic. We all follow human capacities of pattern recognition, among many other basic aesthetic principles. Connecting this to art: artists make use of these formal principles to create works of art. They employ techniques and methods which manage to "creatively express an idea" for others to experience. This is true of course, even for contemporary works which aim to be entirely abstract, accidental, or intentionally noncommittal in terms of content. They are still works of *creation*; they still *express* the intent of their originator—even if the intent was to create a space of silence (as in John Cage's well-known "4'33"). Artists instantiate their ideas through the use of aesthetic principles as commonplace as perception itself. And in turn, we, the audience, perceive and assess these experiences through the same means. Note too, that neither for the artist nor for the audience need this process be witting. It is highly likely that most people never think about occlusion, placement, or relative sizing when seeing the figures of the Sistine Chapel; nor is it necessary to think that Michelangelo had those principles actively in his mind as he painted. Perhaps he simply knew intuitively how to depict them. But in the case of both artist and audience, there is a language, unspoken though it may be, of formal aesthetic communication.

I have used the term "formal" in the last sentence to avoid, until now, conflating formal expression with expression of content. It is also helpful for us to hold in mind the orderliness of form even as we now turn to content once more. Since form is not invented by the perceiver, though it is affected by the perceiver (Voltolini's "weakly mind-dependent"), we cannot peg subjective-determinacy at the level of form. Even there, form has meaning. Gestalt theorists remind us that relationships of forms create understanding, just as letters create words—and even more primally at that, for no one has to teach us how to perceive the environment. But there is a grammar of aesthetic experiences nonetheless. Even the most abstract of our visual stimuli, like color and shade, are found to foreground themselves (warm colors), recede (cool colors), and establish distinctions (edge detection).[36] These formal elements are, of necessity, the vehicle in which content arrives for the observer.

We have already seen in Livingston's writings elements of an argument that intention in artworks, which wed both form and content, is a perfectly acceptable sort of thing to use for interpretation and enjoyment. The intentionality of an artist in their use of formal features is partly what is presented to us in the resulting work. They made decisions to use that color, this note, those arrangements, this style, that figure, and so on and so forth. We are perfectly justified to assess those choices as being meaningful and communicating something to those of us who view their work. I am speaking of minimal communication here, but of course a great deal more than minimal communication takes place. If you are able, spend a few moments looking at the artworks of Käthe Kollwitz, as many as possible, preferably *before* looking up her biographical details. I will not here say anything about this incredible woman that lived through the turn of the nineteenth to twentieth centuries, in the hopes that your own perusal of her artwork may give you an understanding of her life.

Assuming you take me up on such an invitation, you now have a ready-to-mind example of the issues we have been discussing. Without reading anything about the artist, a sense of what they were seeking to express is revealed by observation. All the way, from the barest aesthetic elements of formal choices, up to the figures and feelings described in a work of art, there is creative expression that communicates emotion and ideas. I am not purposefully stacking the cards with a figurative artist. We might look at Mark Rothko's "Orange and Yellow," Piet Mondrian's "Composition with Red, Blue, Yellow," or Dave Brubeck's "Take Five" and still argue that we recognize the artist was making some statement of some sort, a statement which is not born merely from our idea of it. They are "saying" something, sparse though it may be. Nor am I stacking the cards in choosing a rather simplistic set of artworks. Milton's *Paradise Lost*, Jacques-Louis David's "Coronation of Josephine," Beethoven's *Eroica*, Guo Xi's (郭熙) "Early Spring (早春图)", Zhang Zeduan's (张择端) "Along the River During Qingming (清明上河圖)," and countless others are making statements through a multitude of formal features, expressing complex content that is full of intentional expression.

Saying all of this does not cause us to lose sight of the fact that aesthetic experiences are meaningful to us, in part, because of what occurs within us subjectively. The senses, ideas, memories, emotions, and personal perspectives we bring to an aesthetic encounter or work of art also contribute to the experience. But acknowledging this truism in no way diminishes the formal and expressive content that comes to us from the intention of the artist. Whatever happens within us subjectively is provoked, in part, by the objective object of experience. For some readers, all of the foregoing may seem like a long string of truisms about their aesthetic experiences; but such a sentiment is not shared by everyone in the postmodern (and post-postmodern) period.

As noted earlier, for many people trying to think deeply, or philosophically, about art and aesthetics, those Enlightenment-inspired ideas (which have now surpassed their founders' versions) of mere subjectivity threaten to silence the sense the artists may have been seeking to convey. Poor reasoning from the facts that your taste differs from mine, that your idea of a work may not be my idea of a work, that her framework of interpretation is different from his, and such like, results for some people in the conclusion that shared truths about art and aesthetics are inaccessible, or impossible.[37] Rather than there being an illogical situation—namely, that two opposite truth claims are true at the same time—it is likelier that somewhere we have let slip Aristotle's sage advice, and we are no longer talking about the exact same thing at the same time in the same way. Where genuine disagreement arises, we may have recourse to sharing what elements of our own experience we are attending to in comparison with another person's, as good critics. Doing this does not undercut the utility of acknowledging the original meaning of an artist's work. These challenges, raised by an awareness of the impact of our subjective selves in aesthetics, are merely illustrative of the muddied waters we must navigate in reference to aesthetics, artworks, and even texts.

Having sailed fairly far from shore on the murky waters of aesthetics, we now must head back toward a discussion of such textual concerns as this volume treats.

RETURNING TO ORIGINALISM IN HERMENEUTICS

Analytical aestheticians like Livingston, Voltolini, Sibley, Walton, Arnheim, and a host of others have helped us recognize landmarks which let us keep the aesthetic object in view as we pursue our current comparison. But it is not analytic philosophers alone who have sought to counterbalance an overemphasis on solipsistic subjectivity. Although space does not permit an exploration, "continental" philosophers (a catchall for nonanalytical philosophers) from various narratives also champion attention to the object of aesthetic experience and what it has to say to us. A neo-Marxist like Walter Benjamin can insist on rigorous attention to media and means as a way of informing our aesthetic understanding,[38] and a phenomenologist like Maurice Merleau-Ponty can insist on acknowledging the undeniability of discussing our experience of a world which is not entirely a subjective projection of the disembodied mind.[39] So we appear to be in large company with those who would let the artwork or object of aesthetic experience address us as it is, rather than *merely* as we imagine it to be.

Since the argument I am making is meant to be a sort of mild *reductio*, it is really the claim of the opposite party—the objectivity deniers—which I have in view. Those who, for one reason or another, claim that *a work of art or object of aesthetic experience cannot be or should not be appraised with respect to its original form and content.* Preceding authors and arguments notwithstanding, this italicized phrase is descriptive of some theorists today. Such theories overlap with textual concerns of all sorts: historical, fictional, scriptural, and legal. Since we can establish that we *can* and likely *should* appraise works of art with respect to their original form and content, this will mean the same for texts.

The merit in looking at hermeneutics from a position of aesthetics is that the latter field is where subjectivity famously forms a background condition both of the actual experience and of all the prevalent theories (post-Enlightenment) that treat of it. In this last section I briefly touch on a few theories doubting or denying pretenses of objectivity or contact with original intent while highlighting simple dismissals of such, followed by a gathering of insights for use in hermeneutics.

A Few Forms of Denial and How to Deny Them

In the section above, on definitions of art, I mentioned Gordan Graham's excellent aesthetics primer, *Philosophy of the Arts*. In his closing chapter Graham pauses his normative approach to explaining the arts to look at opposing, definitional methodologies. As many of these handily form an "opposing party" to the claims of this argument (that original intent can and should be countenanced), I will use Graham's survey and response to touch on a few in the opposition. Beginning his survey of their theories, the author observes: "The highly influential ideas about *art and literature* described as Marxism, structuralism, deconstructionism or postmodernism purport to have revolutionized the subject in a way that makes philosophical aesthetics outmoded and renders it redundant."[40]

First, Graham assesses the institutional theory of art, which basically claims that art is art because art institutions recognize it to be so. Living in the age of bananas taped to walls as works of art worth hundreds of thousands of dollars, this theory has a certain appeal.[41] But it "suffers from circularity." Apparently there is an "artworld" which defines "art," but what defines the "artworld," other than its relation to "art," as yet undefined? Further, what of instances where such an artworld might be mistaken? Lastly, what of the "wider context" beyond such institutions as we think of them in developed countries—what of art outside galleries and museums?[42] The institutional theory of art might not have immediately evident overlap with scriptural and legal hermeneutics, but Graham himself makes comparison of it alongside of common law legal contexts. If it is true that some institutions (such as legal ones) adjudicate statuses, mightn't it be that art institutions do the same? In art, the quibble remains that there is something *in* the art, or *about* the art which is adjudicated. I might add to Graham's observations that there are also legal texts (statutes, laws, precedents) which also inform those adjudications.

Next, Graham addresses the somewhat nebulous region of Marxist aesthetic theory.[43] In an extensive discussion, the author explains that among Marxist theories of art the proposition was put forward that art was nothing more than a product of underlying sociological conditions (namely economic, and influenced by ideology). In turn, interpretation of art must rid itself of ideology and make use of science—all of which is "science" or "ideology" in Marxist senses of the words. In doing so, Graham points out (and Marxists like Bennet affirm), art itself disappears from view. There is no such thing. All that remains are ideological accretions. This is an odd impasse, and of course not all (or many) Marxist theorists follow through with their convictions. Graham lists those like Terry Eagleton (I would add the Neo-Marxist Walter Benjamin) who manage to wrestle with works of art, though even in doing so they "look beyond" the works to underlying social conditions. The obvious failure of such a view, if ever taken verbatim, is that the arts *must* be saying something for us to recognize some supposed ideology of which they are the products. I would add too that it says nothing of the pragmatic use of art by Marxists to propagandize,[44] giving the lie to the disappearance of art as an independent vehicle of communication. For textual theories, there is no reason why a dual recognition can not take place, in which contextual histories are sought for, while inscripturated meanings are also held sacrosanct. Such is usually the case of most classical hermeneutical practice already, Marxist or otherwise.

Graham then turns to structuralism, of the Levi-Strauss variety.[45] Observing that it had an outsized impact on literature, the author notes that it has similarity with Marxist approaches. The similarity is, in part, that both are seeking a system beyond, or beneath, the actual utterances with which we are dealing. Works of art, or texts, are instances of general structures operating in the various arts. I suppose this has similarities with the project of gestalt theorists, but with less practical precision. Rather than denying original intent, we might say (like Marxism) that it tended for some to distract from original intent, to see forces at work being manifested in works. I say "tended," for, as Graham points out, it has largely been replaced with the last theory.

At the time I am writing this, postmodernism and deconstruction are the favored methodologies which doubt that original intent both matters and is accessible. Graham's treatment of them is largely focused on the writers who promoted them, such as Jacques Derrida, J. Hillis Miller, Paul de Man, and Foucault.[46] Perhaps inspired by their effort to critique structuralism, writers like Derrida suggest that we have reached a point historically where there is a "rupture," or a break in our hermeneutics where we should no longer read or speak in a traditional framework of interpretation, or we are merely operating—trapped—within that traditional framework, and thus speak only of it and not of what we intend. It seems this is what he thought structuralists had done: felt the confines of the structures producing content, and yet remained trapped by the strictures of those structures. Graham has the patience to note that either Derrida's recommendation is impossible to do (to develop a new language without translating it from any preexisting language), or else that, on a more charitable account, Derrida calls us to

> use language in a different way, "knowingly," which is to say, conscious of its limitations. In other words, there is a way out of the linguistic "trap" if we stop trying to devise replacements for old theories and instead understand them in a different way.[47]

While those of us arguing for the role of original intention in texts and artworks likely laud the caution about letting theories determine our experience of the object (rather than the object itself), we likely lament the conclusion of Derrida and the deconstructionists that we must create our own "different way" of encountering the object. Put bluntly, for many in this camp the theories of others have simply been replaced with sheerly idiosyncratic personal theories, playing with the text rather than letting it play out itself, or play with us. I use the term "play" intentionally, for Derrida uses play (as Camus might use *volition* for his Sisyphus) as a rescue from despair: having lost all hope of ever knowing what a text is, in its originally intended self, we may at least enjoy what we make of it. "[T]he joyous affirmation of the play of the world and of the innocence of becoming, the affirmation of a world of signs without fault, without truth, and without origin which is offered to an active interpretation."[48] As Graham notes, such ideas have been taken up with vigor in textual circles in Anglophone spheres, and likely underly much of the current popularity of flatly denying the knowability of texts' original intent. I leave it to the reader to visit Graham's good and obvious responses to such lines of thought. It seems sufficient for the moment that such a view contains an inherent contradiction, as do many forms of applied skepticism: we must have some measure of certainty about a text to declare that our encounter with it is wrong; we must know something about it to claim that we know nothing about it, and that our play is merely *ours* and not the game put forth by the author in the first place. There is a sort of unintended arrogance in insisting that we might do anything with a text *except* read it as it was meant to be read.

A Few Gleanings from the Comparison

What can be gleaned from the foregoing, for the purposes of originalism in texts, both scriptural and legal? First, I believe there is strength in the *reductio* of defending our *ability* to discover original intent in works of art. This defense begins at the understandability and predictability of formal features, based upon objective properties and received with gestalt tendencies (to name a few glosses of such truths of experience). It continues at the level of content revealed in form, admitting awareness of artistic intent as a justified pursuit in understanding and appreciating art. If this can all be said in a field where subjectivity is a necessary feature, then surely it can be said in fields where there is promise of less subjectivity. If we need not shy away from discussions of "what the artists meant" while standing in a museum of modern art, staring at a banana, we need not shy away from discussions of "what the author meant" while reading Paul's letters to Timothy or the constitutional documents of a country.

Second, while the above is a mild *reductio* for the *ability* to make use of original intent, we can also see one here for the *advisability* of making use of original intent. As Livingston continuously reminds us in *Art and Intention*, there is no compulsion for the viewer of a work of art to seek out the originally intended meaning in a work of art. We might even have a very rewarding aesthetic experience without knowing anything about such concerns. But that being said, it is equally easy (for most non-theory-converted thinkers) to acknowledge that learning about original intent is highly enriching for many experiences of art. Consider the examples I requested you familiarize yourself with: the works of Käthe Kollwitz. If you haven't done so yet, the force of the earlier argument is now as risk (last chance, have a look!). You may well have encountered those works from the perspective of a fan of horror movies and the macabre; perhaps Lovecraftian terror is your passion, or body horror, or perhaps death-metal music resonates with your heartstrings. In any case, I can imagine some set of perspectives where you *might* view Kollwitz's works (a) highly personally, and (b) positively and joyfully. Upon realization, from biographical details, that Kollwitz lived through the horrors of war, suffering losses in her country, in her community, and in her own family as a mother, we are introduced to another perspective—that of the artist herself. Bearing this in mind, the intentions, meanings, significance, and signifiers in those artworks become transformed, even for the imaginary person whose initial approach was (a, b). There would be the realization that these works are not merely (a), and not originally (b). They are about *her*, about her experiences, about her human experiences; they are largely focused on the negative, the ugly, the pathos of suffering. Ignore for a moment the case of a selfish person who insists on their own interpretation of Kollwitz's works, or a challenged person who lacks the ability to appreciate their content and significance. For most of us, knowing more about the original intent in such artworks will be enriching. We gain in understanding, and we gain in appreciation. And for some, artworks hold the promise of being personally transformative through the engagement of oneself with an other self. All of this value and promise is lost when we lose sight of or interest in original intent. If this is true in a work of art, where there is neither harm nor foul in being highly (or entirely) subjective, it is also true in works which are written with express purposes of communicating objective truths. Doubtless there are other motivations for interpreting texts with attention to authorial intent, but this is a minimal defense from aesthetics.

Third, identifying the sources of the subjective elements of interpretation in aesthetics allows us to be mindful of them, with expanded awareness, in hermeneutics. Aesthetics treats of the subjective element both in the real, basic level of our phenomenological experience, corralling facts of sensation, perception, and aesthetic cognition. It also treats of the subjective element in the supposed, theoretical level, which seeks to make sense of the manners in which we treat art and aesthetic experience. The role of imagination, intuition, aesthetic distance, intersubjectivity, shared sense, incommunicability and communicability, perspective, association, gestalt, and so on all have fixity in aesthetic discourse because they seek to describe some genuine facets of our subjective experience of an object.[49] But even with these in mind, we need not lose sight of the properties of the object, its form, and the content it communicates, including intentional signs and significance as given by its original creator. Yet, having such conceptual vocabulary, given to us by aesthetic theorists, enables us to identify where our own intentions end and the original intentions begin. In other words, gaining precision in the awareness of the elements of subjective interpretation allows greater precision in the awareness of objective, original elements being interpreted. I suppose that, for some readers in biblical or constitutional hermeneutics, these may be new concepts. However, I also believe there is likely to be much overlap in basic hermeneutic practice. In any case, my hope is that hearing these issues described from another perspective, in another body of literature, will be enriching and will hold a few novelties for those untrained in the study of aesthetics.

Let's look at two brief examples, using the conceptual vocabulary above, of how these terms and concepts from aesthetic theory might fit in a context of biblical or legal texts. With "aesthetic distance" or "disinterest," we speak of the advisability (or inevitability, depending on the theorist) of approaching a work with an initial attitude which is free of selfish interest, or utilitarian aims. This is usually provisional and temporary, for we quickly gain an interest (literal and figurative) in the work. But it is generally recognized that the best initial appreciation and understanding takes place not only without preconceptions, but also without pre-*desires*. Interpreters of a biblical text who wish to find out what a passage *means* must attempt to momentarily divorce that idea from what it *means for them*. Interpreters of legal texts must approach the documents in pursuit of what the text *meant originally*, rather than what it will *mean contemporarily*. Again, this is a commonplace idea, but scholars of textual originalism will be enriched by tracing the insights arising around aesthetic distance and disinterest. And readers of all sorts can keep an eye on reining in their initial personal interest when approaching a text. Note that, in so doing, we are holding in tension both the subjective aspect of interpretation of a text as well as the importance of the original meaning as shaped by its author.

Another example is *gestalt* considerations, as described above. While texts do not always define their terms at the outset (though contemporary legal documents often do), definitions or meanings of individual terms will be partly determined by the context in which they are found. Just as a painting, song, sculpture, advertisement, or another work of art creates an arena or area of self-referential meaning, so do texts. While texts make use of vocabulary which is usually preexistent and thus arrive with meaning associations, so too do artworks and designs make use of formal features which have some preexistent meaning associations. Gestalt, design, and composition theories help us to see how such elements being employed can have their meaning affected by their place within the immediate scheme, composition, or context. There is a tension between the deployment of an element based on its preexistent meaning and its immediate meaning based on the context in which it appears. We can rightly ask what "blue" means in Impressionistic or in Song Dynasty landscapes by referring both to its preexisting meaning and to the meaning given to it in the particular setting of those epochs and their artworks. Turning to biblical interpretation, the term "body" in the New Testament has its own meaning produced by the interaction of its extra-biblical sense with the special use Paul makes of it. Turning to legal interpretation, words like "President" and "State" in the American Constitution have their own meaning produced by the interaction of their extra-constitutional sense and the uses the Constitution makes of them.

Biblical scholars will see this replicated with increasing specificity in biblical genres, individual books, and discrete passages or phrases. Legal scholars will likely find the extent of this application depending largely on the size of the text, whether the relatively brief case of the American Constitution or the relatively lengthier cases of Amendments to that document, but also in the wider context of legal documents crafted in the original's era. The takeaway from aesthetic similarities, especially with an eye toward subjectivity, is that a reader's own vocabulary must be open to a "stable dynamism": stable at the onset in that our preexisting knowledge of terms allows us to make sense of a text and understand why a term was deployed; dynamic in interpretation because we also must ascertain what a term means here; and stable in conclusion as we proceed with originalist/intentionalist confidence that the original author(s) intended to communicate meaning by means of the work as a holistic unit. The commonplace in hermeneutics that "context determines meaning" is true, but only if it retains the gestalt tension that terms are selected for use in a context due to their preexisting meaning yet also receive precise meaning in their immediate context. The balance of these two elements results in our understanding of a text. As in the earlier examples, the principles in which such a balance is discussed in aesthetic theories may enrich hermeneutic discussions. Note, finally, that in balancing the elements of such a gestalt, the individual reader's experience of a text matters alongside the importance of its original meaning as shaped by its author.

As noted throughout, my expectation is a number of aesthetic discussions of intentionalism and interpretation will provide new insights to originalism in textual hermeneutics.[50] While I believe these will parallel or overlap with discussions in both arenas, aesthetic discussions take place within a context where subjectivity is a given, but where it is not terminal. For those interpreters favoring originalism, whose opponents are likely to refer to subjective concerns as precluding such interpretations, aesthetic intentionalists and interpretive optimists should provide a refreshing and enlivening set of resources. Meanwhile, the fact that, even in aesthetics, we must pay attention to authorial contributions to textual meaning indicates that in the interpretation of legal and religious texts we will have to do the same.

CONCLUSION

Suppose someone proffers the casual rebuke that "you can't be sure that's what this text means. After all, it means one thing to you, and another to me. Therefore, there can't be any one meaning in such a text." The opening and closing assertions have nothing to do with the commonplace premise in the middle. That a text has multiple meanings *to us* does not entail that it has unknowable meanings as originally intended. In such a hypothetical rebuke, the word "can't" derails us. A text *can* mean something to you, and something to me, and yet it *can* retain its original meanings, there for the discovering should we choose to pursue it. Such discussion, as we have seen, is a commonplace in aesthetics. In aesthetics, we are well aware that art admits of multiple meanings to viewers, without that admittance having anything to do with the meaning(s) of the original. Intentionalism in aesthetics, as overlapping with concerns of originalism in hermeneutics, develops the language needed for putting these two spheres of meanings in their proper perspective. I think engagement of aesthetic theories of interpretation and hermeneutic theories of interpretation could be a growth area for research, and perhaps some of the ideas indicated briefly above could be explored in more depth in the future.

In fact, I would suggest that this is one of the benefits of engaging aesthetic philosophical theories with the theories of hermeneutics as practiced in theological and legal settings. It is likely that most readers are aware of the continuing impact that philosophers in aesthetics have had in contemporary thinking. What likely appeared to be *mere* aesthetics in the Enlightenment era—Hume's work on taste, Kant's work on aesthetic judgment—has grown (or tumesced, depending on one's perspective) into a subjective shift which has left the world of hermeneutics wrestling with the simplest of suppositions: that a text can be read, that an author can communicate, that ideas as originally conveyed can and should be known. Heading back toward the origins of those aesthetic theories can help clarify the role of subjectivity in interpretation as we navigate the currently muddied waters of interpretation, and diving down into the development of reasonable aesthetic theories, then and now, allows us to discover that there is a solid foundation beneath our understanding after all.

NOTES

1. Interestingly, in aesthetic intentionalism Paisley Livingston has suggested "textualist intentionalism" as a possible position which may overlap somewhat with Boone's textualism. See the discussion in the second section of this chapter as well as Paisley Livingston, *Art and Intention: A Philosophical Study* (Oxford: Oxford University Press, 2005), chapter 6.

2. Future engagement of textual originalism that makes room for amendment with aesthetics would likely benefit from some of the aesthetic discussions of "versions" (What do we mean by something being a "version" of an original? What constitutes version-ality?) and "reproduction" (not merely Neo-Marxist critiques of capital-concerns, but also the effect on audience by means of repetition and surfeit), both of which are treated by Walter Benjamin, "The Work of Art in the Age of Mechanical Reproduction," trans. Harry Zohn. 1935, https://www.marxists.org/reference/subject/philosophy/works/ge/benjamin.htm.

3. Intriguingly, this connection between discernment via the bodily senses is seen clearly in the Greek New Testament, at the Epistle to the Hebrews, chapter 5 and verse 14, in the context of judgments of *taste* as a spiritual metaphor: τελειων δε εστιν η στερεα τροφη των δια την εξιν τα αισθητηρια γεγυμνασμενα εχοντων προς διακρισιν καλου τε και κακου. Westcott and Hort (1881).

4. Alexander Gottlieb Baumgarten's eighteenth-centry *Aesthetica,* a Latin text (*Aesthetica* [Hildesheim: Georg Olms, 1986]), set up aesthetics as a proper field

within philosophy, but any reader of classical philosophy western (e.g., Aristotle's *Poetics*) or eastern (e.g., Liu Xie, *The Literary Mind and the Carving of Dragons : A Study of Thought and Pattern in Chinese Literature*, trans. Yu-chung Shih [New York: Columbia University Press, 1959]) will see aesthetic concerns are a commonplace within philosophy. See also, Kai Hammermeister, *The German Aesthetic Tradition* (New York: Cambridge University Press, 2002), and the excellent discussion at "aesthetic," *Online Etymology Dictionary*; https://www.etymonline.com/word/aesthetic.

5. Jonathan Johnson, "Aesthetics of Play," in *Philosophy's Arena: Play and Players in a Gamified World*, ed. Jeremy Sampson (Delaware: Vernon Press, 2024).

6. In some languages, such as Chinese and Japanese, "aesthetics" could be read literally as the "study of beauty" (美学).

7. Jonathan Johnson, "The Anatomy of Ugliness: Locating the Experience of Aesthetic Negativity," PhD Dissertation, Hong Kong Baptist University, 2019. Stepping out on increasingly personal limbs, I add that "successful art" can "powerfully express the great truths of human experience," and that "great art" should "elevate the observer to ennobling contemplation."

8. Gordon Graham, *Philosophy of the Arts: An Introduction to Aesthetics*, 3rd ed. (London: Routledge, 2005), chapter 9, "Theories of Art."

9. Building on general reasonings about the arts and aesthetic experience, writers like David Hume (e.g., David Hume, "On the Standard of Taste," in *The Philosophical Works of David Hume*, ed. T. H. Green and T. H. Grose, Vol. 3 [1757 reprint London: Longman, Green, 1874–75]); Edmund Burke, *A Philosophical Enquiry into the Origin of Our Ideas of the Sublime and Beautiful* (London: R. and J. Dodsley, 1757, reprinted Harmondsworth: Penguin, 1999); and especially Immanuel Kant, *Critique of the Power of Judgment*, trans. Paul Guyer and Eric Matthews, ed. Paul Guyer (1790, reprint Cambridge: Cambridge University Press, 2000) developed the current vocabulary for how we speak about the arts. Most of the terms italicized above were birthed or inspired in the nativity of modern aesthetics during the eighteenth century. Although Burke's work strived for empiricism, and Hume's was inspired by it, these writers were largely rationalizing our experience of art and aesthetic inputs—proto-phenomenologists, as it were—but without the attention I believe actual artists could have shared. As every beginning art and design student knows, while the subjective description of our aesthetic experience resonates with these writings, our objective practice is readily communicable. More on this in the second section of this article.

10. Kieran Setiya, "Intention," in *The Stanford Encyclopedia of Philosophy* (Winter 2022 Edition), ed. Edward N. Zalta and Uri Nodelman, https://plato.stanford.edu/archives/win2022/entries/intention.

11. G. E. M. Anscombe, *Intention* (Oxford: Oxford University Press, 1957). Soon after Donald Davidson would further frame the discussion in his essay, originally from 1963. For a newer reprint, see Donald Davidson, "Actions, Reasons, and Causes," in *Essays on Actions and Events*, 3–20 (Oxford: Oxford University Press, 1980).

12. For example, see Stoutland's contextual introduction to Anscombe's impact in philosophy of action. Frederick Stoutland, "Introduction: Anscombe's *Intention* in Context," in *Essays on Anscombe's Intention*, ed. Anton Ford, Jennifer Hornsby, and Frederick Stoutland (Cambridge, MA: Harvard University Press, 2011), 1–22.

13. Here it should be acknowledged that texts, when viewed as literary works, may fall under the auspices of aesthetics as well. I address this inevitability in this chapter's close.

14. Livingston, *Art and Intention.* Another analytic aesthetician is Nick Zangwill, as seen in Nick Zangwill, "The Creative Theory of Art," *American Philosophical Quarterly* 32 (1995): 315–332.

15. See too, in Livingston, *Art and Intention*, chapter 1 ("What Are Intentions?") his noting of a few senses of realism (even of the naïve sort, glossed here as relating to a view called by Horgan and Graham "southern fundamentalism") or anti-skepticism (as G. E. Moore's), which, problematic though they may be in themselves, do direct us towards a sense of the burden of comprehensibility or "consistency" for anti-realist, anti-intentional claims. See Terence Horgan and George Graham, "In Defense of Southern Fundamentalism," in *Folk Psychology and the Philosophy of Mind*, ed. Scott M. Christensen and Dale R. Turner (Hillsdale, NJ: Lawrence Erlbaum, 1993), 288–311.

16. Livingston, *Art and Intention.* In the Kindle edition, locations 550–553. In chapter 2, subsection "The Roles of Intention."

17. Cf. Peter Lamarque, "The Death of the Author: An Analytic Autopsy," *British Journal of Aesthetics* 30, no. 4 (1990): 319–331.

18. Representative of this group, he cites William K. Wimsatt and Monroe C. Beardsley, "The Intentional Fallacy," *Sewanee Review* 54, no. 3 (1946): 468–488; reprinted in *On Literary Intention: Critical Essays*, ed. David Newton-De Molina (Edinburgh: Edinburgh University Press, 1976), 1–13. Other members of the taxonomy are given as: *absolute intentionalism, anti-realist absolute intentionalism, fictionalist intentionalism, moderate fictionalist intentionalism, textualist intentionalism, conditionalist intentionalism*, and *moderate, constrained*, or *partial intentionalism.*

19. Some within this position might be called "volitional anti-intentionalists," in that they could be seen as willfully setting aside, ignoring, or choosing to "look beyond" whatever intentions might threaten to derail the aesthetic experience.

20. Structuralism in language was a popular philosophical movement that largely affected linguistics, and eventually the liberal arts—both domains overlapping with hermeneutical concerns. For a concise treatment, see Graham, *Philosophy of the Arts*, 235–238.

21. Livingston's taxonomy here (see note 18, above) and the discussion of each position, may prove further enlightening for the discussion of originalism in theological and legal hermeneutics. It is likely that absolute intentionalism will be attractive to some originalists in the legal realm, both due to the precision and the brevity of legal texts (such as the Constitution) and the judicial weight resting upon the minutiae; alternatively, the attraction for scriptural hermeneutics may be theological, in reference to notions of inspiration or theological value; yet the counterbalance for a text such as the Christian scriptures will be the literary nature of the corpus, incorporating genres of

literature that overlap with artistic and aesthetic considerations. This latter reality may make the aesthetic discussion more germane to the theological than the legal texts.

22. Livingston here echoes Noël Carroll, "Art, Intention, and Conversation," in *Intention and Interpretation*, ed. Gary Iseminger (Philadelphia: Temple University Press, 1992), 97–131.

23. Livingston, *Art and Intention*, Kindle location 1791–1794. From chapter 6, subsection "Claims and Counterclaims." In Livingston's text, the line "*given that the interpretation of art falls within the framework of conversation*" is italicized, which I have undone, so as to let the entire quote share the burden of emphasis, and likely undoing some of the *intention* of the author's immediate emphasis on Carroll's less-than-convincing conversational framework.

24. My italics, for emphasis. Livingston, *Art and Intention*, Kindle location 2469, at the close of "Conclusion," within Chapter 7, "Fiction and Fictional Truth."

25. Kant, *Critique of Judgment*, 40, "On Taste as a Kind of *Sensus Communis*."

26. For example, in practice, see Janet Best, Editor, *Colour Design: Theories and Applications*, 2nd ed. (Cambridge: Elsevier, 2017); in higher theory, see George Pavlidis, *A Brief History of Colour Theory: Foundations of Colour Science* (Cham: Springer International Publishing, 2021).

27. For example, see William Lidwell, Kritina Holden, and Jill Butler, *Universal Principles of Design, Revised and Updated: 125 Ways to Enhance Usability, Influence Perception, Increase Appeal, Make Better Design Decisions, and Teach through Design* (Beverly, MA: Rockport Publishers, 2010), or Colin Ware, *Visual Thinking for Design* (Amsterdam: Elsevier, 2008).

28. I give these two well-known figures as representative only. Consider Plato's *Republic*, Books II and III, in which imitation does not seem to come out so well (yet, contrast Plato's imitative skill everywhere); see also Confucius's love of the arts, utilitarian though we might fear it to be, both in poetry and music as discussed in the *Analects* (论语); see section 阳货 (Yang Huo).

29. Alberto Voltolini, *A Syncretistic Theory of Depiction* (New York: Palgrave Macmillan, 2015).

30. Voltolini, *A Syncretistic Theory of Depiction*, 50.

31. Voltolini, *A Syncretistic Theory of Depiction*, 50.

32. Voltolini, *A Syncretistic Theory of Depiction*, 51.

33. Often Christian von Ehrenfels is identified as one of the leaders in this field of psychology.

34. Frank Sibley, "Aesthetic and Nonaesthetic," *The Philosophical Review* 74, no. 2 (1965): 135–159 and Kendall Walton, "Categories of Art," *The Philosophical Review* 79, no. 3 (1970): 334–367. See also Voltolini, *A Syncretistic Theory of Depiction*, around pages 128 and 242.

35. Rudolf Arnheim, *Art and Visual Perception: A Psychology of the Creative Eye* (Berkeley: University of California Press, 1954) and *The Power of the Center: A Study of Composition in the Visual Arts* (Berkeley: University of California Press, 1982).

36. My own aesthetic training is in studio arts, which are a visual field. But music theorists have much to say about harmonies, disharmonies, and the ways in which

chords, progressions, and musical elements in their smallest groupings still communicate expressively. Note too that our sense of meaning, formally, arrives in relation of elements with one another. Once I heard an apparent aesthetic meaning-nihilist plunk a key on a keyboard and ask something like, "There! What does that mean?" For those of us arguing for meaning in aesthetic elements, our interest begins where all aesthetic experience begins: elements in relation with one another.

37. Although Kant goes to great lengths to establish his own quasi-certainty in aesthetic judgments, based on shared faculties, we may also lay some blame at his feet for setting up antinomies of aesthetics: He argues that on the one hand, we feel aesthetic judgments strongly and surely, with personal certainty; but that on the other hand, we find that discussions with others about the same experience are rife with disagreements. I believe a large amount of clarity in such areas can be found when both disputants are enabled to explain what elements and what gestalts are in view when they are making their judgments, and why. Just because a high level of expertise or experience is called for does not mean the task of clarifying common experiences is impossible.

38. For examples, see Benjamin, "The Work of Art in the Age of Mechanical Reproduction"; Anca Pusca, "Walter Benjamin, a Methodological Contribution," *International Political Sociology* 3, no. 2 (2009): 238–254; Jonathan Johnson, "From Modernity to Memes: Reexamining Visual Culture as a Christian Vessel," in *Religious Change in Asia*, ed. J. Derrick Lemons and Shun-hing Chan (Amsterdam: Amsterdam University Press, forthcoming); or, as a practitioner of Benjamin's methodology, John Berger, *Ways of Seeing* (London: Penguin Books, 1972).

39. Maurice Merleau-Ponty, *The World of Perception*, trans. Oliver Davis (London: Routledge Classics, 2009).

40. My italics, for emphasis on the shared fields of "art and literature." Graham, *Philosophy of the Arts*, 221.

41. At the time of this writing, there is a small uproar in the art world as a university student unwittingly (or wittingly?) ate a banana—"an iconic work by Italian artist Maurizio Cattelan"—that was taped to a museum wall. As the story goes, the student claimed hunger, and not provocation, as a motive. This is the second time the work ("sold for $120,000 at Art Basel Miami Beach in December 2019") has been eaten. Another artist, David Datuna, staged his own performative art by eating an earlier iteration (the bananas are apparently refreshed regularly, and taped back to their various walls). This raises plenty of philosophical fodder for discussion, considering the original intent of the work by Cattelan, the appropriated intent by the performative eater Datuna, and the current master of riposte, an unknown Korean university student. Rob Picheta and Jacqui Palumbo, "Student Eats Artwork of a Banana Duct-taped to a Museum Wall because 'He Was Hungry'," in *CNN Style*, online; May 2023, https://www.cnn.com/style/article/student-eats-maurizio-cattelan-banana-art-south-korea-intl-hnk/index.html.

42. Graham, *Philosophy of the Arts*, 228–229.

43. Graham, *Philosophy of the Arts*, 230–235.

44. See, for example, Mao Zedong's comments on the use of art for revolutionary purposes. Zedong Mao, *Talks at the Yenan Forum on Art and Literature*, 1st ed. (Peking: Foreign Languages Press, 1956).

45. Graham, *Philosophy of the Arts*, 235–238.
46. Graham, *Philosophy of the Arts*, 238–243.
47. Graham, *Philosophy of the Arts*, 240.
48. Jacques Derrida, *Writing and Difference*, trans. Alan Bass (London: Routledge, 1990), 294. As cited in Graham, 241.
49. I have not spelt out what these specialized terms in aesthetics mean, but I do imagine their study could be of use for technical hermeneutics, and seeing how much, and to what extent, they might apply to bodies of scriptural and legal texts.
50. See especially endnotes 2, 13, 18–19, 21, and 49.

WORKS CITED

"aesthetic." *Online Etymology Dictionary*. https://www.etymonline.com/word/aesthetic.

Anscombe, G. E. M. *Intention*. Oxford: Oxford University Press, 1957.

Aristotle. *Poetics*.

Arnheim, Rudolf. *Art and Visual Perception: A Psychology of the Creative Eye*. Berkeley: University of California Press, 1954.

———. *The Power of the Center: A Study of Composition in the Visual Arts*. Berkeley: University of California Press, 1982.

Baumgarden, Gottlieb. *Aesthetica*. Hildesheim: Georg Olms, 1986.

Benjamin, Walter. *The Work of Art in the Age of Mechanical Reproduction*, translated by Harry Zohn, 1935. https://www.marxists.org/reference/subject/philosophy/works/ge/benjamin.htm.

Berger, John. *Ways of Seeing*. London: Penguin Books, 1972.

Best, Janet, Editor. *Colour Design: Theories and Applications*, 2nd ed. Cambridge: Elsevier, 2017.

Burke, Edmund, *A Philosophical Enquiry into the Origin of Our Ideas of the Sublime and Beautiful*. London: R. and J. Dodsley, 1757, reprinted Harmondsworth: Penguin, 1998.

Carroll, Noël. "Art, Intention, and Conversation." In *Intention and Interpretation*, edited by Gary Iseminger, 97–131. Philadelphia: Temple University Press, 1992.

Confucius. *The Analects*.

Davidson, Donald. "Actions, Reasons, and Causes." In *Essays on Actions and Events*, 3–20. Oxford: Oxford University Press, 1980.

Derrida, Jacques. *Writing and Difference*, translated by Alan Bass. London: Routledge, 1990.

Graham, Gordon. *Philosophy of the Arts: An Introduction to Aesthetics*, 3rd ed. London: Routledge, 2005.

Hammermeister, Kai. *The German Aesthetic Tradition*. New York: Cambridge University Press, 2002.

Horgan, Terence and George Graham. "In Defense of Southern Fundamentalism." In *Folk Psychology and the Philosophy of Mind*, edited by Scott M. Christensen and Dale R. Turner, 288–311. Hillsdale, NJ: Lawrence Erlbaum, 1993.

Hume, David. "On the Standard of Taste." In *The Philosophical Works of David Hume*, edited by T. H. Green and T. H. Grose, Vol. 3. 1757, reprint London: Longman, Green, 1874–75.

Johnson, Jonathan. "The Anatomy of Ugliness: Locating the Experience of Aesthetic Negativity." PhD Dissertation, Hong Kong Baptist University, 2019.

———. "Aesthetics of Play." In *Philosophy's Arena: Play and Players in a Gamified World*, edited by Jeremy Sampson. Delaware: Vernon Press, 2024.

———. "From Modernity to Memes: Reexamining Visual Culture as a Christian Vessel." In *Religious Change in Asia*, edited by J. Derrick Lemons and Shun-hing Chan. Amsterdam: Amsterdam University Press, forthcoming.

Kant, Immanuel. *Critique of the Power of Judgment*, translated by Paul Guyer and Eric Matthews, edited by Paul Guyer, 1790, reprint Cambridge: Cambridge University Press, 2000.

Lamarque, Peter. "The Death of the Author: An Analytical Autopsy." *British Journal of Aethetics* 30, no. 4 (1990): 319–331.

Lidwell, William, Kritina Holden, and Jill Butler. *Universal Principles of Design, Revised and Updated: 125 Ways to Enhance Usability, Influence Perception, Increase Appeal, Make Better Design Decisions, and Teach through Design.* Beverly, MA: Rockport Publishers, 2010.

Livingston, Paisley. *Art and Intention: A Philosophical Study.* Oxford: Oxford University Press, 2005.

Mao, Zedong. *Talks at the Yenan Forum on Art and Literature*, 1st ed. Peking: Foreign Languages Press, 1956.

Merleau-Ponty, Maurice. *The World of Perception*, translated by Oliver Davis. London: Routledge Classics, 2009.

The New Testament in the Original Greek. Westcott and Hort edition. 1881.

Pavlidis, George. *A Brief History of Colour Theory: Foundations of Colour Science.* Cham: Springer International Publishing, 2021.

Picheta, Rob and Jacqui Palumbo. "Student Eats Artwork of a Banana Duct-taped to a Museum Wall because 'He Was Hungry'." In *CNN Style*, online, May 2023. https://edition.cnn.com/style/article/student-eats-maurizio-cattelan-banana-art-south-korea-intl-hnk/index.html.

Plato. *Republic*, translated and edited by Chris Emlyn-Jones and William Predd. Cambridge, MA: Harvard University Press, 2013.

Pusca, Anca. "Walter Benjamin, a Methodological Contribution." *International Political Sociology* 3, no. 2 (2009): 238–254.

Setiya, Kieran, "Intention." In *The Stanford Encyclopedia of Philosophy* (Winter 2022 Edition), edited by Edward N. Zalta and Uri Nodelman. https://plato.stanford.edu/archives/win2022/entries/intention/.

Sibley, Frank. "Aesthetic and Nonaesthetic." *The Philosophical Review* 74, no. 2 (1965): 135–159.

Stoutland, Frederick. "Introduction: Anscombe's *Intention* in Context." In *Essays on Anscombe's Intention*, edited by Anton Ford, Jennifer Hornsby, and Frederick Stoutland, 1–22. Cambridge, MA: Harvard University Press, 2011.

Voltolini, Alberto. *A Syncretistic Theory of Depiction*. New York: Palgrave Macmillan, 2015.

Walton, Kendall. "Categories of Art." *The Philosophical Review* 79, no. 3 (1970): 334–367.

Ware, Colin. *Visual Thinking for Design*. Amsterdam: Elsevier, 2008.

Wimsatt, William K. and Monroe C. Beardsley. "The Intentional Fallacy." *Sewanee Review* 54, no. 3 (1946): 468–488, reprinted in *On Literary Intention: Critical Essays*, edited by David Newton-De Molina, 1–13. Edinburgh: Edinburgh University Press, 1976.

Xie, Liu. *The Literary Mind and the Carving of Dragons : A Study of Thought and Pattern in Chinese Literature*, translated by Yu-chung Shih. New York: Columbia University Press, 1959.

Zangwill, Nick. "The Creative Theory of Art." *American Philosophical Quarterly* 32 (1995): 315–332.

Chapter 3

The Torah Is Not in Heaven

Living Originalism and Political Integrity in the Oven of Akhnai

Daniel Weissglass

Constitutions require interpretation.[1] To ensure that some action is coherent with the demands of a text, we need to make an effort to understand what, precisely, that text demands. Developing such an understanding, in turn, requires not just that we interpret the text—but that we interpret it correctly. However, the appropriate interpretation of constitutional texts is not trivial, and long-standing substantive debates about the appropriate methods for constitutional interpretation attest to the complicated relationships between laws, legislators, and the legislated.

In this chapter, I explore a Talmudic story—the Oven of Akhnai—and draw out morals it provides for constitutional interpretation. First, I review the story of the Oven of Akhnai, which will provide an exegetical background from which the remainder of the chapter will be drawn. Second, I will argue that the Torah, in Talmudic discussions, functions as a constitution for the Jewish polity and that the Oven of Akhnai presents a striking rejection of straightforward notions of originalism in the interpretation of that constitution. Third, I show that the context and characters of the Oven of Akhnai does not endorse a simple non-originalism, but instead hews closely to living originalism[2]—a leading contemporary model of constitutional interpretation. Fourth, I argue that, so conceived, the finale of the Oven of Akhnai provides a useful way of understanding constitutional interpretation in living originalism—that constitutional interpretation serves to promote political integrity—and that this understanding is supported by deep similarities in the conceptual frameworks underlying living originalism and political integrity. Finally, I sketch some possible advantages of this way of understanding things for both living originalism and political integrity, with an eye to the promise of future work exploring this intersection.

THE OVEN OF AKHNAI

The Oven of Akhnai is a Talmudic[3] story recording a debate between several great rabbis about whether a certain kind of oven might become ritually impure. During this otherwise unremarkable legal discussion, trees will walk, a voice will ring from heaven, a great rabbi will be forbidden to ever again argue before the Sanhedrin, and another will die as a result of the former's grief and anger.

All of these remarkable events, however, emerge from an astonishingly technical dispute about whether a cooking vessel of a certain construction is capable of becoming ritually impure:

> If one cut an earthenware oven widthwise into segments, and placed sand between each and every segment, Rabbi Eliezer deems it ritually pure. Because of the sand, its legal status is not that of a complete vessel, and therefore it is not susceptible to ritual impurity. And the Rabbis deem it ritually impure, as it is functionally a complete oven. (BM 59a12)[4]

The question is roughly one about whether physical continuity or contribution to a single function make something a single object, a metaphysical dispute given practical importance due to halakhic prescriptions about pure and impure objects.

This otherwise technical and abstract legal issue becomes the center of extraordinary happenings as R. Eliezer, frustrated at the failure of his legal arguments or at the failure of his colleagues to recognize their truth, appeals to a series of miracles to compel his colleagues to see the wisdom of his position.

> And this is known as the oven of akhnai. The Gemara asks: What is the relevance of akhnai, a snake, in this context? Rav Yehuda said that Shmuel said: It is characterized in that manner due to the fact that the Rabbis surrounded it with their statements like this snake, which often forms a coil when at rest, and deemed it impure. The Sages taught: On that day, when they discussed this matter, Rabbi Eliezer answered all possible answers in the world to support his opinion, but the Rabbis did not accept his explanations from him.
>
> After failing to convince the Rabbis logically, Rabbi Eliezer said to them: If the halakha is in accordance with my opinion, this carob tree will prove it. The carob tree was uprooted from its place one hundred cubits, and some say four hundred cubits. The Rabbis said to him: One does not cite halakhic proof from the carob tree. Rabbi Eliezer then said to them: If the halakha is in accordance with my opinion, the stream will prove it. The water in the stream turned backward and began flowing in the opposite direction. They said to him: One does not cite halakhic proof from a stream.

> Rabbi Eliezer then said to them: If the halakha is in accordance with my opinion, the walls of the study hall will prove it. The walls of the study hall leaned inward and began to fall. Rabbi Yehoshua scolded the walls and said to them: If Torah scholars are contending with each other in matters of halakha, what is the nature of your involvement in this dispute? The Gemara relates: The walls did not fall because of the deference due Rabbi Yehoshua, but they did not straighten because of the deference due Rabbi Eliezer, and they still remain leaning.
>
> Rabbi Eliezer then said to them: If the halakha is in accordance with my opinion, Heaven will prove it. A Divine Voice emerged from Heaven and said: Why are you differing with Rabbi Eliezer, as the halakha is in accordance with his opinion in every place that he expresses an opinion? (BM 59b1–4)

The Sanhedrin has held its ground in the face of remarkable happenings, but with this final appeal, R. Eliezer has called the voice of God itself to testify on the matter of the law—and receives a testimony in his support. We might expect that this would settle the matter, but that is not what happens:

> Rabbi Yehoshua stood on his feet and said: It is written: "It is not in heaven" (Deuteronomy 30:12). The Gemara asks: What is the relevance of the phrase "It is not in heaven" in this context? Rabbi Yirmeya says: Since the Torah was already given at Mount Sinai, we do not regard a Divine Voice, as You already wrote at Mount Sinai, in the Torah: "After a majority to incline" (Exodus 23:2). Since the majority of Rabbis disagreed with Rabbi Eliezer's opinion, the halakha is not ruled in accordance with his opinion. The Gemara relates: Years after, Rabbi Natan encountered Elijah the prophet and said to him: What did the Holy One, Blessed be He, do at that time, when Rabbi Yehoshua issued his declaration? Elijah said to him: The Holy One, Blessed be He, smiled and said: My children have triumphed over Me; My children have triumphed over Me. (BM 59b5)

God may speak, but a divine voice has no standing in the Sanhedrin on matters of law. The halakha is not in Heaven, but in the majority opinion of the assembled scholars of the Sanhedrin. Just as remarkable as the rabbis' defiance of God's voice here, God accepts their rejection as wholly appropriate—seemingly endorsing that he does not have the right to rule on halakha.[5]

Despite, then, a truly remarkable performance of miracles, R. Eliezer will lose the debate. Further, he will also lose his position in the Sanhedrin.

> The Sages said: On that day, the Sages brought all the ritually pure items deemed pure by the ruling of Rabbi Eliezer with regard to the oven and burned them in fire, and the Sages reached a consensus in his regard and ostracized him. And the Sages said: Who will go and inform him of his ostracism? Rabbi Akiva, his beloved disciple, said to them: I will go, lest an unseemly person go

and inform him in a callous and offensive manner, and he would thereby destroy the entire world.

What did Rabbi Akiva do? He wore black and wrapped himself in black, as an expression of mourning and pain, and sat before Rabbi Eliezer at a distance of four cubits, which is the distance that one must maintain from an ostracized individual. Rabbi Eliezer said to him: Akiva, what is different about today from other days, that you comport yourself in this manner? Rabbi Akiva said to him: My teacher, it appears to me that your colleagues are distancing themselves from you. He employed euphemism, as actually they distanced Rabbi Eliezer from them. Rabbi Eliezer too, rent his garments and removed his shoes, as is the custom of an ostracized person, and he dropped from his seat and sat upon the ground. (BM 59b6–7)

R. Eliezer is banned from the Sanhedrin, due to his insistence—here and elsewhere—on his own halakhic interpretations over those of the Sanhedrin. This ban would last, according to tradition, until the eve of R. Elizer's death, where it would be removed—despite R. Eliezer's continuing refusal to accept his colleagues' rulings. He would never again sit in the study hall and debate halakha, and even his beloved and devoted students would distance themselves from him—a distance which pained all and involved the loss of great knowledge about the Torah.[6]

Perhaps unsurprising, as we have seen R. Eliezer's ability to summon miracles,[7] R. Eliezer's grief is marked by supernatural happenings:

The Gemara relates: His eyes shed tears, and as a result the entire world was afflicted: One-third of its olives were afflicted, and one-third of its wheat, and one-third of its barley. And some say that even dough kneaded in a woman's hands spoiled. The Sages taught: There was great anger on that day, as any place that Rabbi Eliezer fixed his gaze was burned.

And even Rabban Gamliel, the Nasi of the Sanhedrin at Yavne, the head of the Sages who were responsible for the decision to ostracize Rabbi Eliezer, was coming on a boat at the time, and a large wave swelled over him and threatened to drown him. Rabban Gamliel said: It seems to me that this is only for the sake of Rabbi Eliezer ben Hyrcanus, as God punishes those who mistreat others. (BM 59b8–9)

The effects of R. Eliezer's grief are profound and of global significance; even another great sage—R. Gamliel, the highest-ranking member of the Sanhedrin—is placed at risk of harm as a result:

Rabban Gamliel stood on his feet and said: Master of the Universe, it is revealed and known before You that neither was it for my honor that I acted when ostracizing him, nor was it for the honor of the house of my father that I acted; rather, it was for Your honor, so that disputes will not proliferate in Israel. In response, the sea calmed from its raging. (BM 59b9)

As Gamliel meant not to enhance his honor by humiliating a rival, but to honor God by maintaining the unity of the people of Israel, Gamliel was spared from the wave.[8]

AKHNAI, CONSTITUTIONALISM, AND THE TORAH

The Oven of Akhnai is not only a fascinating and dramatic story, but also the source of significant insights into Jewish jursiprudence.[9] However, to understand the story as one about constitutional interpretation requires that we first establish that the Torah functions, in Talmudic disputes, as a constitution—and that the Oven of Akhnai should be understood as involving a dispute about how best to interpret that constitution. On the way to establishing this, I will introduce important components of the Jewish understanding of the Torah that will help to make sense of the morals of the Oven of Akhnai.

The Torah is the central religious doctrine of Judaism, consisting of both a written text and oral tradition. Both written and oral Torah are understood by orthodox believers to have been presented to Moses during the revelations which occurred on Mount Sinai. The division between the written and oral portions of the Torah is itself significant, with the written portions having been commanded to be written, and the oral portions having been expressly forbidden to be so.[10]

Those familiar with the Torah may find it strange to consider the possibility of its being a constitution. Certainly, the Torah does contain within it a great many laws and rules. However, it also contains stories—a mythohistorical account of the Jewish people and their origins. Even where it does include laws, some of these laws seem far too narrow and particular to be aptly considered constitutional, such as Lev. 19:19, which forbids cross-breeding cattle, planting more than one kind of seed in a given field, and wearing mixed fabrics.

However, the Torah accomplishes two important things which are sometimes taken to be definitive of constitutions as such. First, a constitution legislates the political and governmental practices of a polity by defining the powers and limitations of its governmental organs as well as the legal status of persons. The Torah clearly satisfies these substantive requirements of a constitution. It addresses the relative authority of the components of the state, including monarchs, priests, judges, and prophets. In doing so, it goes so far as to establish some degree of a separation of powers. Likewise, it establishes the legal status of various categories of people. Second, it contains laws which are fundamental to the polity, as well as in some sense prior to most everyday laws.[11] While there may be a number of particular and peculiar laws which are far too specific to satisfy constitutional considerations in the Torah, it is also the source of the basic laws—such as the Ten Commandments, as well as those structuring the polity mentioned above—that ground Jewish practice. That is, despite the large amount of nonconstitutional content and the nonconstitutional roles it may play in establishing a mythological core, the Torah also serves a constitutional function by constituting and structuring the Jewish polity.

Given that the Torah functions as the constitution of the Jewish polity, we can see that the Oven of Akhnai provides a somewhat surprising verdict about the authority of the founder of that constitution (i.e., God). During a debate about the proper interpretation of the Torah, God directly explains that the interpreting authorities are making a mistake. This, however, is set aside as irrelevant to the proper interpretation of halakha. That is, the founder has no say in interpreting the constitution of the Jewish people.

The Oven of Akhnai, then, is a straightforward rejection of straightforward originalisms—positions which argue that the proper interpretation of a constitution requires fidelity to the work of the founders. This fidelity might require that we respect the intent of the founders when they wrote the law, the meaning that the law would have had to its intended audience, or some other interpretive practice which seeks to find the founders within the text. However, all originalisms share a prioritization of the purposes and practices of the founders in determining what a constitution requires.[12]

Especially remarkable is that the Oven of Akhnai presents circumstances which are immune to the sorts of worries usually used to object to originalist approaches. Originalism, especially original intent originalism, has suffered due to concerns that the relevant facts about the founders' intent or meaning might be irrecoverable, or that the founders may have erred and written a law which means something other than their intention.[13] These concerns do not apply with an infallible founder speaking directly to the judiciary. We know what God intended, we know that God did not err in writing the law or in interpreting what was written, and we need not worry about any crosscurrents of conflicting authorial intentions muddying interpretive waters. And yet, the story tells us, the matter is decided against the founder—a decision which even the founder deems appropriate. In this regard, we can take the Oven of Akhnai to present a limit case against which to test originalist ideas in Jewish jurisprudence. Even when the evidence of the original meaning is absolute, and when the founder cannot possibly be wrong, we are not bound to it. Whatever God might have meant or said is secondary to the decision of the Sanhedrin.

A natural interpretation of this story is as an endorsement of a sort of formalist non-originalism: any interpretation made in the appropriate way is the correct one, even if it knowingly undermines the original intent of the text. Such interpretations, in fact, have been made.[14] By such an account, that the rabbinical council has followed the appropriate interpretive practice, through majority decision, is all that matters for determining the correct interpretation. Even with the support of all other things, including the voice of God, R. Eliezer's position fails because it does not conform to proper legal practice.

However, this interpretation struggles to make sense of the emphasis which the rabbis of the Sanhedrin place on citing Torah passages in the defense of their view. Were they arguing that the text has no status in limiting interpretation, it is unclear why they would turn to the text to defend this view. It is worth, then, a deeper exploration of the passages cited.

The first passage cited is Deuteronomy 30.[15] The most relevant part of this passage seems to be lines 9 through 14, copied below with the cited phrase italicized:

> You, however, will again heed God and obey all the divine commandments that I enjoin upon you this day. And your God will grant you abounding prosperity in all your undertakings, in your issue from the womb, the offspring of your cattle, and your produce from the soil. For God will again delight in your well-being as in that of your ancestors, since you will be heeding your God and keeping the divine commandments and laws that are recorded in this book of the Teaching—once you return to your God with all your heart and soul.
>
> Surely, this Instruction which I enjoin upon you this day is not too baffling for you, nor is it beyond reach. *It is not in the heavens*, that you should say, "Who among us can go up to the heavens and get it for us and impart it to us, that we may observe it?" Neither is it beyond the sea, that you should say, "Who among us can cross to the other side of the sea and get it for us and impart it to us, that we may observe it?" No, the thing is very close to you, in your mouth and in your heart, to observe it.

This passage arises in context of prolonged discussion of the terms in which the commandments of the Torah are given to the Israelites in their covenant with God. It suggests that the keeping of the commandments does not, itself, require more than is humanly possible.

R. Yehoshua cites this passage to demonstrate the divine revelation is irrelevant to matters of halakha. A fairly straightforward way to understand his reasoning is that the fact that the commandments can be humanly obeyed requires that they can be humanly understood. As such, we can know that divine revelation is not necessary to understand the Torah—and so may have no place in the discussion of halakha. Importantly, this passage as a whole might be taken as a rejection specifically of the need for persons to perform supernatural acts to clarify halakha. Interpreted in this way, the passage undermines the significance of R. Eliezer's summoning of the divine voice, preventing it from standing as evidence in halakhic debate.

The second passage cited is Ex. 23:2 and occurs in context of a number of prohibitions and commandments relating to fair and just conduct. The passage can be translated as follows, with the text cited in the Talmudic story italicized: "You shall neither side with the multitude[16] to do wrong—you shall not give perverse testimony in a dispute so as to pervert it *in favor of the multitude*."

The use to which R. Yirmeya puts this passage is somewhat perplexing, as it seems to contradict the obvious meaning of the text—which seems to reject precisely the sort of majoritarian principle which R. Yirmeya wishes to establish. One interpretation of the text which makes sense of this citation is by interpreting the passage from Exodus as establishing limits on a general majoritarian principle, rather than as rejecting majoritarianism. We can find such an interpretation in another Talmudic passage:

> From the implication of that which is stated: "You shall not follow a multitude to convict" (Exodus 23:2), I would derive that I may not convict a person on the basis of a majority but I should follow the majority to exonerate. If so, why is it stated in the same verse: "To incline after a multitude," from which it can be understood that the majority is followed in all cases? In order to resolve the apparent contradiction it must be explained: Your inclination after the majority to exonerate is not like your inclination after the majority to convict. Your inclination after the majority to exonerate can result in a verdict by a majority of one judge. But your inclination after the majority to convict a transgressor must be by a more decisive majority of at least two. (San 2a16)

This passage suggests that we take the phrase in Ex. 23:2 translated alternatively above as "side with the multitude" and "in favor of the multitude," to express an endorsement of majoritarianism in its second mention—where it does not include the negation contained in the first. The rest of the passage is then taken to insist that we limit ourselves to following the majority when they incline us toward gentler or less troubling ends. Similarly, we might think the passage should be understood chiefly as placing limits on a general principle of majoritarianism—specifically meaning joining evil majorities or bearing false witness to serve a majority. Understood in this way, R. Yirmeya cites this passage expressly to acknowledge the limits of majoritarianism while still insisting on the importance of the majoritarian principle in the current case.[17] In either case, the decision of the Oven of Akhnai seems unlikely to fall into the sort of case where we should reject majoritarianism—there is no clear reason to think their decision is itself an evil, the court itself doesn't seem evil, and no one is giving false testimony.[18]

If the Sanhedrin simply wished to establish total freedom in interpreting the text of the Torah, the turn to the text seems peculiar. Instead, this suggests that the Sanhedrin's interpretive authority is, in fact, grounded in the text itself.[19] This has been likened to a position in the theory of constitutional interpretation called "living originalism," which aims to square intuitions about fidelity to the original text with those about the need for flexibility and adaptation.[20] A key piece of living originalism, and the source of its analogy to the Oven of Akhnai, is that the founders of the US intentionally created a system in which later generations would be responsible for interpreting the content of constitutional law, and in which much of their own views would be disregarded in favor of those of present generations.[21] In the following section, I will argue that this analogy in fact goes deeper than has been previously noted, and that living originalism and the jurisprudence expressed in the Oven of Akhnai are deeply and meaningfully similar.

LIVING ORIGINALISM AND THE OVEN OF AKHNAI

Living originalism holds that the provisions of the US Constitution can be divided into three categories: rules (e.g., the minimum age of the president), standards (e.g. a prohibition on arbitrary search and seizure), and principles (e.g., the free exercise of religion). Rules are concrete, and are concrete precisely because constitutional authors wish to constrain future generations. In the interpretation of rules, we should lean toward originalism—interpreting the text as closely as possible as we might to the understanding of the founders. Standards and principles are abstract, and are abstract precisely because constitutional authors wish to leave the implementation of those standards and principles flexible enough to adapt to changing circumstances and values. In interpreting standards and principles, we should lean toward a view of the Constitution as "living"—interpreting the text as closely as possible in line with the contemporary understanding of the concepts which underly them.[22]

Critically, and in sharp contrast with other originalist positions, living originalism suggests that we ought to interpret standards and principles in line with the moral attitudes of the present, even when such interpretation results in something which might have been rejected by the founders. This, however, is true because it was the will of the founders that the text be interpreted in this way, so even this is carrying forward a form of originalist thinking.[23] We can see, then, thc similarity to the argument of the Sanhedrin in Oven of Akhnai: they are entitled to interpret the Torah, even contrary to God, because this is precisely what the Torah charges them to do.

Previous work has suggested that there is an important disanalogy between living originalism and the jurisprudential implications of the Oven of Akhnai in that the first has a clear position with respect to the status of precedent, while the second does not.[24] Living originalism views precedent as being only weakly binding and takes an evolving interpretation of the law to be a fulfillment of—rather than a rejection of—the relevant constitution. In contrast to originalisms which focus on the original expected applications of constitutions and their provisions, living originalisms see the exercise of interpretation in line with contemporary values and serving as a fundamental enaction of the constitution.[25] The Oven of Akhnai, this work suggests, has no such implication.[26] However, there is good reason to take the Oven of Akhnai to imply such an approach to precedent, and to think that such an approach to precedent is appropriate to Jewish jurisprudence more broadly.

Talmudic stories are not strictly historical. In the case of the Oven of Akhnai, for instance, the inclusion of R. Yirmeya is a certain anachronism, as he was from a much later period than the other speakers.[27] This suggests that we need to understand these stories not merely as legal debates, but as literary devices in which figures represent not (only) their historical views but also broader ideological positions. If we consider this literary element, then the ostracization of R. Eliezer carries clear consequences for the significance of precedent—as R. Eliezer is consistently represented as a masterful scholar, a scrupulous moralist, a stubborn opponent, and—most importantly—a staunch traditionalist. A brief review of Talmudic accounts of his character will demonstrate how closely identified he became with traditionalist thinking.

R. Eliezer is said to have modeled his conduct after his teacher (Suk28a4), R. Yohanan ben Zakkai, about whom it is said:

> In all his days he never engaged in idle conversation; and he never walked four cubits without engaging in Torah study and without donning phylacteries; and no person ever preceded him into the study hall; and he never slept in the study hall, neither substantial sleep nor a brief nap; and he never contemplated matters of Torah in alleyways filthy with human excrement, as doing so is a display of contempt for the Torah; and he never left anyone in the study hall and exited; and no person ever found him sitting and silent, i.e., inactive; rather, he was always sitting and studying; and only he opened the door for his students, disregarding his own eminent standing; and he never said anything that he did not hear from his teacher; and he never said to his students that the time has arrived to arise and leave the study hall except on Passover eves, when they were obligated to sacrifice the Paschal lamb, and Yom Kippur eves, when there is a mitzva to eat and drink abundantly. (Suk28a4)

R. Eliezer does not seem to reject such characterization. When pressed to describe his own character—notably as an explanation for his refusal to answer questions about halakha regarding issues that his teacher had not spoken on—R. Eliezer uses much of the same language to describe himself that the Talmud uses to describe his teacher:

> Now you forced me to say a matter that I did not hear from my teachers, as I must describe my character traits and the manner in which I conduct myself.

> In all my days, no person ever preceded me into the study hall, as I am always first to arrive; and I never slept in the study hall, neither substantial sleep nor a brief nap; and I never left anyone in the study hall and exited, as I was always last to leave; and I never engaged in idle conversation; rather, I discussed only necessary matters or matters of Torah; and I never said anything that I did not hear from my teacher. (Suk28a3)

Together, these passages convey several important themes of R. Eliezer's character. R. Eliezer is established as a dedicated scholar, enamored with his teacher, who is devoted to developing only what his master has taught. He aims to mirror his teacher not just in belief but also in his very character.

This thorough effort at emulating his teacher was noticed, and R. Eliezer's teacher says of R. Eliezer that he is "a plastered cistern which loses not a drop" (PA 2.8). Even from his teacher's view, R. Eliezer is a remarkable receptacle of tradition. This earns R. Eliezer great esteem in his teacher's eyes, with his teacher saying that "if all the sages of Israel were on one scale of the balance and Rabbi Eliezer ben Hyrcanus on the other scale, he would outweigh them all" (PA 2.8).

R. Eliezer makes clear, in other passages, that his traditionalism is not merely the idiosyncrasy of a worshipful student, but a moral expectation he has of students in general:

> One who prays behind his rabbi and one who greets his rabbi without waiting for his rabbi to greet him first, one who returns his rabbi's greeting without saying: Greetings to you, rabbi, one who rivals his rabbi's yeshiva, i.e., establishes a yeshiva of his own and teaches during his rabbi's lifetime without his consent (Rambam), and one who says something in the name of his rabbi which he did not hear directly from his rabbi, causes the Divine Presence to withdraw from Israel. (Ber 27b2)

This imparts a clear moral message—that one must defer to one's master on all matters of halakhot and tradition, and that the role of a student is to capture the wisdom of their masters and carry it forward. In doing so, it shows that R. Eliezer isn't simply a thorough traditionalist, but that he sees being such a traditionalist as an essential demand of a student. Students, R. Eliezer contends, ought humbly to absorb the teachings of their teacher. That he holds such a view is reinforced in R. Eliezer's discussion with his former students on his deathbed, at the end of a long period of ostracization which would have prevented his students from studying with him:

> Rabbi Eliezer said to them: Why have you come? They said to him: We have come to study Torah, as they did not want to say that they came to visit him due to his illness. Rabbi Eliezer said to them: And why have you not come until now? They said to him: We did not have spare time. Rabbi Eliezer said

> to them: I would be surprised if these Sages die their own death, i.e., a natural death. Rather, they will be tortured to death by the Romans. Rabbi Akiva said to him: How will my death come about? Rabbi Eliezer said to him: Your death will be worse than theirs, as you were my primary student and you did not come to study.
>
> Rabbi Eliezer raised his two arms and placed them on his heart, and he said: Woe to you, my two arms, as they are like two Torah scrolls that are now being rolled up, and will never be opened again. I have learned much Torah, and I have taught much Torah. I have learned much Torah, and I have not taken away from my teachers, i.e., I have not received from their wisdom, even like a dog lapping from the sea. I have taught much Torah, and my students have taken away from me, i.e., they have received from my wisdom, only like the tiny amount that a paintbrush removes from a tube of paint. (San 68a4–5)

Here, in a short space, we see R. Eliezer convey several remarkably traditionalist ideas: that past generations have greater wisdom than the present, that failing to learn from your teacher is a failure, and that this failure is so severe as to warrant a death painful in proportion to the failure.

This emphasis on tradition extended, as we might expect, to matters of interpretation. When, during his ostracization, R. Eliezer inquires with a former colleague about what has been happening in the Sanhedrin, he is told that the Sanhedrin has voted on a matter of tithing. To this, R. Eliezer responds:

> Go and tell them: Don't worry about your voting. I received a tradition from Rabbi Yohanan ben Zakkai who heard it from his teacher, and his teacher from his teacher, and so back to a halachah[28] given to Moses from Sinai, that Ammon and Moab must give tithe for the poor in the seventh year. (Yad 4.3)

That is, tradition decided matters of halakha, and the votes of the Sanhedrin are irrelevant.[29]

R. Eliezer, then, is persistently portrayed as a traditionalist in all ways. Students should seek chiefly to emulate their teachers, who are superior to them in wisdom. Failure to do so is a moral failure, and one which should be punished. And we can know the meaning of halakha from tradition alone, without any need for the Sanhedrin to make its interpretations.

It is no stretch to interpret R. Eliezer, then, as a representative and embodiment of a jurisprudence which depends on submission to tradition received from previous generations. His ostracization from the community in the Oven of Akhnai, then, can be understood as a repudiation of such traditionalism. Current generations, in interpreting the Torah, must be free to go beyond what was taught to them by their teachers and to seek out new understandings.

This conclusion is compatible with the broader tradition of Jewish jurisprudence, where a high value is given to flexibility in the law. The prohibition against the writing of oral Torah, itself probably a rabbinic invention,[30] is often justified by arguing that oral transmission allows greater flexibility for (re)interpretation of the halakhot,[31] and a protection against "a static, rigid posture that may stem from fixed textual formulations that may impede dynamic implementation."[32] Such a position seems deeply compatible with the position of living originalism, which holds that "precedents should be modified or discarded if they are no longer reasonable constructions of text and principle, and especially if they have become deeply unjust and unworkable."[33] The broader interpretive tradition of Jewish law also suggests a preference for seeing the revision of precedent as being in line with basic halakhic practice. The authority of past interpretation during ongoing interpretations remained a controversial thing throughout most of the Jewish history, with some arguing that more recent scholars should be considered more authoritative—as they have access to both the reasoning of the ancients and their own thoughts.[34]

All of this suggests that Jewish jurisprudence, especially as communicated in the story of the Oven of Akhnai, is amenable to something very much like living originalism. The founders (God) have delegated authority in interpreting the constitution (the Torah) to the current generation (the Sanhedrin). While those interpretations should be informed by precedent and history (tradition and past interpretations), they need not comply with them—and might overturn them when necessary. This is not a process of practical concession to the needs of governance, but a fundamental feature of the system of governance itself. That is, these are not just useful mistakes in interpretation, but the proper function of the interpretive system developed by the founders—the development of which was the key function of the constitution.

Of course, it is worth noting significant disanalogies between the jurisprudential position of the Oven of Akhnai and living originalism. Living originalism has several commitments which are either contrary to or unsupported by the context of the Oven of Akhnai. One key difference is that living originalism is meant to be a theory of interpretation aimed at the general population,[35] while the Oven of Akhnai explores interpretation in context of a formal court—the Sanhedrin. The Oven of Akhnai itself, then, seems to provide relatively little guidance about a critical focus of living originalism.

A second key difference is that living originalism is meant to operate within a purportedly secular, sovereign state, while the Oven of Akhnai operates chiefly within a religious community governed by Roman imperial authorities. Living originalism is deeply interested in "state-building" constructions, whereby the constitution would be interpreted not just through judicial decisions but through the development of the various institutions and powers of the state.[36] While the Sanhedrin, at various points, was entrusted with secular authority—and the boundary between religious and secular authority is itself vague—it was not, at the time of the Oven of Akhnai, an organ of a sovereign power and was therefore unable to engage in such constructions. This might result in the Sanhedrin's rulings seeming a rather narrow and limited set of constitutional interpretations, leaving us without much of the surrounding context which living originalism is well-designed to explore. At the least, this leaves us not able to take full advantage of the insights of living originalism in this context.

Finally, a key component of living originalism is the role of constitutional interpretation in promoting democratic legitimacy, meaning that "it allows the members of the political community to govern themselves and makes government action accountable to the public will, public values, and public opinion."[37] Even if we make the necessary changes to adapt this concept to a system with the limited secular authority exhibited by the Sanhedrin, we ought not read such a democratic commitment into the Oven of Akhnai—or Talmudic jurisprudence writ large. While the Oven of Akhnai endorses a majoritarian principle, that is a principle for determining debates among an elite group, not among the general population—and it would be a mistake to take the story to indicate a broader democratic spirit in Talmudic Judaism.

However, despite these differences, living originalism's conception of constitutions is one that would likely recognize the Torah as such. Living originalism focuses on constitutions as legal constructs which have served as "basic," "higher," and "our" law. "Basic" law resembles the substantive demands made of constitutions above; they dictate a stable structure and framework for governance that " allocates rights, duties, powers, and responsibilities."[38] It requires a system of laws which will allow the polity to continue to function. We have already seen, above, that the Torah satisfies the demands of basic law. "Higher" law is "a source of inspiration and aspiration, a repository of values and principles."[39] The Torah certainly serves such a function in Jewish culture broadly, and so it seems also to satisfy this criterion. For something to be "our" law, we must "view it as our achievement and the product of our efforts as a people, which involves a collective identification with those who came before us and with those who will come after us."[40] It is hard to imagine anything more central to Jewish identity than the Torah, and its role in creating a sense of cultural continuity within Judaism is undeniable. Accordingly, it seems that the Torah does satisfy the requirements of a constitution as laid out by living originalism.

TALMUDIC INSIGHTS: INTEGRITY AND LIVING ORIGINALISM

A key challenge is how to make sense of living originalism stripped of this commitment to democratic legitimacy. Some hope for doing so is that living originalism does not take democratic legitimacy to be the peculiar end of constitutional interpretation. Constitutional interpretation is only one component of a larger set of political institutions which promote democratic legitimacy.[41] To the extent that we might separate practices by their intended ends, then we might say that constitutional interpretation—to be distinct from the broader political practices of democratic legitimacy—must have some distinct end of its own. An alternative candidate for the end of constitutional interpretation is fidelity, the keeping with the intent of the founders. As understood by living originalists, fidelity implies strict interpretations of rules and creative interpretations of principles and standards—because the choice of a strict rule implies an intent to restrict discretion, while the choice of vaguer standards or principle implies an intent to direct future discretion without restricting it.[42] However, fidelity is presented chiefly as a limit on the bounds of acceptable interpretations, not the goal of interpretation itself. Given that the living originalist's conception of fidelity is one in which there may be multiple fidelitous interpretations of a given passage, it is, in fact, hard to see how it would function as the end of constitutional interpretation—as it could not seem to guide interpretation in such cases.

This, however, only reveals a second problem—it isn't entirely clear, on the living originalist's conception—what constitutional interpretation is meant to do. It is clear that the interpretation of the US Constitution is meant to promote democratic legitimacy, and that good interpretations are bound by principles of fidelity. However, none of this provides a distinct account of the ends of constitutional interpretation itself.

Here, the Oven of Akhnai is again a helpful source. When, on the sea, R. Gamliel is confronted with a great storm because of his ostracization of an honored colleague, Gamliel calls out to God that he knows this storm has come upon him as a result of his ostracizing R. Eliezer, but that he did not ostracize R. Eliezer out of vanity or pride, but that so "disputes would not proliferate in the land of Israel." The storm then subsides, indicating that God took R. Gamliel's justification to be sufficient.

In this passage, R. Gamliel can be understood not simply as speaking in his own defense, but of offering an account of the demands of jurisprudential practice—an account which God finds at least sufficiently compelling to halt the storm. If R. Gamliel's relatively extreme course of action with respect to R. Eliezer is justified, it seems that the urgent need to prevent the "proliferation of disputes" is sufficient to limit the boundaries of acceptable jurisprudential practice. R. Eliezer was ostracized not due to his refusal to accept a particular ruling—but because his dependence on divine revelation and refusal to accept majority rule represented a threat to the unity of the Jewish people.

We can understand R. Gamliel's concern for the unity of the Jewish people more clearly in context of the historical moment in which they were made.[43] At this point in Jewish history, the Jewish community was under serious threat. In this period after a failed revolt of the Jewish people against Roman authority, the Jewish polity was at risk of dissolution. The temple had been destroyed, the people scattered, authorities killed, and political systems destroyed. Disputes had become common, severe, and difficult to resolve. The Jewish polity was under threat from without by Roman imperial power, within by sectarianism, and—in a twilight space between within and without—the rise of Christianity as both a distinct faith and an alternative interpretation of Jewish texts.[44] If we construe R. Gamliel and the Sanhedrin as responding to these threats, we can see that what he is suggesting is not an end to debate—an objective impossible to achieve and contrary to the scholarly tradition of Judaism—but to preserve the unity of the Jewish polity. We can permit disagreement about the halakhot, but we cannot permit the leaders of the community to promulgate different Torahs—and thereby create different Judaisms. So the matter must be settled, and majority rule is the way that settlements will be reached.

We might consider this concern as being one chiefly of the survival of the Jewish polity. Were disputes to continue and sectarianism to worsen, the Jewish community might simply collapse and be absorbed by surrounding political systems. However, I do not think it likely that survival by any means and with any creed would be considered sufficient by R. Gamliel. It is not just the maintenance of any polity which concerns R. Gamliel, but the maintenance of the Jewish polity. The survival of the Jewish polity as such requires not simply the survival of its constituents nor the continuation of secular power structures or systems of government but rather the persistence of its character as a *Jewish* polity. Were this not his concern, R. Gamliel and the Sanhedrin might have discarded prohibitions and principles which placed them in opposition to Roman rule and enforced an acculturation. However, this did not happen, and much of the Talmudic work focuses on retaining and refining Jewish distinctness.

R. Gamliel, we can say, aims to preserve the integrity of the Jewish polity—and it is precisely this which I take to be the distinctive function of constitutional interpretation. "Integrity" generally describes a property of agents who act according to those projects, commitments, values, beliefs, and so on which they take to ground their identity. Maintaining one's integrity is taken by proponents of the concept to be itself normative, and we may find that one rightly pursues a course of action which fails some other standard—utilitarianism being one prominent in recent work,[45] though deontological reasoning is not less vulnerable—because doing so is essential for maintaining integrity. Recent work has generalized the concept of integrity to include the notion of political integrity.[46] By taking polities to be collective agents, we can apply nearly the same standards to determine their integrity as we do in the individual case.[47]

To make sense of what integrity demands of a polity, we need to specify the identity-grounding commitments of the polity, and this is the function I recommend we understand constitutions—of the sort described by living originalism—to have. In providing basic and higher law, a constitution specifies the procedures and values which become identity-grounding commitments as the constitution is recognized by the polity as "our" law. That is, we can take a constitution to specify a set of potential identity-grounding commitments, which are made the grounds of an actual identity through the recognition of the law by the polity as being their own. Constitutional interpretation, including not just legal determinations but also the project of carrying out the constitution, then becomes a matter of maintaining political integrity. As the constitution creates a polity and defines its character through the articulation of principles, the establishment of powers, the demarcation of citizens, and so on—the end of constitutional interpretation is to preserve and advance the integrity of the polity so constituted.

There are two reasons I believe that the notion I am here attributing to R. Gamliel—that the integrity of the polity should be understood as the end of, and guide for, jurisprudential practice—provides a worthwhile perspective on living originalism. The first of these is a deep compatibility between the two, powerfully demonstrated by the fact that living originalism and recent work on political integrity share core commitments, foundational assumptions, and even general ways of speaking. The second is that each may usefully clarify the other—living originalism provides a useful way of understanding the identity-grounding commitments of a polity, while integrity provides a useful way of understanding the proper limits of interpretive practice within a living originalist framework.

The compatibility between living originalism and political integrity is demonstrated in several ways. Work on living originalism makes repeated reference to particularly important commitments and takes remaining in touch with those commitments a key demand on successful interpretation. The structural features of the US judicial system to which living originalists credit interpretive constraint are considered valuable because they keep "judicial decisions in touch with popular understandings of our Constitution's basic commitments,"[48] suggest that "[t]he conversation between past commitments and present generations is at the heart of constitutional interpretation,"[49] and argue that for a constitution to be "our law" requires that it "allow us to identify our present principles and commitments with the principles and commitments of those who lived before us"[50] and that "[it] must be more than a law created by framers that binds us in the present; it must also be a law that connects our present political aspirations and commitments with the aspirations and commitments of previous generations."[51]

While work on political integrity has less to say about constitutional interpretation, due in large part to its being interested in a broader set of political concerns for a broader set of polities (i.e., not restricted to those having a constitution of the sort specified by living originalists), it does mention that one way for a polity to articulate its commitments is for them to be "enshrined . . . in its current constitution."[52] This work also argues that "a U.S. President who has not bothered to master even the U.S. constitution fails integrity's requirement of reflectiveness to a truly extraordinary extent,"[53] where the reflectiveness required of a politician is that they think carefully about whether the policy principles for which they stand are justified.[54] This suggests that any US president ought to stand for, and consider themselves as standing for, the principles of the US Constitution, and thereby suggests that these principles are central commitments of the US polity. It is not unreasonable, then, to take those working on political identity to be open to a constitutional account of the identity-grounding commitments of a polity.

The connection goes rather deeper, in fact. Living originalists talk about the importance of political institutions in building out the Constitution, while proponents of political identity discuss the importance of identity-grounding institutions—institutions which include legal protections which are, at least in the United States, established by the Constitution. Both theorists make much of the success of recent generations in creating more liberal societies, and emphasize the importance of understanding these as being fulfillments of the Constitution (for living originalists) or political integrity (for proponents of political integrity). Both are chiefly interested in liberal democracies, and both are interested in the impact of larger political movements in bringing changing notions of our constitutional/identity-grounding commitments.[55] This all suggests to me that living originalists and proponents of political integrity would, or should, find plausible that constitutional interpretation should and does aim at the promotion of political integrity.

INTEGRITY AND INTERPRETATION: FUTURE WORK

I have argued here that the Oven of Akhnai suggests a jurisprudence broadly in line with a form of living originalism which takes constitutional interpretation to be directed toward political integrity. In this process, I have shown a number of aspects of the Talmudic story which suggest that this is a reasonable interpretation and argued that the overall frameworks of living originalism and political integrity have a great deal in common. However, perhaps the most interesting result is the possibility that the Oven of Akhnai provides us with a useful way of thinking about the relationship between constitutional interpretation and political integrity, one which might be applied to resolve challenges faced by both theories.

For the proponent of political integrity, finding a connection between living originalism and political integrity carries a number of benefits. Living originalism provides a clear case where integrity can and should be understood as having a distinct moral significance, helping to respond to so-called "fifth-wheel" objections about the value of integrity as independent of other moral considerations. Notably, "all-things-considered morality" would seem to provide an implausible account of constitutional interpretation. Taking an all-things-considered morality approach to constitutional interpretation would amount to suggesting that we ought to interpret the Constitution in whatever way it might have the best overall moral consequences, regardless of the consequences of doing so for political integrity.[56] This, however, seems deeply implausible as it discards the significance of historical and textual factors in constitutional interpretation. Even Dworkin's "moral reading" of the Constitution, understood in its most unoriginalist formulations, is more constrained than this—it asks us to interpret the Constitution in light of abstract moral principles expressed by the document itself, and there only where doing so is necessitated by the use of abstract moral language.[57] To take the task of constitutional interpretation to demand fidelity only to "all-things-considered morality" is to completely negate the importance of fidelity to the text and to liberate us—for better or worse—from anything which might genuinely be considered "interpretation." The core concept of integrity, then, seems to capture a normatively significant aspect of constitutional language which fifth-wheel objections simply cannot. We might see this benefit most clearly, however, by turning to the benefits that integrity would grant to the living originalist.

The first benefit of joining living originalism to political integrity for the living originalist is that integrity highlights an important feature of constitutional interpretation which might otherwise be neglected—its connection to political identity. At least for polities with constitutions satisfying the tripartite constitutional standard of living originalism (i.e., that it provide basic, higher, and "our" law),[58] placing integrity at the center of constitutional interpretation reinforces that constitutional interpretation is not just a practice of interpreting a legal text important to a polity, but a matter of interpreting and constructing that polity's identity. This helps to make sense of the fervor surrounding constitutional interpretation in such polities, especially when that fervor may seem excessive in comparison to the consequences of the interpretive question. While constitutional interpretation often has exceptional practical significance for the polity and its constituents, the role of constitutional interpretation in determining the identity of a polity gives it a separate significance which is retained even where practical consequences are not obvious.

A second, and particularly intriguing, possible benefit for living originalism of this fusion is that taking integrity as the central objective of constitutional interpretation may be useful for clarifying the "originalist" component of living originalism. Living originalism has become a popular approach to constitutional interpretation in US legal theory in part because it purports to wed the originalist intuition that we are in fact interpreting a text with a fixed meaning—a meaning which is determined at least in part by the practices, policy, and intent of the founders—and the living constitutionalist intuition that for a constitution to function and for a government to continue it must be adaptable. However, living originalism leaves the significance of its originalist commitments unclear, a fact noted by critics and companions alike.[59] The limit given by early formulations of living originalism on the interpretation of constitutional passages is "whether a proposed construction is one that the text can bear and makes the most sense of the clause in the context of the larger constitutional plan."[60] If we take the "larger constitutional plan" to refer exclusively to the intent of the founders with respect to whether a given constitutional passage is a rule (concrete, specific, and binding) or a standard/principle (abstract, vague, and guiding), then this passage seems to license a great deal of freedom—especially as whether a passage is concrete and specific or abstract and vague may depend on our interpretive choices.[61] Critics have suggested that this limit amounts to nearly no limit at all, and that living originalism licenses almost total freedom in our interpretive practices, making any claim to substantive originalism rather flimsy.[62] Friendlier readers have raised questions about whether this apparent originalism might rest on a confusion regarding how we determine the interpretive framework of the Constitution and how we determine the proper interpretation of Constitutional passages, as well as larger questions as to whether the originalist component of the theory has any real value in motivating the interpretive position stated by living originalism.[63]

Taking political integrity as the end of constitutional interpretation might help clarify the importance of historical considerations. Integrity suggests, at least, a stronger connection to the past than does "what the text can bear" through its requirement that a polity see itself as furthering its identity-grounding commitments. The literature on political integrity is particularly committed to the idea that historical facts can result in a polity possessing more powerful integrity-based reasons for or against certain actions. For instance, the possession of a history of now-rejected practices of racial discrimination gives a polity a good reason to avoid certain engagements with any polity engaged in practices similar to those they have rejected—in particular suggesting that the US government had strong integrity reasons to reject engagement in South Africa during Apartheid due to the comparatively central role that the United States' struggle against its own history of racism plays in US identity. Critically, it is not just a polity's subjective understanding of their history which is of importance to such commitments—the objective history of the polity must also be considered.[64] Likewise, the close connection of integrity with steadfastness—a general requirement that one stand by their moral convictions, and that they not surrender them arbitrarily and easily—would seem to suggest that most cases of interpretation would require fidelity to earlier understandings. A polity that surrenders their convictions readily, or simply reinterprets them when they become inconvenient, is not likely to have much integrity. While identity-grounding commitments can change, largely through (identity-grounding) moral struggles, that change cannot be easy and arbitrary without raising some questions about the depth of that polity's integrity.[65]

A reasonable first pass at the weight of integrity in reinforcing the originalist commitments of living originalism suggests that the particular history of a polity which includes a constitution creates an integrity-grounded reason to remain true to the commitments established therein, as the constitution both reflects and informs the identity of the polity. This can be understood in context of an important motivation of originalisms—that too-great interpretive freedom allows a judicial elite to wrongfully set aside principles established by democratic practices of popular sovereignty[66]—as suggesting that a judiciary which acts to reinterpret the constitution without employing the proper democratic mechanisms (e.g., amendment, etc.) may be attempting to unilaterally redefine the identity of the polity. Such a redefinition would likely fail, weakening the identification of the constituents of that polity with the formal political system, and would be apparently reprehensible even if successful. At the same time, this interpretation would seem to make sense of the living originalist emphasis on popular political movements informed and underwritten by constitutional interpretations: such movements indicate popular interests and may, under some circumstances, be usefully considered indications of the will of the sovereign populace.[67] The rough outline, then, of the interpretive consequences of a commitment to integrity would be a default to originalist understandings of the relevant constitution, overruled when the polity indicates that such interpretations are no longer in line with predominant understandings of the polity's self-image.

This proposed fusion opens a range of interesting question. What methods should any given polity accept as demonstrations of the will of the populace on matters of constitutional interpretation? How should we understand the commitments and status of oppressed or ignored constituents in a polity, especially as relates to their furthering or rejecting given constitutional interpretations? How does a *de jure* recognition of formerly merely *de facto* constituents of the polity (e.g., members of groups so thoroughly oppressed that they were prohibited from political participation), and the resulting change in the constitution of the polity, impact its political identity? Where should we find political identity in polities without a constitution satisfying the tripartite structure proposed by living originalism, and which consequences of the analysis here will carry over to those polities? These questions will need to be thoroughly considered in future work. However, the fusion of living originalism and political integrity—as I argue we can take to be suggested by the Oven of Akhnai—suggests a productive and valuable path for future work.

That is, I believe that the interpretation of the Oven of Akhnai which I have proposed here points to a promising intersection between theoretical work in constitutional interpretation and political practice more broadly. The degree to which this promise bears out, of course, remains a question to be determined by future work—some of which is ongoing. However, by inviting the readers to consider constitutional interpretation in context of its larger functions, I believe that the Oven of Akhnai provides a powerful incitement toward a deeper and more thorough assessment of the legal and political functions of constitutions, their interpretations, and their impacts for the identity of polities.

NOTES

1. I would like to thank two parties for their support while I worked on this chapter. First, I would like to thank the editors of this volume, who have worked tirelessly with me through multiple revisions of the text—a text considerably improved by their efforts. Second, I would like to thank the Institute of Philosophy at the Research Centre for the Humanities located in Budapest, Hungary. Much of the text was written while visiting that institute, and their generous provision of a workspace was vital to its completion.

2. Balkin, the author initially putting forward living originalism, uses the term "framework originalism." I prefer that term as well, but "living originalism" appears to have won out in popular use. If only in the spirit of this chapter, I will concede to this majoritarian terminological convention.

3. I will give here some definitions for Jewish legal concepts which are important to the discussion to follow, and which may not be familiar to all readers. These definitions are largely taken from Suzanne Last Stone, "In Pursuit of the Counter-Text: The Turn to the Jewish Legal Model in Contemporary American Legal Theory," *Harvard Law Review* 106, no. 4 (1993), https://doi.org/10.2307/1341644, chiefly in footnotes 13 and 78.

Halakha: A term which refers to Jewish law, both in reference to particular laws and to the system of law as a whole. "Halakha" is the singular noun form, with "halakhot" the plural, and "halakhic" the adjectival form.

Sanhedrin: Here, as in many places, used as a reference to the "Great Sanhedrin"—the highest authority on matters of halakha in the Jewish tradition. The Great Sanhedrin was the supreme judicial body of the Jewish polity, and had authority over lesser sanhedrins which had narrower jurisdiction. Portrayed inconsistently as a religious and political court, a chiefly political court, a chiefly religious court, or as referring to two separate bodies—one religious and one political, the nature and composition of the Great Sanhedrin is unclear. It did appear to have powers beyond the judicial—including the ability to appoint a king, declare war, and so on. It also oversaw critical rituals. These powers, however, likely varied across Jewish history. At the time the Talmud was written, and at which this story was meant to have taken place, the Sanhedrin was operating out of Yavneh; and the Nasi, the president of the Sanhedrin, was taken by the Romans to be the political leader of the Jewish polity. The Sanhedrin would dissolve in 425 CE. See, for further information, "Sanhedrin," *Britannica* (June 3, 2023). https://www.britannica.com/topic/sanhedrin.

Talmud: A compilation of discussion and decisions about halakha had by sages and later commentaries on those discussions and decisions. The initial discussions and decisions are collectively referred to as the "Mishna," and the scholars who produced them called "tannaim." The Mishna was assembled in roughly 200 C.E. The later commentaries are called the "Gemarah," and the scholars who produced them called the "amoraim." The Gemarah, and the Talmud as a whole, took final shape sometime around 500 C.E. There are two versions of the Talmud, a less comprehensive version called the "Palestinian" or "Jerusalem Talmud," and the more comprehensive "Babylonian Talmud." Sefaria places the composition of the Babylonian Talmud, on which I will be relying in this chapter, from about 450 to 500 CE. Note that this places the composition of the Talmud well after many of the events recorded, though portions of the Talmud may well have been written or transmitted orally from an earlier time.

4. Unless otherwise noted, all included passages of Talmudic texts are from the William Davidson Edition of the Koren Noé Talmud, with commentary by Rabbi Addin Even-Israel Stensaltz (License: CC-BY-NC); *Koren Talmud Bavli*, Copyright © Koren Publishers Jerusalem Ltd. and The Steinsaltz Center. They were accessed through "Sefaria: A Living Library of Jewish Texts Online," through which any reader may access these materials without charge. These passages are reproduced here with the permission of Koren Publishers. I am grateful to Koren Publishers for this permission, without which I fear much of the charisma of the chapter may have been lost.

I will refer to Talmudic texts using abbreviated names for the book, and line numbers associated with this version of these texts. The abbreviations, and the texts they cite, are as listed below, roughly in order of their prominence in this chapter.

BM—Bava Metzia, a text primarily centered on civil laws, especially those not dealing with damages.

San—Sanhedrin, a text describing the Jewish court system.

Suk—Sukkah, a text chiefly devoted to discussing the holiday of Sukkot

PA—Pirkei Avot, a text of the Mishna consisting of aphorisms and moral stories.

Yad—Mishna Yadayim, a text of the Mishna discussing questions of purity chiefly pertaining to hands. This text uses the Dr. Joshua Kulp translation, as it is not available in the William Davidson Edition. The Dr. Joshua Kulp translation is shared, via Sefaria, under a CC-BY license.

5. Note: Some interpreters take God's laughter here to be sarcastic, a rebuke of rabbinical arrogance, but most take it to be a genuine acceptance of the rabbinical position which thereby affirms the jurisprudential principles—the rejection of revelation as evidence and the assertion of majority rule on matters of interpretation—expressed by the Sanhedrin (Stone, "In Pursuit of the Counter-Text.")

6. Jeffrey L. Rubenstein, "The Death of Rabbi Eliezer: Bavli Sanhedrin 68a," in *Hakol Kol Yaakov*, ed. Robert A. Harris and Jonathan S. Milgram (Leiden: Brill, 2021), 303–343, https://doi.org/10.1163/9789004420465_013.

7. R. Eliezer's apparent magical abilities are a matter of Talmudic discussion, where it is discussed that his mastery of sorcery was permissible precisely because he had learned it not to perform sorcerous acts, but to learn halakha (San 68a13).

8. Despite God's acceptance of this reasoning, it appears the Eliezer's grief would prove too much, and Gamliel would die shortly as a result of Eliezer's sorrowful prayers (BM 59b10–12). This is the source of halakhic positions which suggest that verbal mistreatment is of a special moral category subject to strong punishments, and that victims of such mistreatment are in a special position to seek divine retribution. It is in this context that the story is introduced within the Talmud, citing R. Eliezer's status as the victim of such mistreatment as the cause of the unusual potency of his prayers in bringing about the death of R. Gamliel (see BM 59a12, 59b11–12). However, I will focus on interpretations which emphasize the jurisprudential claims made in the text.

9. I will not presume to provide an authoritative interpretation of the Oven of Akhnai. This story, as might be expected of any which has garnered so much attention, has been variously interpreted in a range of contradictory ways. The classic review of these interpretations, which may be of interest to those who wish to see the broader range of possible interpretations of this story, is Izhak Englard, "Majority Decision vs. Individual Truth: The Interpretations of the 'Oven of Achnai' Aggadah," *Tradition* 15, no. 1–2 (1975): 137–152.

10. An interesting history of this ban may be found in Yair Furstenberg, "The Invention of the Ban against Writing Oral Torah in the Babylonian Talmud," *AJS Review: The Journal of the Association for Jewish Studies* 46, no. 1 (2022): 131–150. https://doi.org/10.1353/ajs.2022.0007.

11. Jonathan Burnside, "Old Testament: Torah and Constitutionalism," in *Christianity and Constitutionalism*, ed. Nicholas Aroney and Ian Leigh (Oxford: Oxford University Press, 2022), 33–57. https://doi.org/10.1093/oso/9780197587256.003.0002.

12. See, for an efficient review of Originalist positions, which vary chiefly in their understanding of what fidelity entails, Jeffrey Goldsworthy, "Constitutional Interpretation: Originalism," *Philosophy Compass* 4, no. 4 (2009): 682–702. https://doi.org/10.1111/j.1747-9991.2009.00207.x.

13. Goldsworthy, "Constitutional Interpretation: Originalism."

14. Englard, "Majority Decision vs. Individual Truth."

15. Passages from the Torah are also taken from Sefaria.org. Except where noted, all passages quoted are from The Contemporary Torah, with the Hebrew removed for brevity. See The Contemporary Torah, JPS, *Sefaria: A Living Library of Jewish Texts Online* (2006), https://www.sefaria.org/texts/Tanakh. Paragraph breaks are my own, for legibility.

16. Note: I have modified the translation here. The Hebrew phrase translated here as "the multitude" is translated by The Contemporary Torah as "the mighty." Either translation is appropriate, but the use to which R. Yirmeya puts the phrase appears to be that meaning "the multitude," and this is how it is translated in the Talmudic text, so I have adjusted the translated text to reflect that meaning.

17. Avital Hochstein, "Mishpatim: Does the Majority Rule?" *Shalom Hartman Institute* (January 30, 2019). https://www.hartman.org.il/mishpatim-does-the-majority-rule/.

18. Regardless of the interpretation we favor, I will take the apparent implication of the Talmudic text—that R. Yirmeya's citation is correct and appropriate—to be the case.

19. Hochstein, "Mishpatim."

20. Gideon Sapir, "Living Originalism—The Jewish Version," *Jerusalem Review of Legal Studies* 7, no. 1 (June 2013): 49–56, https://doi.org/10.1093/jrls/jlt003.

21. Sapir, "Living Originalism—The Jewish Version" and Jack M. Balkin, *Living Originalism* (Cambridge, MA: Harvard University Press, 2011), http://ebookcentral.proquest.com/lib/duke/detail.action?docID=3301022.

22. Balkin, *Living Originalism.*

23. Balkin, *Living Originalism.*

24. Sapir, "Living Originalism—The Jewish Version."

25. Balkin, *Living Originalism* and Sapir, "Living Originalism—The Jewish Version."

26. Sapir, "Living Originalism—The Jewish Version."

27. Stone, "In Pursuit of the Counter-Text."

28. A variant transliteration of "halakha."

29. Note that it is not obvious, from prior Talmudic discussions, that majority decision should outweigh reported traditions. Arguments of this sort—"my teacher told me such-and-such"—were common and well-respected in Talmudic discourse. Some hold that the Oven of Akhnai may be the first implementation of majority rule as a hard jurisprudential principle. See Judah Goldin, "On the Account of the Banning of R. Eliezer Ben Hyrqanus: An Analysis and Proposal," *Journal of the Ancient Near Eastern Society* 16, no. 1 (January 1984): 85–97.

30. Furstenberg, "The Invention of the Ban against Writing Oral Torah in the Babylonian Talmud."

31. Sapir, "Living Originalism—The Jewish Version," 56.

32. Michael Rosensweig, "Creativity as a Foundation of Torah Life," *Tradition* 53, no. 3 (Summer 2021): 1831.

33. Balkin, *Living Originalism*, 129.

34. Stone, "In Pursuit of the Counter-Text," 853.

35. Balkin, *Living Originalism*, 23.
36. Balkin, *Living Originalism*, 33.
37. Balkin, *Living Originalism*, 65.
38. Balkin, *Living Originalism*, 59.
39. Balkin, *Living Originalism*, 60.
40. Balkin, *Living Originalism*, 60.
41. Balkin, *Living Originalism*, 64.
42. Jack M. Balkin, "Nine Perspectives on *Living Originalism*," *University of Illinois Law Review* 2012, no. 3 (2012): 103–104.
43. Note that the Gamliel of the Oven of Akhnai is not the same as that mentioned in the Christian New Testament—called Gamliel the Elder or R. Gamliel I. The R. Gamliel referenced here, sometimes called Rabban Gamliel of Yavneh, or R. Gamliel II, was active from about 80–110 CE, after the destruction of the Temple and the move of the Sanhedrin to Yavneh. The events of this story, then, take place in Yavneh in this context.
44. Goldin, "On the Account of the Banning of R. Eliezer," 91–95; Stone, "In Pursuit of the Counter-Text," 856–857.
45. J. J. C. Smart and Bernard Williams, *Utilitarianism: For and Against* (Cambridge: Cambridge University Press, 1973).
46. This is chiefly developed with respect to liberal democracies, as the features of these polities make it especially apt to describe them as collective agents in virtue of their "sovereign body politic." As mentioned above, such a democratic conception is not appropriate for Talmudic Judaism. However, I think that the importance of liberality and democracy in grounding collective agency is somewhat overstated in the original context. While a "sovereign body politic" may be one way to constitute a collective agent, it is likely not the only way. It may be enough, for instance, for a polity to consist of individuals who endorse the projects of the polity and see themselves as a part of it. If that is the case, then we can take Talmudic Judaism to have its own form of integrity, with the acknowledgment that it would be binding to and on only that portion of those who might have been called Jewish at the time who would satisfy the appropriate requirements for collective agency. The nature of collective agency is, itself, a rather substantive question, and one that cannot be fully addressed here.
47. Shmuel Nili, "Integrity, Personal and Political," *The Journal of Politics* 80, no. 2 (April 2018): 428–441, https://doi.org/10.1086/694786; and Shmuel Nili, *Integrity, Personal, and Political* (Oxford: Oxford University Press, 2020).
48. Balkin, *Living Originalism*, 19.
49. Balkin, *Living Originalism*, 20.
50. Balkin, *Living Originalism*, 64.
51. Balkin, *Living Originalism*, 268.
52. Nili, *Integrity, Personal, and Political*, 60.
53. Nili, *Integrity, Personal, and Political*, 118.
54. Nili, *Integrity, Personal, and Political*, 106.
55. Nili, "Integrity, Personal and Political"; Balkin, *Living Originalism.*
56. Nili, *Integrity, Personal, and Political*, 70–72.

57. Connie S. Rosati, "The Moral Reading of Constitutions," in *The Legacy of Ronald Dworkin*, ed. Wil Waluchow and Stefan Sciaraffa (Oxford University Press, 2016), 323–352, https://doi.org/10.1093/acprof:oso/9780190466411.003.0014.

58. I make this qualification because constitutions do not play this role in all cases (see Balkin, "Nine Perspectives on *Living Originalism*," 130.). In governments without such a constitutionally centered government, it may be that the constitutional interpretation and political integrity do not align in the way I am suggesting here. How integrity relates to the processes of legal interpretation in such polities remains a question for the future.

59. Nelson Lund, "Living Originalism: The Magical Mystery Tour," *Texas A&M Law Review* 3, no. 1 (2015): 31–43; Hugh Baxter, "Why the 'Originalism' in Balkin's *Living Originalism*?" *Boston University Law Review* 92, no. 4 (2012): 1213–1224; and Barak Medina, "'Foundational' Originalism? On Jack Balkin's *Living Originalism*," *Jerusalem Review of Legal Studies* 7, no. 1 (June 1, 2013): 1–16, https://doi.org/10.1093/jrls/jlt002.

60. Balkin, *Living Originalism*, 254.

61. Medina, "'Foundational' Originalism?" 12.

62. Lund, "Living Originalism."

63. Baxter, "Why the 'Originalism'"; Medina, "'Foundational' Originalism?"

64. Nili, *Integrity, Personal, and Political*, 57.

65. Nili, "Integrity, Personal and Political"; Nili, *Integrity, Personal, and Political*, 19–20.

66. Goldsworthy, "Constitutional Interpretation: Originalism."

67. Balkin, *Living Originalism*, 54–58, 70–99.

WORKS CITED

Balkin, Jack M. *Living Originalism*. Cambridge, MA: Harvard University Press, 2011. http://ebookcentral.proquest.com/lib/duke/detail.action?docID=3301022.

———. "Nine Perspectives on *Living Originalism*." *University of Illinois Law Review* 2012, no. 3 (2012): 101–159.

Baxter, Hugh. "Why the 'Originalism' in Balkin's *Living Originalism*?" *Boston University Law Review* 92, no. 4 (2012): 1213–1224.

Burnside, Jonathan. "Old Testament: Torah and Constitutionalism." In *Christianity and Constitutionalism*, edited by Nicholas Aroney and Ian Leigh, 33–57. Oxford: Oxford University Press, 2022. https://doi.org/10.1093/oso/9780197587256.003.0002.

The Contemporary Torah, JPS. *Sefaria: A Living Library of Jewish Texts Online*. 2006. https://www.sefaria.org/texts/Tanakh.

Englard, Izhak. "Majority Decision vs. Individual Truth: The Interpretations of the 'Oven of Achnai' Aggadah." *Tradition* 15, no. 1–2 (1975): 137–152.

Furstenberg, Yair. "The Invention of the Ban against Writing Oral Torah in the Babylonian Talmud." *AJS Review: The Journal of the Association for Jewish Studies* 46, no. 1 (2022): 131–150. https://doi.org/10.1353/ajs.2022.0007.

Goldin, Judah. "On the Account of the Banning of R. Eliezer Ben Hyrqanus: An Analysis and Proposal." *Journal of the Ancient Near Eastern Society* 16, no. 1 (January 1984): 85–97.

Goldsworthy, Jeffrey. "Constitutional Interpretation: Originalism." *Philosophy Compass* 4, no. 4 (2009): 682–702. https://doi.org/10.1111/j.1747-9991.2009.00207.x.

Hochstein, Avital. "Mishpatim: Does the Majority Rule?" *Shalom Hartman Institute* (January 30, 2019). https://www.hartman.org.il/mishpatim-does-the-majority-rule/.

Lund, Nelson. "Living Originalism: The Magical Mystery Tour." *Texas A&M Law Review* 3, no. 1 (2015): 31–43.

Medina, Barak. "'Foundational' Originalism? On Jack Balkin's *Living Originalism*." *Jerusalem Review of Legal Studies* 7, no. 1 (June 1, 2013): 1–16. https://doi.org/10.1093/jrls/jlt002.

Mishna Daytime. *Sefaria: A Living Library of Jewish Texts Online*, translated by Joshua Kulp. www.sefaria.org/Mishnah_Yadayim.

Nili, Shmuel. "Integrity, Personal and Political." *The Journal of Politics* 80, no. 2 (April 2018): 428–441. https://doi.org/10.1086/694786.

———. *Integrity, Personal, and Political*. Oxford: Oxford University Press, 2020.

Rosati, Connie S. "The Moral Reading of Constitutions." In *The Legacy of Ronald Dworkin*, edited by Wil Waluchow and Stefan Sciaraffa, 323–352. Oxford University Press, 2016. https://doi.org/10.1093/acprof:oso/9780190466411.003.0014.

Rosensweig, Michael. "Creativity as a Foundation of Torah Life." *Tradition* 53, no. 3 (Summer 2021): 182–191.

Rubenstein, Jeffrey L. "The Death of Rabbi Eliezer: Bavli Sanhedrin 68a." In *Hakol Kol Yaakov*, edited by Robert A. Harris and Jonathan S. Milgram, 303–343. Leiden: Brill, 2021. https://doi.org/10.1163/9789004420465_013.

"Sanhedrin." *Britannica* (June 3, 2023). https://www.britannica.com/topic/sanhedrin.

Sapir, Gideon. "Living Originalism—The Jewish Version." *Jerusalem Review of Legal Studies* 7, no. 1 (June 1, 2013): 49–56. https://doi.org/10.1093/jrls/jlt003.

Smart, J. J. C. and Bernard Williams. *Utilitarianism: For and against*. Cambridge: Cambridge University Press, 1973.

Stone, Suzanne Last. "In Pursuit of the Counter-Text: The Turn to the Jewish Legal Model in Contemporary American Legal Theory." *Harvard Law Review* 106, no. 4 (1993): 813–894. https://doi.org/10.2307/1341644.

William Davidson Edition of the Koren Noé Talmud; with commentary by Rabbi Addin Even-Israel Stensaltz. *Koren Talmud Bavli*. Koren Publishers Jerusalem Ltd. and The Steinsaltz Center. Sefaria: A Living Library of Jewish Texts Online. https://www.sefaria.org/texts/Talmud.

Chapter 4

Sacred Scripture, Sacred Constitution

Individual Religious Hermeneutics and Constitutional Interpretation

Nicholas Higgins and Micah Allred

Explaining how Trump was able to win the religious vote, with 81 percent of the white evangelical voters, and 56 percent of those who attend worship weekly or more, supporting him in the 2016 election,[1] has become a cottage area of study in empirical political science. Some have offered the general political explanation that these religious voters tend to be the most conservative.[2] Others have identified qualities such as concern over status threat,[3] or having racial resentment or significant negative partisanship toward the Democratic party (or Hillary Clinton specifically),[4] which is argued to specifically affect female Trump supporters.[5] Others have argued that the concept of Christian Nationalism was a driving factor to support Trump.[6] It is important to recognize that Christian Nationalism is different than evangelicalism, as many people who do not identify as evangelical or even as Christians hold to Christian nationalist beliefs,[7] with continued research showing that non-attending Christian nationalists were more likely to support Trump.[8]

During the heat of the 2016 campaign, some reporters and political commentators saw the choice of Mike Pence as running mate as bringing religiously faithful credibility to the ticket[9] and thereby explaining Trump's appeal to religious voters. This thought is likely derived from Pence's oft-repeated phrase, used when he accepted the Vice Presidential nomination: "I am a Christian, a conservative, and a Republican—in that order."[10] He sought to appeal to the Christian conservative base by emphasizing the centrality of his Christian identity, which precedes both his ideological and party identification. While Pence has used this phrase for years given the tumultuous 2016 election and the nomination of a thrice-divorced, self-professedly greedy,[11] and self-assertedly unrepentant man[12] as president, the presence of a man like Pence on the Republican ticket may have been selected in order to calm many religious voters. Yet most research has shown that vice presidential candidates have minimal effects on general vote share,[13] even in their home state.[14] There is even less evidence for a vice president who identifies with a specific religious community to increase his ticket's vote share of that group.[15]

The reality is that the above explanations, though offering important research and information, forget the specific political environment of the 2016 and 2020 elections, and the fight over the Supreme Court. Antonin Scalia's death on February 13, 2016, in the heat of the primary campaign season may have changed a latent idea to a critical one in voters' minds. With President Obama's nominee, Merrick Garland, languishing in the Republican-controlled Senate, in March 2016 Senate Majority Leader Mitch McConnell noted that it was the Senate's right to withhold its consent from the President's nominee.[16] Such delay was a moment of pride for McConnell, who at a campaign rally stated, "One of my proudest moments was when I looked Barack Obama in the eye and I said, 'Mr. President, you will not fill the Supreme Court vacancy'."[17] This active delay further emphasized the centrality of the 2016 election as decisive for the future of the Supreme Court. As Trump seemed to be wrapping up the Republican Primary, he recognized that the plurality of votes which he won in the crowded field might need to be solidified and expanded. So on May 18, 2016, he published a list of potential Supreme Court nominees that would increase his conservative and religious support.[18] After the 2016 election religious leaders believed that Trump would keep his promises, particularly on the Supreme Court,[19] and with the appointments of Neil Gorsuch and Brett Kavanaugh Trump and his advisors seemed to recognize the political value of this issue, because the same playbook was used for the 2020 election. When Ruth Bader Ginsberg died on September 18, 2020, with only 38 days until the election, and through the raucous complaints of the Democrats of Republican hypocrisy, Trump nominated and appointed Amy Coney Barrett to fill the seat. As John Fea, a Professor of History at Messiah College whose research focuses on American Evangelicalism, noted, this time "it's less about trying to win over the evangelicals . . . . It's a matter of upholding them—not losing them. It's a matter of securing that 80%."[20] News outlets frequently cited the general judicial action, and this one specifically, as influential in evangelical support for Trump's 2020 election.[21]

This latter claim that religious support for Trump is derived because of his stated plan, and eventual fulfillment, of nominating originalist members of the Court is based upon a critical presumption that there is a link between religious belief and a particular style of constitutional interpretation. This paper seeks to address that presumption and offer a theory of why religious individuals (whether Christian or not, whether evangelical or not) might be likely to adhere to a specific method of constitutional interpretation. We offer a theory which argues that support for originalist positions is not merely a consequentialist desire for policy outcome, but rather is rooted in adherence to a methodological way of reading and reasoning. Specifically, we assert that the hermeneutical method utilized to read the Bible is a heuristic method of reading which is applied to other sources that are held in high esteem. That is to say, readers who seriously want to understand the text they are considering ask certain questions while they are reading. Questions like: "What was the author trying to communicate to the audience at the time?" or "What were the public meanings of the words at the time?" These sorts of textual questions help the reader to truly understand what is being said. Most people of course read non-controversial texts like this in a studious and rational manner that can be distinguished from reading meaning into the text. After offering a brief overview of some scholarship on the relationship between public opinion and the Supreme Court, with specific emphasis on the way citizens' constitutional views impact broader political beliefs, we offer a theoretical explanation of why we think there is a connection between individual hermeneutics and a specific constitutional theory. We then prove that theory through our data analysis, offering comments on what it does and does not show, as well as potential limits and additional areas that can be examined.

THE CURRENT DISCUSSION

To analyze the methodological relationship between the reading of sacred texts and the reading of the Constitution, it is important to survey the current incomplete scholarship, showing how our argument builds upon the broader research, but seeks to bring new information and support in the realm of constitutional interpretation. When examining the discussion of the citizens' relation to the judicial system, most academic research has been focused on how public opinion has affected the Supreme Court, with most scholars saying it does[22] though not all agree on the empirical relationship, at least in the past fifty years.[23] Some scholars also examine the causes of citizens' ideological perceptions of the court.[24] Some scholars have tracked the specific religious responses to the Court's rulings particularly in the landmark religious decisions like *Engel* and *Schempp*.[25] These findings report significant impact on public opinion and subsequent political action by religious groups to counteract many of the Court's decisions. Perhaps the most profound example of this was after the *Smith* decision in the 1990s. Lobbying groups took Congress by storm to pass the Religious Freedom Restoration Act (RFRA).[26]

Further, when scholars have examined the citizens' perception of the Court, they have found that citizens' opinions are affected by their (the citizens') own political ideology. Scheb II and Lyons found support for the Court depends on the individual's ideological proximity to the perceived ideology of the court.[27] Similarly, after *Bush v. Gore* data was collected on public perception and knowledge of the court. It showed a strong approval/disapproval rating based on party affiliation.[28] While distinguishing by party affiliation or ideology can be useful, because of the Court's role in constitutional interpretation there is an opportunity to see how an individual's view of constitutional interpretation influences their views of court and other political issues.

In one of the few published empirical studies examining the potential influences upon individuals' adherence to specific forms of constitutional interpretation, Greene, Persily, and Ansolabehere seek to determine what factors influence individual citizens' support of an originalist view of constitutional interpretation.[29] Specifically, they note that demographic qualities such as age and political identity—such as ideology, party identification, and support for the tea party, as well as policy views on limiting abortion, gay rights, and supporting gun rights—all correspond to supporting an originalist interpretation of the Constitution. Interestingly, in addition to these broad sociodemographic and political influences, the authors note that religion also has a significant influence on predicting someone's likelihood to hold to an originalist interpretation. They note,

> The starkest differences in the cross-tabulations, however, appear concerning religiosity, where 52% of originalists describe themselves as born-again or evangelical, as compared to only 17% of nonoriginalists. Similarly, 57% of originalists attend religious services at least once per week, as compared to 18% of nonoriginalists. Also, 76% of originalists believe in the literal truth of the Bible, whereas only 35% of nonoriginalists do.[30]

However, despite this appearance in the data, upon further statistical analysis controlling for other explanations, they find that religious belief, i.e. identifying as an evangelical as well as frequency of religious attendance, has no statistically significant influence upon a citizen's theory of constitutional interpretation.[31] However, they do note that, when controlling for numerous factors, holding to a literal interpretation of the Bible is a statistically significant factor in predicting whether an individual holds to originalism.[32] It is interesting that the prediction is not based upon a set of religious beliefs or even a frequent form of religious attendance, but specifically is linked to a specific interpretive method of the Bible, showing that there is a hermeneutical link between interpretation of religious text and interpretation of the Constitution. As Lund notes, "for both our religious traditions and our constitutional tradition, issues of hermeneutics and the solving of various exegetical problems lie at the heart of the interpretative enterprise."[33] Recently Lewis, Blake, Mockbee, and Friesen[34] have sought to further examine this link, using a novel survey which created a Biblical Interpretive Scale and a Constitutional Interpretive Scale based upon multiple questions in their proprietary data. Lewis *et al* echo Greene *et al*, noting "the findings from this last model suggest that biblical and constitutional interpretive approaches are directly related, as well as that the biblical hermeneutical approach's influence outweighs that of traditional measures of religious affiliation."[35]

Scholars focused less on empirical data and more on historical and intellectual influences have noted the close alignment between these ideas: Sanford Levinson in his book *Constitutional Faith* breaks down the debate over the Constitution as a religious one, fundamentally:

> The Constitution is a discrete document that can be taken off the shelf, like the Bible, and perused. Its writtenness supplies a tangibility, an ability quite literally to take the Constitution into one's own hands and read it with one's own eye.[36]

Charles Lamb has argued for Judicial Restraint from the perspective of John Marshall, citing the "common sense" of anyone reading a text.[37] At times the Court has also been surrounded by competing views of its obligations to the public in terms of religious freedom, for example. Scholars have rightly noted that entire schools of thought have formed around the power of the Court to create policy outcomes on a given religious issue. Furthermore, those favoring separationism have argued that "government and religion will better achieve their ends if they remain independent of each other."[38] On the other side of the coin, prominent hermeneutical scholars like Moisés Silva have argued that hermeneutics is a serious study needed in more areas than just the biblical text: "Why should such a discipline be needed at all? We never had to take a class on 'How to interpret the Newspaper'."[39] Silva responds to this question, explaining that "we do need hermeneutics for texts other than the Bible."[40] This scholar goes on in the book to make clear the point that everyone has been taught hermeneutics at least subconsciously by the way the rest of society deals with the text.

THEORY

In order to best understand our hypothesis and the data we use to analyze this relationship, it is important to understand the theoretical foundation and reason for the connection between religious hermeneutics and constitutional interpretation. We begin by assuming that all readings utilize some heuristic mechanism to interpret texts and that such models can be used as a basis for predicting future behavior in textual interpretation. This assumption is rational and useful for a few reasons. First, by virtue of reading any specific text, the reader has already had to put it into a framework of understanding in order to communicate with others or contemplate the meaning internally.

Second, this framework if not actively thought of is at least subconsciously employed by the reader to even make a basic analysis of the text and to show comprehension of it. Since we are specifically presenting the connection between religious text interpretation and civil text, we begin by examining the categories of religious interpretation.

Religious hermeneutics has offered numerous different categories of interpretations (such as literal, devotional, allegorical), yet using a word that is commonly appealed to can be difficult.[41] We have tried to identify in this section what exactly is meant by the socially used term "literal" and how we understand it for this analysis. The simplest definition that we could formulate captures what we believe to be the essence of the most basic hermeneutical training: taking the text seriously as written. Many people in society would be comfortable calling this version of interpretation "literal" even though of course there would be times that one would not use a "strictly literal" approach in a given text. What is meant by this term largely speaking is something more along the lines of believing what the author is saying and reading it seriously. As the definition becomes more detailed and precise, it may start to look like originalism as it is known today.

One reason we hesitate to use the term "originalism" when speaking of the religious hermeneutic is because "originalism" (as coined by the late, influential Justice Antonin Scalia) was and still is associated with a high "legal" connotation and is not typically used in churches or in sermons preached anywhere to religious peoples. Notwithstanding this prudential measure of labeling accuracy, originalism could be a very useful title for the concept we are trying to define. After all, "literal," to some, implies strict use of the words for exactly what they mean. To correct this faulty accusation, Scalia once wrote:

> I don't like the term 'strict construction.' I do not think the Constitution, or any text, should be interpreted either strictly or sloppily; it should be interpreted reasonably. . . . I do believe, however, that you give the text the meaning it had when it was adopted.[42]

Scalia correctly justified his position against opponents that would mischaracterize his originalist approach as strict, and in the religious context the term strict is often expressed as legalistic. Ironically enough, Justice Stephen Breyer uses this term to categorize the originalist position when arguing that his own "living constitution" model would disavow "a contrary constitutional approach, a more 'legalistic' approach that places too much weight upon language, history, tradition, and precedent alone while understating the importance of consequences."[43]

The causal factor we propose for a preference for legal originalism on the part of many religious people is the hermeneutical training that one has received by virtue of religious practice. This may be as simple as sitting through a sermon or two that taught how to read a religious text, the practice of personal Bible study, or a more careful study into the mechanics. Regardless, many religious systems, such as Christianity and Judaism (it should be noted that Scalia was a Catholic and Breyer Jewish) historically have taught their young these basic principles for centuries. Within Christianity, for example, their own text testifies to the implied hermeneutic: complete trust for life and wisdom. Peter quotes the prophet Isaiah in his epistle: "All flesh is like grass and all its glory like the flower of grass. The grass withers, and the flower falls, but the word of the Lord remains forever" (1 Pet. 1:24–25, ESV). The hypothesis for our study is: people who profess a "literal" interpretation of a holy book should be found also to profess an originalist interpretation of the Constitution.

The reason we argue the same method can be applied to the Constitution and should be in scholarly studies is for two reasons. First, scholarly literature has previously recognized a similar hermeneutic to the Constitution and the Holy Scripture. Second, modern evangelical, religious authorities have advocated that their followers maintain a similar hermeneutic regarding both the Bible and the Constitution. The first point we showed previously in the "current discussion." The second, we believe, is just as clear. The primary supporting arguments for the ratification of the Constitution, the Federalist papers, seek to show that the Constitutional Convention's ability to agree on a structure was an act of divine providence. James Madison, writing under the pseudonym Publius, states,

> The real wonder is that so many difficulties should have been surmounted, and surmounted with a unanimity almost as unprecedented as it must have been unexpected. It is impossible for any man of candor to reflect on this circumstance without partaking of the astonishment. It is impossible for the man of pious reflection not to perceive in it a finger of that Almighty hand which has been so frequently and signally extended to our relief in the critical stages of the revolution. (*Federalist* 37)

Scholars such as Jaroslav Pelikan argue that from the beginning the Constitution was treated by prominent figures as having the same utility of the Bible and participating in the same role. Citing 2 Tim. 3:16–17, which states that the Bible is taken to be "profitable for teaching, for reproof, and for training in righteousness that the man of God may be complete, equipped for every good work," Pelikan claims that "the Constitution was likewise" and quotes Chief Justice John Marshall as stating that it was "intended to endure for ages to come, and consequently to be adapted to the various *crises* of human affairs."[44] Pelikan also observes that the Constitution is American Scripture and should be historically seen to have a similar weight in society: "both texts are centuries old by now, whether two or twenty, and both are 'venerable' and even venerated and enshrined."[45] Scholars like Gregory Kalscheur agree with Pelikan's analogy and even posit that this community-based interpretive model "might best be understood as a sort of developmental originalism."[46] While Kalscheur is doubtful about the application of this analogy as a tool for lawyers and judges, he recognizes the important questions that arise in communities that are founded and ruled by documents when it comes to creative interpretation: "Is the proposed textual interpretation an authentic, healthy development manifesting creative continuity-in-identity, or is it a malignant corruption of the identity of the community given life by the text?"[47] Even our founders advocated an understanding of the Constitution as an act of divine Providence. The idea that hermeneutics is a transferrable system from one document of importance to another is not a novel concept—rather, it has been shown by previous scholarly work to have been advocated by prominent figures in the early republic, and advocated by religious authorities in recent decades.

Scholars have long recognized that political actors utilize informational shortcuts called "heuristics" to process information for decision-making. Given limited time, resources, or knowledge, individuals often look for ways to help them intellectually process complex or varied information. Using "cues," that is, guidance from other areas, prior knowledge, or other trusted actors, individuals can utilize that information as a rubric or heuristic to process new ideas.[48] While this is a known psychological processing action, it has been widely applied to political science helping voters make political decisions for which they are uninformed.[49] According to Popkin, this low-information reasoning "is by no means devoid of substantive content, and is instead a process that economically incorporates learning and information from past experiences, daily life, the media, and political campaigns."[50] Lau and Redlawsk note five important heuristics that political scientists recognize in guiding vote choice: party affiliation, ideology, endorsements, viability (polls), and candidate appearance.[51] This popular use of heuristics is not to be considered a negative judgment on the ability of the voter but rather a rational strategy to "keep the information processing demands of the task within bounds."[52] Popkin says that voters reason by using low-cost shortcuts that allow them to "evaluate complex information."[53] When information is too costly or inconvenient for the person needing to make a decision, they will use a proxy for the actual information. For example, a voter may conclude based on a candidate supporting the voter's views on abortion that that candidate is likely to support the voter's views on euthanasia as well. The voter may deem a candidate with the same views as the voter on the national debt as someone likely also to agree on tax policy. A candidate's previous personal behavior can also serve as a shortcut for information about their past political choices. The use of heuristics, though it sometimes can be active conscious choice, also can arise from unconscious or intuitive use.[54] Additionally, religious belief has also been recognized as central to understanding voters' actions.[55] This impact is because the individual internalizes the "fundamental beliefs, ideas, ethical codes, and symbols associated with a religious tradition including what others call theology or a belief system."[56] Thus, religious stereotypes are often used as a heuristical shortcut for candidate evaluation,[57] with religious language serving as indicative of shared outlook[58] affecting Latinos and Catholics[59] as well as white evangelical Protestants.[60]

We contend that Biblical interpretation is yet another heuristic particularly utilized when reasoning through sacred and semi-sacred texts. Biblical interpretation becomes a heuristic when Christians are trying to sort out legitimacy in preaching, spiritual counsel, and so on. For instance, a Christian that hears a sermon preached on Sunday morning might evaluate it based not on the technical handling of the text (of which they may have little training), but on the teaching itself. If the listener hears doctrines being taught that do not agree with what they have heard from other "Bible-believing" or "literal interpretation" pastors, they may be inclined to criticize the sermon, bring a complaint to the elders, or even leave the congregation. This informational shortcut provides an accessible way for laypeople to practice orthodoxy in their own participation in the church.

This same heuristic is also sometimes applied to the interpretation of the Constitution. As Pelikan notes, ''Both the New Testament and the Constitution are set within historical periods that are endowed with a special aura by their traditions and that carry a unique authority for their communities."[61] As noted previously, scholarship has established that historically the Bible and the Constitution have been regarded in high esteem, often side by side in the religious quarter of society. Furthermore, popular evangelical leaders have advocated to their followers that to have an originalist interpretation of the Constitution is comparable to having a "literal" interpretation of the Bible. Moral Majority spokesperson Jerry Falwell wrote: "We have seen that the goal of the framers of our Constitution was to govern the United States of America under God's laws."[62] The president of the Southern Baptist Theological Seminary, Al Mohler, has advocated on his radio show that originalism is a corollary to biblical faithfulness. When praising Justice Thomas for a recent decision Mohler was clear to point out the necessity of amending the Constitution in order to change it: "Don't just try to make the Constitution say what it clearly doesn't say."[63] Other leaders in the evangelical community, such as Pat Robertson, James Dobson, and Eric Metaxas, have all repeatedly taught on various programs and media that constitutional originalism is critical to preserving the honor and morality of the document—much like holy scripture. Some scholars have seen critical similarities in interpretive methods between originalists of the Constitution and historical Protestant interpretation (particularly exemplified by Anglican Richard Hooker and

English and American Puritans).[64] Because these citizens rightly perceive the Constitution as the supreme authority in the sphere of American law, they understand the Constitution is the functional equivalent in the national place to what the Bible is in the religious place. Because of this, the method of interpretive processing of an individual's holy book becomes a heuristic shortcut in understanding the meaning of the Constitution.

HYPOTHESIS

Given that religious leaders have made statements about the semi-divine nature of the Constitution and the reverence it is due, we would expect individuals to use a similar cognitive heuristic in interpreting their religious holy book and the Constitution.

We hypothesize that individuals who hold to a literal interpretation of their holy book will be more likely to adhere to an originalist or strict constructionist view of the Constitution.

DATA AND METHODOLOGY

The data used in this paper are taken from a 2014 Political Polarization and Typology Survey performed by the Pew Research Center.[65] This is an individual-level analysis performed via telephone calls over three distinct phases with non-overlapping date intervals and distinct questions. While the total sample size of the whole survey is 10,013 adults living in the United States, this study will be focused on phase b, with an N of 3,337.

Dependent Variable: Constitutional Interpretation

The primary dependent variable for this study is a question related to the individual belief on constitutional interpretation methodology. A dichotomous variable was created based upon Question B55, with those who say the

Table 4.1 Completed Interviews by Data Collection Phase and Sampling Frame

Phase	Dates of Data Collection	*Completed Interviews*		
		Landline Sample	*Cell Sample*	*Total*
A	1/23/14 – 2/9/14	1,671	1,670	3,341
B	2/12/14 – 2/26/14	1,671	1,666	3,337
C	2/27/14 – 3/16/14	1,668	1,667	3,335
		5,010	5,003	10,013

Supreme Court should "base its rulings on the understanding of what the U.S. Constitution meant as it was originally written" as 1. Responses that said the Supreme Court should "base its rulings on its understanding of what the U.S. Constitution means in current times," as well as those who chose an answer "somewhere between" the originally written and the current-times meaning, were coded as 0.

Independent Variable: Literal Hermeneutic

The primary independent variable we wish to examine is the individual's hermeneutic of religious texts. To do this, we created a variable from two questions. QB139 asked respondents if their holy book "is the word of God" or "a book written by men." If they replied that it "is the word of God," they were then asked a follow-up question (QB139a) whether the holy book "is to be taken literally, word for word" or if "not everything should be taken literally word for word." Those who responded that the holy book is the Word of God and is to be taken literally, word for word, were coded as 1. Those who said the holy book was written by men, or that it was the word of God but not to be taken literally, were coded as 0.

Control Variables

While there are few previous studies that examine individual-level data on personal opinion of constitutional interpretation, one recent study did seek to profile individuals who hold to originalist interpretation and found that rule of law, cultural values, and political beliefs all impact originalism.[66] While the present data do not allow examination of personal adherence to or belief in the rule of law, it is possible to control for both political and cultural qualities.

Religious Qualities. As our main independent variable is about Biblical interpretation, recognizing that evangelicals and those who attend church more frequently are more likely to have a literal biblical interpretation, we control for this by a dichotomous variable identifying evangelicals as those Christians who self-identify as evangelical/born again. We also create a three-point variable into those who attend weekly or more (3), those who attend monthly to a few times per year (2), and those who seldom/never attend (1).

Political Qualities. Greene *et al* found that political party, ideology, and Tea Party support all influenced support for originalism. Thus, we control for political party on a 7-point scale, accounting for strength of party identification and leaning of independents, with Strong Republican identification at 1 and Strong Democrat identification at 7. We control for ideology using Pew's 5-point scale of ideological consistency with Consistently Liberal, Mostly Liberal, Mixed, Mostly Conservative, and Consistent Conservative (1–5) to determine ideological adherence. Additionally, following Greene, Persily, and Ansolabehere and recognizing that the Tea Party was influential at the time of the survey in 2014, particularly in the conservative and Republican arenas, we use a 3-point scale to measure agreement with the Tea Party: 1 as disagree, 2 as no opinion/either way, 3 as agree.

Socioeconomic Status. While previous studies, depending on the model, have mixed results concerning whether age is correlated to adherence to originalism (see Greene, Persily, and Ansolabehere for positive correlation and Lewis *et al* for mixed results by model), we thought it necessary to include the individual's self-reported age. We also control for sex, education (5-point scale from less than high school (1), some college (3), and some postgraduate (5)) and income on a 9-point scale (less than $10,000 (1); $50,000–75,000 (6); $150,00 or more (9)).

Cultural Qualities. Because originalism is tied to ideals and values established in the past, we think that individuals who have a retrospective orientation to the principles of the American ideal will be more likely to support originalism. We determine whether they have a retrospective or prospective orientation through a dichotomous variable examining whether "this country has been successful because of its ability to change or reliance on long-standing principles" (Question B26). We code the retrospective view of holding to long-standing principles as 2 and the prospective view of the ability to change as 1.

Importantly, Lewis *et al* note, "because originalism often (but not always) leads to conservative judicial decisions, it is possible that evangelicals only support originalism instrumentally in the hopes that the Supreme Court will decide cases consistent with their policy preferences."[67] This concept is echoed by the findings of Greene, Persily, and Ansolabehere who note that opposition to *Roe v. Wade*, resistance to expansion of gay rights, and support for gun rights are linked with the support of originalism. As mentioned above, this survey was done in three phases, and questions on gun rights and abortion were in other phases; thus they can not be compared to the Originalism question, which was only in phase b. Because we cannot simultaneously control for originalism as policy outcome through a variety of measures, we offer a model with a dichotomous control for opposition/support of gay marriage and a model without such control (see Table 4.2).

Table 4.2 Summary Statistics

Variable	*N*	*Mean*	*Std. Dev.*	*Min Max*
Originalism	3,248	.491	.499	0 1
Literal Hermeneutic	3,144	.327	.469	0 1
Frequency of Attendance	3,312	2.08	.812	1 3
Born Again/Evangelical	3,264	.326	.468	0 1
Ideological Consistency	3,337	2.91	1.19	1 5
Party	3,110	4.10	2.06	1 7
Tea Party Support	3,230	1.86	.726	1 3
Sex	3,337	1.50	.5	1 2
Income	3,337	5.13	2.4	1 9
Age	3,273	52.11	17.9	18 97
Education	3,317	4.87	1.85	1 8
Gay Marriage	3,086	.571	.494	0 1
Retrospective Principles	3,154	1.47	.499	1 2

ANALYSIS

As previous studies have noted, there are numerous correlative influences upon an individual's adherence to a literal constitutional interpretation. When examining the socioeconomic variables, while education has no significant impact upon adherence to originalism, both sex and income had a correlation, finding that men and those with lower incomes are more likely to adhere to originalism. This was just within the acceptable levels of statistical significance ($p = .10$) and in the second model, which added additional cultural controls, their significance increased to the 0.05 level. Consistent with previous studies, we also found that an increase in age is statistically correlated to the adherence to the originalist methodological interpretation of the Constitution. Given this, there was a question of whether originalism was viewed as superior because of a time preference that prefers things in the past. It could be argued that older people have fonder memories for their younger days, and as such may associate older things with good things. Thankfully, the data we had allowed us to control for a temporal focus asking whether it is the country's long-standing principles or ability to change that makes it successful. As one may expect, those who have a fondness for the long-standing principles are significantly more likely to adhere to an originalist view of the Constitution, yet, even when controlled for this retrospective view, older individuals still statistically supported originalism.[68]

Table 4.3 Literal Bible Interpretation: Logistic Regression of Originalism (Originally Written +)

Variable Names	*Model 1*	*Model 2*
Religious		
Literal Biblical Interpretation	.356***(.124)	.302** (.131)
Frequency of Attendance	.043 (.068)	.035 (.071)
Evangelical/Born Again	.296** (.121)	.266** (.12)
Political		
Party	-.154***(.029)	-.153*** (.030)
Ideological Consistency	.628***(.061)	.588*** (.065)
Tea Party Agreement	.529***(.088)	.500***(.091)
SES Variables		
Age	.008***(.002)	.007***(.002)
Sex	-.199* (.102)	-.177* (.106)
Income	-.049** (.023)	-.043* (.024)
Education	.011(.032)	.009 (.033)
Cultural Variables		
Retrospective Principles	.669***(.104)	.691***(.108)
Gay Marriage		-.271** (.124)
Constant	-3.49***(.418)	-3.14***(.458)
N	**2,452**	**2,334**
R2	**.285**	**.291**

Entries are a Logistic Regression of Originalism
*p ≤ .10 **p ≤ .5 ***p ≤ .01 (two-tailed test)

Entries Are a Logistic Regression of Originalism

Ability to control for this retrospective view is important because it allows us to disaggregate our results to more accurately determine whether our theoretical model stands. While those who are older and those who think American founding principles are critical to her success may hold to originalism, our theoretical framework argues that hermeneutical methodology is transferable between one's religious belief and one's political beliefs, regardless of cultural or political adherents. As noted in the first model of table 4.3, when controlling for both political, religious, and temporal outlook, those who adhere to a literal interpretation of the Bible are statistically more likely to adhere to originalism at the .01 level, and this has a marginal effect of a 6 percent increase in adherence to originalism. Thus, the null hypothesis from H1 can be rejected, lending credence to our theory.

However, previous scholars and popular press have raised a possibility that would undermine our theory, specifically that originalism is not rooted in any consistent or desired methodological understanding but rather is truly a utilitarian method of seeking specific policy outcomes. Particularly, originalism is associated with specific stances and key issues in the culture wars, such as abortion and gay marriage. In order to assess whether literalism is merely a proxy for the issue of policy outcomes for issues of the culture war, or, as we assert, it is linked with a specific interpretive methodology, we ran a second model in which we controlled for whether the individual opposes or supports gay marriage.[69] While model 2 does indicate that support for gay marriage is negatively associated with originalism ($p=.03$) with a negative marginal effect of 4 percent on originalism, originalism is not merely a proxy for policy outcome because those who held to a literal biblical interpretation still statistically significantly held to originalism ($p=.02$). This means that Biblical literalists are likelier to be constitutional originalists whether or not they support same-sex marriage. When examining the marginal effects of model 2 we find that moving from nonliteral to a literal Biblical hermeneutic increases the likelihood that one adheres to originalism by 5 percent, nearly the same as model 1. Further, when we look at the effect for only those who support gay marriage, the marginal effect of a literal hermeneutic is also 5 percent. While there may be some relationship between constitutional adherence and policy position, there is still statistical evidence for our theory that hermeneutics as an interpretive methodology is consistent even in the face of those who adhere to a position for pure policy.

Because our primary variable is based in religious hermeneutics, we wanted to control for other important religious influences on political beliefs. While we found no statistical evidence for frequency of religious attendance being linked to originalism, there is some evidence, consistent with earlier studies, that evangelical belief is also associated with originalism. Finally, we also controlled for political variables and found that in both models, Political Party, Ideological Consistency, and agreement with the more conservative Tea Party are all significant predictors of adherence to originalism.

CONCLUSION

Ultimately, these findings will hopefully prove to be valuable to an understanding of the hermeneutical demographics of the country and how to understand public opinion as it relates to the Court and its rulings. Our argument adds important context to the broader research because this study provides evidence for the theory that constitutional decision-making may have a methodological basis, in this case rooted in their religious belief, rather than merely being a choice of policy outcomes; such recognition would critically influence future studies of constitutional decision-making and argue that a more nuanced position than mere attitudinal policy agreement may be at work by individual decision-makers. While this study may not be the final word on the issue, it provides an important nuance in the discussion. Further, while this is an assessment of the individual opinion of the American public, it would be interesting to determine if the theoretical basis would apply to elites and judges. It is important to note that we are not asserting that this evidence will be found in elite decision-makers (in particular, as judges are trained in legal interpretation methods as such the heuristic theory would no longer be as applicable), only that this evidence indicates the need for future study and a nuanced assessment of the evidence. Nevertheless, the rational ground of consistent interpretation of texts should be something scholars pay more attention to, especially with regard to religious people in the American political system.

NOTES

1. Jessica Martínez and Gregory A. Smith, "How the Faithful Voted: A Preliminary 2016 Analysis," *Pew Research Center* (2016), https://www.pewresearch.org/short-reads/2016/11/09/how-the-faithful-voted-a-preliminary-2016-analysis.

2. Janelle S. Wong, *Immigrants, Evangelicals, and Politics in an Era of Demographic Change* (New York: Russell Sage Foundation, 2018).

3. Diana C. Mutz, "Status Threat, Not Economic Hardship, Explains the 2016 Presidential Vote," *Proceedings of the National Academy of Sciences* 115, no. 19 (2018): E4330–E4339.

4. Alan Abramowitz and Jennifer McCoy, "United States: Racial Resentment, Negative Partisanship, and Polarization in Trump's America," *The ANNALS of the American Academy of Political and Social Science* 681, no. 1 (2019), 137–156.

5. Mark Setzler and Alixandra B. Yanus, "Why Did Women Vote for Donald Trump?" *PS: Political Science & Politics* 51, no. 3 (2018), 523–527.

6. Philip Gorski, "Why Evangelicals Voted for Trump: A Critical Cultural Sociology," *American Journal of Cultural Sociology* 5 (2017): 338–354 and Andrew L. Whitehead, Samuel L. Perry, and Joseph O. Baker, "Make America Christian Again: Christian Nationalism and Voting for Donald Trump in the 2016 Presidential Election," *Sociology of Religion* 79, no. 2 (2018), 147–171.

7. Ruth Braunstein and Malaena Taylor, "Is the Tea Party a 'Religious' Movement? Religiosity in the Tea Party Versus the Religious Right," *Sociology of Religion* 78, no. 1 (2017), 33–59 and Andrew L. Whitehead and Samuel L. Perry, *Taking America Back for God: Christian Nationalism in the United States* (Oxford: Oxford University Press, 2020).

8. Samuel Stroope, Paul Froese, Heather M. Rackin, and Jack Delehanty, "Unchurched Christian Nationalism and the 2016 US Presidential Election," *Sociological Forum* 36, no. 2 (2021), 405–425.

9. Ben Jacobs, David Smith, and Alan Yuhas, "Trump's VP: Mike Pence Brings Political and Evangelical Credibility to the Ticket," *The Guardian* (July 15, 2016), https://www.theguardian.com/us-news/2016/jul/15/mike-pence-donald-trump-vice-president-conservative-christian.

10. Catherine Garcia, "Mike Pence: 'I'm a Christian, a Conservative, and a Republican—in that Order'," *The Week* (July 21, 2016), https://theweek.com/speedreads/637487/mike-pence-im-christian-conservative-republican--that-order.

11. Bradford Richardson, "Trump: 'I'm Very Greedy'," *The Hill* (January 9, 2016), https://thehill.com/blogs/ballot-box/gop-primaries/265335-trump-im-very-greedy.

12. Eugene Scott, "Trump believes in God, but hasn't sought forgiveness," *CNN.com* (July 18, 2015), https://www.cnn.com/2015/07/18/politics/trump-has-never-sought-forgiveness/index.html.

13. Bernard Grofman and Reuben Kline, "Evaluating the Impact of Vice Presidential Selection on Voter Choice," *Presidential Studies Quarterly* 40, no. 2 (2010), 303–309.

14. Robert L. Dudley and Ronald B. Rapoport, "Vice-Presidential Candidates and the Home State Advantage: Playing Second Banana at Home and on the Road," *American Journal of Political Science* 33, no. 2 (1989), 537–540 and Christopher J. Devine and Kyle C. Kopko, "Presidential Versus Vice Presidential Home State Advantage: A Comparative Analysis of Electoral Significance, Causes, and Processes, 1884-2008," *Presidential Studies Quarterly* 43, no. 4 (2013), 814–838. See, for an opposite finding with different model specifications, Heersink, Boris and Brenton D. Peterson, "Measuring the Vice-Presidential Home State Advantage with Synthetic Controls," *American Politics Research* 44, no. 4 (2016), 734–763.

15. Cammie Jo Bolin, Ted G. Jelen, and Clyde Wilcox, "'Can We Get the Catholic Vote?': The Effects of Catholic Running Mates in Presidential Elections," in *Catholics and US Politics After the 2020 Elections: Biden Chases the "Swing Vote"*, ed. Marie Gayte, Blandine Chelini-Pont, Mark J. Rozell (New York: Macmillan, 2022), 187–213.

16. Amita Kelly, "McConnell: Blocking Supreme Court Nomination 'About a Principle, Not a Person'," *NPR Politics* (March 16, 2016), https://www.npr.org/2016/03/16/470664561/mcconnell-blocking-supreme-court-nomination-about-a-principle-not-a-person.

17. Alex Roarty, "Tea Party-Aligned Kentucky Gov May End 95-Year Democratic Reign," *Roll Call* (August 6, 2016), https://rollcall.com/2016/08/06/tea-party-aligned-kentucky-gov-may-end-95-year-democratic-reign/.

18. Ben Kamisar and Lydia Wheeler, "Trump soothes the right with list of Supreme Court picks," *The Hill* (May 18, 2016), https://thehill.com/blogs/ballot-box/presidential-races/280381-trump-unveils-list-of-11-potential-supreme-court-nominees/.

19. Laurie Goodstein, "Religious Right Believes Donald Trump Will Deliver on His Promises," *The New York Times* (November 11, 2016).

20. Oma Seddiq, "'Barrett is Like Jesus' for Evangelical Voters: Why Confirming a New Supreme Court Justice before the Election Mattered More to Republicans than Another Coronavirus Stimulus," *Business Insider* (October 28, 2020), https://www.businessinsider.com/confirming-barrett-mattered-more-to-republicans-than-stimulus-package-2020-10?utm_source=reddit.com.

21. J. P. Keenan and Ivan Pereira, "For Many White Evangelicals, the Supreme Court Makeup Solidifies their Support for President Trump," *ABC News* (October 16, 2020), https://abcnews.go.com/Politics/white-evangelicals-supreme-court-makeup-solidifies-support-president/story?id=73153818.

22. William Mishler and Reginald S. Sheehan, "The Supreme Court as a Countermajoritarian Institution?: The Impact of Public Opinion on Supreme Court Decisions," *American Political Science Review* 87, no. 1 (1993), 87–101; Micheal W. Giles, Bethany Blackstone, and Richard L. Vining, Jr., "The Supreme Court in American Democracy: Unraveling the Linkages between Public Opinion and Judicial Decision Making," *The Journal of Politics* 70, no. 2 (2008), 293–306; and Christopher J. Casillas, Peter K. Enns, and Patrick C. Wohlfarth, "How Public Opinion Constrains the US Supreme Court," *American Journal of Political Science* 55, no. 1 (2011), 74–88.

23. Ben Johnson and Logan Strother. "Does the US Supreme Court Respond to Public Opinion?," in *Open Judicial Politics*, ed. Rorie Spill Solberg and Eric Waltenburg (Corvallis, OR: Oregon State University, 2021), 751–767.

24. Michael A. Zilis, "Cognitive Heuristics, Inter-institutional Politics, and Public Perceptions of Insulated Institutions: The Case of the U.S. Supreme Court," *International Journal of Public Opinion Research* 33, no. 1 (2021), 76–98.

25. Kenneth D. Wald and Allison Calhoun-Brown, *Religion and Politics in the United States* (Lanham: Rowman & Littlefield, 2014), 102.

26. Amy Adamczyk, John Wybraniec, and Roger Finke, "Religious Regulation and the Courts: Documenting the Effects of *Smith* and RFRA," *Journal of Church and State* 46, no. 2 (2004), 37–62.

27. John M. Scheb II and William Lyons, "Judicial Behavior and Public Opinion: Popular Expectations Regarding the Factors that Influence Supreme Court Decisions," *Political Behavior* 23, no. 2 (2001), 190.

28. Herbert M. Kritzer, "The Impact of Bush v. Gore on Public Perceptions and Knowledge of Supreme Court," *Judicature* 85, no. 1 (2001), 32–38.

29. Jamal, Greene, Nathaniel Persily, and Stephen Ansolabehere, "Profiling Originalism," *Columbia Law Review* 111 (2011), 356–418.

30. Greene, Persily, and Ansolabehere, "Profiling Originalism," 373.

31. Greene, Persily, and Ansolabehere, "Profiling Originalism," 408–409.

32. Greene, Persily, and Ansolabehere, "Profiling Originalism," 408.

33. Christopher C. Lund, "Scriptural Interpretation and Constitutional Interpretation: An Introduction," *Michigan State Law Review* 2009, no. 1 (2009), 273.

34. Andrew R. Lewis, William D. Blake, Stephen T. Mockabee, and Amanda Friesen, "American Constitutional Faith and the Politics of Hermeneutics," *Politics and Religion* 13, no. 1 (2020), 57–88.

35. Lewis, Blake, Mockabee, and Friesen, "American Constitutional Faith and the Politics of Hermeneutics," 76.

36. Sanford Levinson, *Constitutional Faith* (Princeton: Princeton University Press, 1988), 30.

37. Charles M. Lamb, "Judicial Restraint on the Supreme Court," in *Supreme Court Activism and Restraint*, ed. Stephen C. Halper and Charles M. Lamb (Lanham: Lexington, 1982), 7–36, 16.

38. Arlin. Adams, "Is the Supreme Court Making a Significant Shift in Church-State Jurisprudence?" In *Government Intervention in Religious Affairs, II*, ed. D. M. Kelly (New York: Pilgrim Press, 1986), 69–78.

39. Walter C. Kaiser Jr. and Moisés Silva, *Introduction to Biblical Hermeneutics: The Search for Meaning* (Grand Rapids, MI: Zondervan Academic, 2009), 17.

40. Kaiser and Silva, *Introduction to Biblical Hermeneutics*, 18.

41. The categories of biblical interpretation are divided into a variety of different genera: While the Allegorical and Literal are the primary historical methods, there are also the Devotional, Liberal (i.e., Hobbes/Spinoza), Neo-Orthodox, and New/Critical Hermeneutics (see, for a lengthy discussion, Bernard Ramm, *Protestant Biblical Interpretation: A Textbook of Hermeneutics* (Ada, MI: Baker Books, 1999, 45–106). While there are subgroups and nuances to each of these genera, there often seem to be misconceptions over the precise meaning of "literal" interpretation. Thomas Horn notes that "The Literal Sense of any place of Scripture is that which the words signify, or require, in their natural and proper acceptation, without any trope, metaphor, or figure, and abstracted from mystic meaning" (cited in Ramm, *Protestant Biblical Interpretation*, 121). E. R. Craven seeks to modify the idea of literal to the concept of *normal*, noting that "Normal is used instead of literal . . . as more expressive of the correct idea. . . . the prophecies are to be *normally* interpreted (i.e., according to the received laws of language) as any other utterances are interpreted—that which is manifestly literal being regarded as literal, and that which is manifestly figurative being so regarded" (cited in Ramm, *Protestant Biblical Interpretation*, 121–122). Literal interpretation is seeking to understand the meaning of the words, as written, recognizing the importance of the style they were written in. Thus, knowledge of the genre, leading to interpreting poetry differently than narrative—see Robert Alter, *The Art of Biblical Narrative* (New York: Basic Books, 1981) and *The Art of Biblical Poetry* (New York: Basic Books, 1985)—is important, as also are the original language and its connotations and denotations.

42. Antonin Scalia, "Constitutional Interpretation the Old-Fashioned Way," Speech at the Woodrow Wilson International Center for Scholars in Washington, DC (March 14, 2005), 1, https://www.bc.edu/content/dam/files/centers/boisi/pdf/Symposia/Symposia%202010-2011/Constitutional_Interpretation_Scalia.pdf.

43. Stephen Breyer, "Our Democratic Constitution," in *The Enduring Debate: Classic and Contemporary Readings in American Politics*, ed. David T. Canon, John J. Coleman, and Kenneth R. Meyer (New York, Norton & Company, 2002), 302–314, 303.

44. Jaroslav Pelikan, *Interpreting the Bible and the Constitution* (Yale University Press, 2008), 8.

45. Pelikan, *Interpreting the Bible and the Constitution*, 7.

46. Gregory A. Kalscheur, "Christian Scripture and American Scripture: An Instructive Analogy?" *Journal of Law and Religion* 21, no. 1 (2006): 105 and 141.

47. Kalscheur, "Christian Scripture and American Scripture," 142.

48. Cheryl Boudreau, "Heuristics and Cues," in *Handbook on Politics and Public Opinion*, ed. Thomas J. Rudolph (2022), 272–282.

49. Samuel L. Popkin, excerpt from *The Reasoning Voter*; in *Principles and Practice of American Politics: Classic and Contemporary Readings*, ed. Samuel Kernell and Steven S. Smith (Los Angeles: Sage, 2013), 533–540; Arthur Lupia, "Shortcuts Versus Encyclopedias: Information and Voting Behavior in California Insurance

Reform Elections," *American Political Science Review* 88, no. 1 (1994), 63–76; Henry E. Brady and Paul M. Sniderman, "Attitude Attribution: A Group Basis for Political Reasoning," *American Political Science Review* 79, no. 4 (1985), 1061–1078; Ruth Hamill, Milton Lodge, and Frederick Blake, "The Breadth, Depth, and Utility of Class, Partisan, and Ideological Schemata," *American Journal of Political Science* 29, no. 4 (1985), 850–870; Victor C. Ottati, "Determinants of Political Judgments: The Joint Influence of Normative and Heuristic Rules of Inference," *Political Behavior* 12, no. 2 (1990), 159–179; John T. Scholz, "Trust and Taxpaying: Testing the Heuristic Approach to Collective Action," *American Journal of Political Science* 42, no. 2 (1998), 398–417; and Paul M. Sniderman, Richard A. Brody, and Phillip E. Tetlock, *Reasoning and Choice: Explorations in Political Psychology* (Cambridge: Cambridge University Press, 1991).

50. Popkin, excerpt from *The Reasoning Voter*, 534.

51. Richard R. Lau and David P. Redlawsk, "Advantages and Disadvantages of Cognitive Heuristics in Political Decision Making," *American Journal of Political Science* 45, no. 4 (2001), 951–971.

52. Robert P. Abelson and Ariel Levi, "Decision Making and Decision Theory," in *The Handbook of Social Psychology*, vol. 1, 3rd ed., ed. Gardner Lindzey and Elliot Aronson (New York: Random House, 1985), 231–309, 255.

53. Popkin, excerpt from *The Reasoning Voter*, 535.

54. Daniel Kahneman, *Thinking, Fast and Slow* (New York: Macmillan, 2011).

55. Geoffrey C. Layman, "Religion and Political Behavior in the United States: The Impact of Beliefs, Affiliations, and Commitment from 1980 to 1994," *Public Opinion Quarterly* 61, no. 2 (1997), 288–316 and John C. Green, *The Faith Factor: How Religion Influences American Elections* (Westport, CT: Praeger, 2007).

56. Wald and Calhoun-Brown, *Religion and Politics in the United States*, 25.

57. Monika L. McDermott, "Religious Stereotyping and Voter Support for Evangelical Candidates," *Political Research Quarterly* 62, no. 2 (2009), 340–354.

58. Brian Robert Calfano and Paul A. Djupe, "God Talk: Religious Cues and Electoral Support," *Political Research Quarterly* 62, no. 2 (2009), 329–339.

59. Nicholas Higgins, "Religious Influences on Latino Ideology and Vote Choice: Are Evangelical Catholics Different?," *Politics, Groups, and Identities* 2, no. 3 (2014), 402–421.

60. Calfano and Djupe, "God Talk."

61. Pelikan, *Interpreting the Bible and the Constitution*, 85.

62. Jerry Falwell, *Listen, America!* (New York: Bantam Books, 1980), 53.

63. Albert Mohler, "Thursday, March 21, 2019," *The Briefing* (March 21, 2019), AlbertMohler.com, https://albertmohler.com/2023/05/19/briefing-3-21-19.

64. Keith Bartholomew, "Biblical and Constitutional Interpretation and the Role of Originalism in Sixteenth- and Twentieth-Century Societies," *Anglican Theological Review* 82, no. 3 (2000), 537–545.

65. "Political Polarization in the American Public: How Increasing Ideological Uniformity and Partisan Antipathy Affect Politics, Compromise and Everyday Life," in *Pew Research Center*, Washington, DC (2014), https://www.pewresearch.org/politics/2014/06/12/political-polarization-in-the-american-public/.

66. Greene, Persily, and Ansolabehere, "Profiling Originalism."

67. Lewis, Blake, Mockabee, and Friesen, "American Constitutional Faith and the Politics of Hermeneutics," 66.

68. This table is presented in the standard form of empirical research. In examining this, there are three main parts to the statistical model: the Coefficient, which is the first number, either positive or negative; the P-Value, which is represented by asterisks (*); and the Standard Error, a number in parentheses. The Coefficient shows the change in the dependent variable (Originalism) with one step in that independent variable. If the number is positive, then the step is up (meaning that those variables are positively correlated with Originalism. If it is negative, then the step is down (meaning that those variables are negatively correlated with Originalism). The number in the parentheses is the standard error, which seeks to quantify the uncertainty in the relationship of the Coefficient. These two numbers are then used to create the P-Value, which is represented by the asterisks (*). P-value is a statistical way to indicate what is the possibility that the relationship between variables is merely by chance. A single asterisk means that there is 10% chance the relationship is by chance, double asterisks mean a 5% chance, and three asterisks mean a 1% chance or less. (The "Originally Written +" simply reminds us that we are coding responses in favor of reading the Constitution that way using a positive integer, 1.)

69. While we would have preferred to use a more complex variable of cultural wars, or use both issues like abortion and gay marriage, the survey did not gather data on abortion from the phase B participants who were asked about constitutional interpretation. Thus, we are left with only gay marriage as our control.

WORKS CITED

Alter, Robert. *The Art of Biblical Narrative*. New York: Basic Books, 1981.

———. *The Art of Biblical Poetry*. New York: Basic Books, 1985.

Abelson, Robert P. and Ariel Levi. "Decision Making and Decision Theory." In *The Handbook of Social Psychology*, Vol. 1, 3rd ed., edited by Gardner Lindzey and Elliot Aronson, 231–309. New York: Random House, 1985.

Abramowitz, Alan and Jennifer McCoy. "United States: Racial Resentment, Negative Partisanship, and Polarization in Trump's America." *The ANNALS of the American Academy of Political and Social Science* 681, no. 1 (2019): 137–156.

Adamczyk, Amy, John Wybraniec, and Roger Finke. "Religious Regulation and the Courts: Documenting the Effects of *Smith* and RFRA." *Journal of Church and State* 46, no. 2 (2004): 237–262.

Adams, Arlin. "Is the Supreme Court Making a Significant Shift in Church-State Jurisprudence?" In *Government Intervention in Religious Affairs, II*, edited by D. M. Kelly, 69–78. New York: Pilgrim Press, 1986.

Bartholomew, Keith. "Biblical and Constitutional Interpretation and the Role of Originalism in Sixteenth- and Twentieth-Century Societies." *Anglican Theological Review* 82, no. 3 (2000): 537–545.

Bolin, Cammie Jo, Ted G. Jelen, and Clyde Wilcox. "'Can We Get the Catholic Vote?': The Effects of Catholic Running Mates in Presidential Elections." In *Catholics and US Politics After the 2020 Elections: Biden Chases the "Swing Vote"*, edited by Marie Gayte, Blandine Chelini-Pont, Mark J. Rozell, 187–213. New York: Macmillan, 2022.

Boudreau, Cheryl. "Heuristics and Cues." In *Handbook on Politics and Public Opinion*, edited by Thomas J. Rudolph, 272–282 (2022).

Brady, Henry E. and Paul M. Sniderman. "Attitude Attribution: A Group Basis for Political Reasoning." *American Political Science Review* 79, no. 4 (1985): 1061–1078.

Braunstein, Ruth and Malaena Taylor. "Is the Tea Party a 'Religious" Movement? Religiosity in the Tea Party Versus the Religious Right." *Sociology of Religion* 78, no. 1 (2017): 33–59.

Breyer, Stephen. "Our Democratic Constitution." In *The Enduring Debate: Classic and Contemporary Readings in American Politics*, edited by David T. Canon, John J. Coleman, and Kenneth R. Meyer, 302–314. New York: Norton & Company, 2002.

Calfano, Brian Robert and Paul A. Djupe. "God Talk: Religious Cues and Electoral Support." *Political Research Quarterly* 62, no. 2 (2009): 329–339.

Casillas, Christopher J., Peter K. Enns, and Patrick C. Wohlfarth. "How Public Opinion Constrains the US Supreme Court." *American Journal of Political Science* 55, no. 1 (2011): 74–88.

Devine, Christopher J. and Kyle C. Kopko. "Presidential Versus Vice Presidential Home State Advantage: A Comparative Analysis of Electoral Significance, Causes, and Processes, 1884-2008." *Presidential Studies Quarterly* 43, no. 4 (2013): 814–838.

Dudley, Robert L. and Ronald B. Rapoport. "Vice-Presidential Candidates and the Home State Advantage: Playing Second Banana at Home and on the Road." *American Journal of Political Science* 33, no. 2 (1989): 537–540.

Falwell, Jerry. *Listen, America!* New York: Bantam Books, 1980.

Garcia, Catherine. "Mike Pence: 'I'm a Christian, a conservative, and a Republican—in that order'." *The Week* (July 21, 2016). https://theweek.com/speedreads/637487/mike-pence-im-christian-conservative-republican--that-order.

Giles, Micheal W., Bethany Blackstone, and Richard L. Vining, Jr. "The Supreme Court in American Democracy: Unraveling the Linkages between Public Opinion and Judicial Decision Making." *The Journal of Politics* 70, no. 2 (2008): 293–306.

Goodstein, Laurie. "Religious Right Believes Donald Trump Will Deliver on His Promises." *The New York Times* (November 11, 2016).

Gorski, Philip. "Why Evangelicals Voted for Trump: A Critical Cultural Sociology." *American Journal of Cultural Sociology* 5 (2017): 338–354.

Green, John C. *The Faith Factor: How Religion Influences American Elections.* Westport, CT: Praeger, 2007.

Greene, Jamal, Nathaniel Persily, and Stephen Ansolabehere. "Profiling Originalism." *Columbia Law Review* 111 (2011): 356–418.

Grofman, Bernard and Reuben Kline. "Evaluating the Impact of Vice Presidential Selection on Voter Choice." *Presidential Studies Quarterly* 40, no. 2 (2010): 303–309.

Hamill, Ruth, Milton Lodge, and Frederick Blake. "The Breadth, Depth, and Utility of Class, Partisan, and Ideological Schemata." *American Journal of Political Science* 29, no. 4 (1985): 850–870.

Heersink, Boris and Brenton D. Peterson. "Measuring the Vice-Presidential Home State Advantage with Synthetic Controls." *American Politics Research* 44, no. 4 (2016): 734–763.

Higgins, Nicholas. "Religious Influences on Latino Ideology and Vote Choice: Are Evangelical Catholics Different?" *Politics, Groups, and Identities* 2, no. 3 (2014): 402–421.

Jacobs, Ben, David Smith, and Alan Yuhas. "Trump's VP: Mike Pence Brings Political and Evangelical Credibility to the Ticket." *The Guardian* (July 15, 2016). https://www.theguardian.com/us-news/2016/jul/15/mike-pence-donald-trump-vice-president-conservative-christian.

Johnson, Ben and Logan Strother. "Does the US Supreme Court Respond to Public Opinion?" In *Open Judicial Politics*, edited by Rorie Spill Solberg and Eric Waltenburg, 751–767. Corvallis, OR: Oregon State University, 2021.

Kahneman, Daniel. *Thinking, Fast and Slow*. New York: Macmillan, 2011.

Kaiser Jr., Walter C. and Moisés Silva. *Introduction to Biblical Hermeneutics: The Search for Meaning*. Grand Rapids, MI: Zondervan Academic, 2009.

Kalscheur, Gregory A. "Christian Scripture and American Scripture: An Instructive Analogy?" *Journal of Law and Religion* 21, no. 1 (2006): 101–142.

Kamisar, Ben and Lydia Wheeler. "Trump Soothes the Right with List of Supreme Court Picks." *The Hill* (May 18, 2016). https://thehill.com/blogs/ballot-box/presidential-races/280381-trump-unveils-list-of-11-potential-supreme-court-nominees/.

Keenan, J. P. and Ivan Pereira. "For many white evangelicals, the Supreme Court makeup solidifies their support for President Trump." *ABC News* (October 16, 2020). https://abcnews.go.com/Politics/white-evangelicals-supreme-court-makeup-solidifies-support-president/story?id=73153818.

Kelly, Amita. "McConnell: Blocking Supreme Court Nomination 'About a Principle, Not a Person'." *NPR Politics* (March 16, 2016). https://www.npr.org/2016/03/16/470664561/mcconnell-blocking-supreme-court-nomination-about-a-principle-not-a-person.

Kritzer, Herbert M. "The Impact of Bush v. Gore on Public Perceptions and Knowledge of Supreme Court." *Judicature* 85, no. 1 (2001): 32–38.

Lamb, Charles M. "Judicial Restraint on the Supreme Court." In *Supreme Court Activism and Restraint*, edited by Stephen C. Halper and Charles M. Lamb, 7–36. Lanham: Lexington, 1982.

Lau, Richard R. and David P. Redlawsk. "Advantages and Disadvantages of Cognitive Heuristics in Political Decision Making." *American Journal of Political Science* 45, no. 4 (2001): 951–971.

Layman, Geoffrey C. "Religion and Political Behavior in the United States: The Impact of Beliefs, Affiliations, and Commitment from 1980 to 1994." *Public Opinion Quarterly* 61, no. 2 (1997): 288–316.

Levinson, Sanford. *Constitutional Faith*. Princeton: Princeton University Press, 1988.

Lewis, Andrew R., William D. Blake, Stephen T. Mockabee, and Amanda Friesen. "American Constitutional Faith and the Politics of Hermeneutics." *Politics and Religion* 13, no. 1 (2020): 57–88.

Lund, Christopher C. "Scriptural Interpretation and Constitutional Interpretation: An Introduction." *Michigan State Law Review* 2009, no. 1 (2009): 273–275.

Lupia, Arthur. "Shortcuts Versus Encyclopedias: Information and Voting Behavior in California Insurance Reform Elections." *American Political Science Review* 88, no. 1 (1994): 63–76.

Madison, James. *Federalist* 37.

Martínez, Jessica and Gregory A. Smith. "How the Faithful Voted: A Preliminary 2016 Analysis." *Pew Research Center* (2016). https://www.pewresearch.org/short-reads/2016/11/09/how-the-faithful-voted-a-preliminary-2016-analysis.

McDermott, Monika L. "Religious Stereotyping and Voter Support for Evangelical Candidates." *Political Research Quarterly* 62, no. 2 (2009): 340–354.

Mishler, William and Reginald S. Sheehan. "The Supreme Court as a Countermajoritarian Institution?: The Impact of Public Opinion on Supreme Court Decisions." *American Political Science Review* 87, no. 1 (1993): 87–101.

Mohler, Albert. "Thursday, March 21, 2019." *The Briefing* (March 21, 2019), AlbertMohler.com. https://albertmohler.com/2023/05/19/briefing-3-21-19.

Mutz, Diana C. "Status Threat, Not Economic Hardship, Explains the 2016 Presidential Vote." *Proceedings of the National Academy of Sciences* 115, no. 19 (2018): E4330–E4339.

Ottati, Victor C. "Determinants of Political Judgments: The Joint Influence of Normative and Heuristic Rules of Inference." *Political Behavior* 12, no. 2 (1990): 159–179.

Pelikan, Jaroslav. *Interpreting the Bible and the Constitution.* Yale University Press, 2004.

"Political Polarization in the American Public: How Increasing Ideological Uniformity and Partisan Antipathy Affect Politics, Compromise and Everyday Life." In *Pew Research Center.* Washington, DC, 2014. https://www.pewresearch.org/politics/2014/06/12/political-polarization-in-the-american-public/.

Popkin, Samuel L. "Excerpt from *The Reasoning Voter.*" In *Principles and Practice of American Politics: Classic and Contemporary Readings*, edited by Samuel Kernell and Steven S. Smith, 533–540. Los Angeles: Sage, 2013.

Ramm, Bernard. *Protestant Biblical Interpretation: A Textbook of Hermeneutics.* Ada, MI: Baker Books, 1999.

Richardson, Bradford. "Trump: 'I'm Very Greedy'." *The Hill* (January 9, 2016). https://thehill.com/blogs/ballot-box/gop-primaries/265335-trump-im-very-greedy.

Roarty, Alex. "Tea Party-Aligned Kentucky Gov May End 95-Year Democratic Reign." *Roll Call* (August 6, 2016). https://rollcall.com/2016/08/06/tea-party-aligned-kentucky-gov-may-end-95-year-democratic-reign/.

Scalia, Antonin. "Constitutional Interpretation the Old-Fashioned Way." Speech at the Woodrow Wilson International Center for Scholars in Washington, D.C. March

14, 2005. https://www.bc.edu/content/dam/files/centers/boisi/pdf/Symposia/Symposia%202010-2011/Constitutional_Interpretation_Scalia.pdf.

Scheb II, John M. and William Lyons. "Judicial Behavior and Public Opinion: Popular Expectations Regarding the Factors that Influence Supreme Court Decisions." *Political Behavior* 23, no. 2 (2001): 181–194.

Scholz, John T. "Trust and Taxpaying: Testing the Heuristic Approach to Collective Action." *American Journal of Political Science* 42, no. 2 (1998): 398–417.

Scott, Eugene. "Trump believes in God, but hasn't sought forgiveness." *CNN.com* (July 18, 2015). https://www.cnn.com/2015/07/18/politics/trump-has-never-sought-forgiveness/index.html.

Seddiq, Oma. "'Barrett is Like Jesus' for Evangelical Voters: Why Confirming a New Supreme Court Justice before the Election Mattered More to Republicans than Another Coronavirus Stimulus." *Business Insider* (October 28, 2020). https://www.businessinsider.com/confirming-barrett-mattered-more-to-republicans-than-stimulus-package-2020-10?utm_source=reddit.com.

Setzler, Mark and Alixandra B. Yanus. "Why Did Women Vote for Donald Trump?" *PS: Political Science & Politics* 51, no. 3 (2018): 523–527.

Sniderman, Paul M., Richard A. Brody, and Phillip E. Tetlock. *Reasoning and Choice: Explorations in Political Psychology*. Cambridge: Cambridge University Press, 1991.

Stroope, Samuel, Paul Froese, Heather M. Rackin, and Jack Delehanty. "Unchurched Christian Nationalism and the 2016 US Presidential Election." *Sociological Forum* 36, no. 2 (2021): 405–425.

Wald, Kenneth D. and Allison Calhoun-Brown. *Religion and Politics in the United States*. Lanham: Rowman & Littlefield, 2014.

Whitehead, Andrew L. and Samuel L. Perry. *Taking America Back for God: Christian Nationalism in the United States*. Oxford: Oxford University Press, 2020.

Whitehead, Andrew L., Samuel L. Perry, and Joseph O. Baker. "Make America Christian Again: Christian Nationalism and Voting for Donald Trump in the 2016 Presidential Election." *Sociology of Religion* 79, no. 2 (2018): 147–171.

Wong, Janelle S. *Immigrants, Evangelicals, and Politics in an Era of Demographic Change*. New York: Russell Sage Foundation, 2018.

Zilis, Michael A. "Cognitive Heuristics, Inter-institutional Politics, and Public Perceptions of Insulated Institutions: The Case of the U.S. Supreme Court." *International Journal of Public Opinion Research* 33, no. 1 (2021): 76–98.

Chapter 5

Originalism and Judicial Restraint

Lessons from the Lutheran Reformation

John Ehrett

ORIGINALISM AND THEOLOGICAL CRISIS

For theologians working in the Lutheran tradition, few concepts are more freighted with meaning than "law." Most famously, "law" is the first element of the Christian law-gospel dialectic, the "curb, mirror, and guide" by which God convicts human beings of their sin and drives them to the gospel.[1] And, secondarily, "law" in Lutheran theology refers to the moral coherence of creation as such, the natural order of Romans 1 that all human beings are capable of apprehending by their own epistemic lights.[2]

It is here that much Lutheran reflection on law qua law tends to peter out. Questions of legal order that are further downstream—such as the proper role and method of interpretation of the positive (written) law—have not often received sustained attention from Lutheran thinkers, especially in recent centuries. In particular, distinctively Lutheran perspectives have been largely absent from academic debates involving constitutional and statutory interpretation in the American context. This is unfortunate, given that Lutheran theological insights can help lay the groundwork for a unique approach to present challenges.

While the relationship between the civil state and the Christian Church—Luther's "two kingdoms" through which God governs human affairs—is always a potentially fraught subject, the present condition of this relationship has recently become increasingly controversial among leading lawyers and legal philosophers belonging to traditional Abrahamic faiths. Most notably, disturbed by the apparent ideological trajectory of the nation's elite, a number of prominent Roman Catholic thinkers have articulated what they see as a profound incompatibility between the norms of the contemporary American regime and the demands of Christian faith.[3] For such critics, the

Enlightenment-influenced inner logic of the American Founding could only ever lead in one direction—toward the marginalization of the spiritual in the name of technological advancement, and toward a pervasive moral dissensus lacking any possibility of ultimate resolution.[4]

As a particularly obvious example of this inexorable trajectory, these observers have pointed to the failure of the modern "conservative legal movement" to deliver anything close to the string of Supreme Court decisions that have so profoundly transformed the nation's cultural values in years past—*Roe v. Wade*, *Planned Parenthood of Southeastern Pennsylvania v. Casey*, *Lawrence v. Texas*, *Obergefell v. Hodges*, and *Bostock v. Clayton County*, just to name a few.[5] In place of a legal philosophy cognizant of natural law and human nature, these decisions have enshrined a decidedly liberal metaphysics valuing personal autonomy *über alles*—and for the most part, there has seemed to be little judicial appetite for revisiting any of them. The cultural ratchet seems to move in only one direction.

Not surprisingly, Christian thinkers of a traditionalist bent had expected more from judges and justices purportedly committed to the constitutional theory commonly known as "originalism"—a prioritization of "the meaning [the Constitution] was understood to have when adopted"[6]—over against theories of interpretation that would treat the document as a flexible expression of evolving American values. Once primarily associated with the political right, over the past several decades originalism has emerged from the margins of academic life to enjoy pride of place in the American judicial system, with even liberal Supreme Court justices like Elena Kagan admitting that, in some sense, "we are all originalists."[7] Given that originalist methodology claims to value a fixed public meaning of the text, binding upon judges for centuries, the widespread embrace of originalism *should* slow down or reverse the law's "secularizing" (for lack of a better word) trajectory. But this redemptive *cultural* payoff has simply never materialized, notwithstanding even major decisions like the Supreme Court's 2022 reversal of *Roe v. Wade*. The Court's decision in *Dobbs v. Jackson Women's Health Organization* studiously declined to resolve metaphysical debates about the status of unborn life—and so a surge of state constitutional amendments establishing a new legal right to abortion swiftly followed in *Dobbs*'s wake.[8]

In light of this history of apparent failure, some have called for a wholesale abandonment of originalism and its (at least surface-level) concern with judicial restraint, urging that this method be replaced by a judicial philosophy far more frank about wielding power in the service of a particular social vision. Most prominently, Harvard Law School professor Adrian Vermeule called last year for "an *illiberal legalism* that is not 'conservative' at all, insofar as standard conservatism is content to play defensively within the procedural rules of the liberal order."[9] For Vermeule, the constitutional text doesn't factor much into the picture at all: in his words, "thinking that the common good and its corollary principles have to be grounded in *specific* texts is a mistake; they can be grounded in the general structure of the constitutional order and in the nature and purposes of government."[10] The ultimate goal of constitutional law, on this view, is "to ensure that the ruler has the power needed to rule well."[11] Originalism, on this view, has had its day. After all, might it not be time to jettison a philosophy of interpretation that, *at best*, can only enshrine the societal values of 1789, rather than leading the public onward and upward to a higher good? As Vermeule put it, any attempt to defend the American Founding as a manifestation of the common good necessarily "leaves originalism in ultimate control, hoping that the original understanding will happen to be morally appealing."[12] Vermeule's proposed approach, conversely, pulls no such punches.

To be sure, Vermeule's project points toward a throne-and-altar vision of law largely unfamiliar to the contemporary Western world. But although Vermeule writes from a Catholic perspective, one might reasonably wonder whether his approach more logically follows from *Protestant* premises. After all, traditionally minded Catholic thinkers regularly charge Luther's Reformation with shattering the great edifice of medieval political order, in which kings and emperors could be called to public account by a higher spiritual authority.[13] The collapse of that church-state relation gave rise to the principle of *cuius regio, eius religio* ("whose land, his religion"), which necessarily collapsed spiritual authority into temporal authority and gave the state a kind of *de facto* theological monopoly.[14] Allegedly, when coupled with the Protestant turn toward theological nominalism—which separated the exercise of divine power from rationality—this shift laid the groundwork for various totalitarianisms to come.[15] And so, ideologically speaking, shouldn't Lutheran jurists be the *swiftest* to endorse something like Vermeule's "illiberal legalism"? Given their fealty to the secular state, mightn't they be the first to submit to the arbitrary will of a sovereign like Vermeule's post-constitutional ruler?

With that hypothetical looming in the background, an important question confronts the Lutheran judge, justice, or other magistrate working today: *Should* he or she be an originalist? Classically speaking, after all, jurisprudential and theological considerations are not two wholly alienated disciplines, but simply two ways of approaching the common subject of metaphysical order.[16] Setting aside secondary considerations—such as whether the judicial oath of office itself compels some version of originalism[17]—can an originalist methodological approach be intelligibly grounded according to Lutheran theological premises?

This chapter answers that question with *a qualified yes*. First, it provides a brief sketch of the development of originalism as a modern theory, before turning to how the historic Lutheran tradition—epitomized by Martin Luther himself and by Lutheran legal philosophers Johannes Eisermann and Johann Oldendorp—approached the question of legal interpretation. Building on these insights, it subsequently develops the outline of an account of legal interpretation that proceeds by analogy to the Lutheran theology of preaching, in which written text and context go hand in hand. In so doing, this account suggests the potential need for a revision—but not an abandonment—of certain standard originalist assumptions, such as the role of practical reasoning in judging and the relation between public meaning and authorial intention. "Originalist" modes of interpretation require that the text in question be taken as a unity, and intention is the conceptual cornerstone of that unity.

ORIGINALISM IN TRANSITION

Originalism as a theory of interpretation emerged primarily as a response to the controversial decisions of the "Warren Court"—a period of legal history in which the Supreme Court, under the leadership of Chief Justice Earl Warren, adopted expansive interpretations of constitutional rights-claims without offering much of a grounding in the text of the document.[18] Mainline constitutional theory, in the hands of almost uniformly progressive faculties at leading law schools, had evolved far beyond serious engagements with the Founding period. For those opposed to this legal revolution, a new intellectual organizing principle was required. Enter originalism.

Originalism as a method has evolved over time. Early theories of originalism stressed the "original intent" of the Constitution's Framers, but following a string of criticisms from those who found "original intent" too opaque, originalists shifted to defending the concept of "original public meaning," or the way in which the constitutional text would have been understood by those in the political communities that originally received and ratified it.[19] "Original public meaning" remains the dominant formulation of the originalist creed to the present day; in practice, the originalist method of constitutional interpretation looks principally to Founding-era documents and resources in an effort to ascertain what constitutional language would have meant to those among whom it was initially disseminated and by whom it was ratified.

The years following this shift to a concept of "public meaning" have been marked by a proliferation of "originalisms" of various sorts. One thinks of—just to name a few—John McGinnis and Michael Rappaport's view that the Constitution should be read according to "original legal methods,"[20] Randy Barnett's natural rights-based theory that the Constitution should be read with a "presumption of liberty" in view,[21] and Jack Balkin's "living originalism" that seeks to affirmatively account for democratic phenomena such as "equal rights for women, greater freedom of speech, federal power to protect the environment, and federal power to pass civil rights laws," among others.[22] These different proponents of "originalism" do not always agree with one another, to say the least—and this is saying nothing of those debates between originalists who employ the *same* methods and reach divergent conclusions. "Originalist" arguments have even been marshaled in support of results—such as the legalization of same-sex marriage—that would likely be utterly alien to the Founding generation or the public that ratified the Fourteenth Amendment's equal-protection guarantee.[23]

For most observers, though, this condition of *academic* fragmentation was masked by a surprising degree of *political* cohesion. Originalism (and the corresponding theory of statutory interpretation, often termed "textualism" in shorthand, which was heavily influenced by the writings of Antonin Scalia[24]) have become watchwords of the judicial nomination process among conservatives, though the precise nuances of nominees' originalist commitments are rarely probed in depth. And this "big-tent" approach has led to a string of apparent victories. Most significantly, the appointment of a succession of Supreme Court justices who at least pay lip service to originalist values has transformed the intellectual landscape of the nation's highest court, forcing litigants to rely more extensively on arguments from constitutional history than on more recent legal precedents or appeals to public policy.[25] The consequences of this shift are reflected in the heavily historical tenor of the Court's output in recent years.

But any complacency within the "originalist" movement was shattered by the Court's 2020 decision in the case of *Bostock v. Clayton County*—which held that existing proscriptions on sex-based employment discrimination *already extended* to employment discrimination against individuals on the basis of their sexual orientation or transgender status.[26] In other words, there was no need for Congress to amend the employment discrimination statutes to prohibit discrimination against LGBT individuals; by parsing the words of the law in a particular way, the purportedly originalist and textualist Justice Neil Gorsuch "discovered" that this discrimination was already prohibited. While *Bostock* did not involve the Constitution, but rather a federal statute, the central methodological objection of its critics was essentially an objection to textual interpretation done badly: *There's no plausible way this was what the law meant when it was enacted.* Surely, this was the sort of outcome that the ascendance of philosophies like originalism was meant to foreclose, wasn't it?[27] It is against this backdrop that more avant-garde theories of constitutional interpretation, such as Vermeule's "illiberal legalism," have come to fire the imaginations of traditionally minded lawyers and scholars.

Originalism today thus stands at a crossroads.[28] What internal resources can it possibly draw upon to keep from lapsing into the very subjectivity and indeterminacy that it was developed to combat? And how should a Lutheran jurist seeking to exercise his or her office faithfully confront this methodological debate? In examining this question, a careful exploration of the history of Lutheran jurisprudential thought is likely to prove especially fruitful.

HISTORICAL LUTHERAN APPROACHES TO LAW AND JURISPRUDENCE

Originalism, of course, did not emerge as a discrete interpretive method until hundreds of years after Luther first nailed his *Ninety-Five Theses* to the Wittenberg church door. One would search in vain through the corpus of historic Lutheran literature for any explicit interventions into modern debates about constitutional theory. Nevertheless, one can still ask questions relevant to today's debates: How did the leading figures of early Lutheranism understand the task of legal interpretation in general, and what insights might they offer to theologians and "magistrates" working today? The answer is multifaceted.

At bottom, early Lutheran writings on the subject reflect an account of legal interpretation that is consistent with the basic originalist commitment to the authority of written law over sovereign will or judicial preference, but that unabashedly incorporates consideration of context and circumstances in ways that many modern originalists might find discomfiting. To that end, a major theme that pervades historical Lutheran writings on the subject is the distinction between "law" and "equity"—a fundamental principle of Roman law, and dating back before that at least to Aristotle.[29] Here, "law" refers to the written text or fixed standard governing a particular subject, while "equity" refers to the application of principles of natural justice to circumstances not covered by the written text, even to the point of creating an exception to the written law.[30] It is this relationship between law and equity that forms the backbone of many early Lutheran musings on the proper role of legal authorities.

Luther: More Than "Lawyers' Law"

Why have a concept of "equity" in the first place? Equity is required because bare text, in short, cannot do justice to the full complexities of governance. In *On Civil Authority*, Luther himself stresses the inherent limitations of any legal system that would seek to govern a populace through the mechanistic application of texts, without room for any flexibility.

> [If] a prince is not wiser than his lawyers and does not have deeper understanding than is in his law books, he will surely rule after the saying in Proverbs xxviii: "A prince who lacks wisdom will unjustly oppress many." . . . For however good and proper laws are, they are all subject to one limitation, that they

> cannot make head against necessity. Hence a prince must have the law firm in his hand in the form of the sword, and measure with his own reason when and where the law is to be administered with severity or to be mitigated, so that reason may always dominate the law and be the supreme law and master of all law. . . . I say this that it may not be considered enough and a commendable course to follow the written law, the lawyers' law; something more is needed.[31]

While Luther is plainly critical of those who would try to make legal interpretation a strictly mechanistic endeavor, it is significant that nothing in Luther's remarks *denies* or *disparages* the need for "the lawyers' law."[32] Rather, the role of the "prince" in wisely executing the law is treated as intrinsically complementary to the existence of the law as such. The reasoning process by which a wise "prince" applies the text to real-world circumstances is, in essence, what now goes by the name of "prosecutorial discretion"—an expression of Aristotelian *phronesis*, or practical reason. The precise nature of the relationship between the sovereign and the written law, however, is left undefined by Luther. More comprehensive expositions of legal philosophy would later come from two Lutheran jurists teaching at the Evangelical University of Marburg—Johannes Eisermann (a former student of Philip Melanchthon) and Johann Oldendorp.[33]

Eisermann: Stability of Textual Meaning

Eisermann's lengthy work *On the Good Ordering of a Commonwealth*, which explores a wide range of topics ranging from human anthropology to natural law, is particularly relevant to the question of originalism and the judicial role. Most significantly, in the course of a discussion of the formation of ancient cities by plowing, as in the case of the legendary founding of Carthage, Eisermann makes a seemingly offhand observation that is highly relevant to the question of interpretive methodology:

> Now saying "the city reaches no further than the walls," it is to be understood that, when we give and bequeath by legacy to any, "all our goods in the city," that the law means "all that is within the wall, and not that [which] is in the suburbs."[34]

Murky though this observation may be, it is not unintelligible. In other words, if a law provides that "the city reaches no further than the walls," a subsequent will or testament of an individual that makes reference to "all our goods in the city" is to be interpreted according to the plain, literal sense of that law: Goods located in the suburbs (i.e., outside the city) are not covered by the will. For Eisermann, the phrase "walls" here refers to the outer physical walls of the city *at its original founding*; they do *not* refer to the more abstract idea of the boundaries of the settlement as they may have expanded over time. Eisermann, then, rejects a view of legal interpretation that would permit an open-ended, ahistorical interpretation of key legal terms: laws are generally to be read according to their historic meaning.

Elsewhere, Eisermann offers the rudiments of a normative justification for this rule by arguing that individuals need stable legal guidance in order to function in society:

> When judicial sentences must be pronounced, when offenders must be punished according to laws, when brotherhoods must be established, that the establishment be not contrary to laws, when statutes must be ordained without the injury or detriment of others—shall they do this well who know not what by law is forbidden, and what permitted?[35]

In other words, judges should avoid upending settled expectations about how the law works (reliance interests, as we call them now). In order to meaningfully make decisions about how to behave in the world, individuals ought to have a clear sense of what conduct is permitted and what is proscribed.

Consistent with this set of commitments—that the written, positive law retains meaning over time and is not infinitely elastic—Eisermann sharply rejects the view that the sovereign is in any sense above the law or otherwise not subject to it. In his words, "such laws as a city must be governed by ought to be kept by all men, and it is a thing that gives a harmful precedent if magistrates offend against the same."[36] Indeed, Eisermann explains that a polity's failure to practice this maxim must necessarily give rise to the despotism warned against in Plato's *Republic*:

> For so much as a commonwealth is a certain means to join men together in honesty of living, grounded upon laws, which ought to touch the profit of all, and the common advancement, not the subjects only ought to obey the same, but also the magistrates, who have no prerogative but such as is honest of itself and profitable to all, whereby each man has his own [that which he is owed] given unto him and others be not harmed: You are not permitted to do to others what you will not have done to yourself. And therefore Plato did well say that such a commonwealth must needs decay where the magistrate rules the law, and not the law the magistrate.[37]

None of this is to deny, however, the need for wise authorities to enforce the law. Indeed, Eisermann is supportive of the role of the magistrate in governing a society profoundly damaged by human sin. Because, in Eisermann's words, "there is no law of such penalty, none so surely established, but as soon as it is made there is one collusion or other found against it," some individuals must be tasked with the "accomplishing of laws, whose charge must be to see that the laws be kept, which is the duty of counselors or Magistrates, whom

I therefore call a living Law. For indeed the Law is dead which is not put in execution."[38] Here, he is aligned with Luther's view: without a civil authority to administer the law in real-world situations, the law becomes toothless.

For Eisermann, this process of putting the law into practice, of course, requires recourse to equitable principles: as he writes, "nothing [must] be done by pretense of law against equity."[39] Instead, "the state of the time, the place, and men" ought to be always "set before the[] eyes" of those exercising political authority.[40] Just as "one shoe is not meet for every man's foot," a legal rule should not always be applied acontextually, but rather take into account the background beliefs and practices of the community within which the law was promulgated.[41] This approach, for Eisermann follows from the fact that "everywhere they use no written laws, but instead . . . they have customs of Boroughs brought in by old manners, usages, and statutes, most profitable for the government of the commonwealth, the punishment of offenders, and defense of good men"; such norms are "of no less authority than the written Law is."[42] In the absence of what would be called today "statutory law," the "common law" of longstanding custom and practice is to be taken as authoritative, and this "common law" forms the backdrop against which "statutory law" is administered.

Oldendorp: Equity as Ubiquitous

The precise character of the relationship between law and equity came to the fore in the work of Johann Oldendorp, who

> insist[ed] that every application of a legal rule required a judge to apply equity . . . because every law by its nature is general and abstract. No lawmaker can anticipate perfectly the circumstances in which the rule will be applied. Thus every application of every rule has to be governed by equity.[43]

As John Witte explains further:

> Equity, for Oldendorp, was the capacity or faculty of a judge to make a reasoned and conscientious judgment in each particular case. Equity was an exercise of both civil reason and natural reason, of both the mind and soul, of the judge. On the one hand, equity required careful examination of the concrete circumstances of the particular case, enabling the judge properly to apply the general rule to those particular circumstances. It included earnest study, analysis, and comparison of comparable cases and legal authorities, as any good jurist and judge is trained to do. This was an exercise of civil reason, which was essential to every legal judgment.[44]

It would seem that on Oldendorp's view, properly speaking it is impossible to conceive of law without equity or equity without law; something akin to the dialectic of rule and application necessarily pervades all possible political regimes. A ruler or magistrate who focuses on the written law too closely—to the exclusion of the development of those faculties of reasoning necessary for faithful application of the text—engages in imbalanced and disordered behavior, rather like weight training only a single arm in the gymnasium.

Interpretation and Proclamation

There is an analogical relation here between this early Lutheran conception of legal authority (as the integrated, symbiotic relation between law and equity) and Luther's concept of the "Word of God" (as the biblical text in the event of proclamation to particular hearers at a particular time). Luther was quite keen to stress that words on a page are not properly equivalent to the Word preached:

> The apostles wrote very little, but they spoke a lot. . . . Notice: it says let their voices be heard, not let their books be read. The ministry of the New Testament is not engraved on dead tablets of stone; rather it sounds in a living voice . . . . Through a living Word God accomplishes and fulfils his gospel.[45]

Likewise, Luther emphasized that "Christ Himself has not written anything, nor has He ordered anything to be written, but rather to be preached by word of mouth."[46]

Just as proclamation of the Word does not displace the Scriptural text, but contextualizes it and is always accountable to it, so too the historic Lutheran conception of "equity" does not entail a displacement of the legal text, but rather (at least in Eisermann and Oldendorp's conception) reflects the fact that all meaningful laws entail circumstantial applications, which themselves ought to be faithful to the texts authorizing them. Moreover, the analogy rests on the presumption of intentional agency "behind" the written texts that are operationalized, and a regime in which the actor is accountable to that agency. The pastor who preaches is accountable to God, the Author of the Scriptures; the sovereign who executes the law is accountable to the original lawmakers and violates the public trust if he contravenes their purposes.

As has been shown, Lutheran jurisprudential thought has spoken of fidelity to the original meanings of texts alongside a robust consideration of circumstances relevant to application. But what if this fidelity to original textual meaning is not itself normatively defensible on theological grounds—such that none of this history *should* really matter for the future of judging? To date, the most comprehensive argument that Lutheran jurists should *not* be originalists—a lengthy essay by W. Bradley Wendel in the 2016 volume *On Secular Governance*—makes something like that claim.[47]

Against originalism, Wendel argues that "what rightly constrains [interpretive] subjectivity is not the literal words of a text, nor an institutional authority, but the community-bound practice of interpreting and putting the text into effect in the life of the community."[48] In so arguing, Wendel seeks to distinguish this "Lutheran" approach to texts from what he views as the errors made in fundamentalist and Catholic accounts of biblical interpretation; the fundamentalist emphasis on the literal words of the text, on his account, parallels the originalist move.[49]

What exactly this means pragmatically, for the magistrate attempting to exercise his or her office, is left unclear. For Wendel,

> [t]he resolution of questions of constitutional interpretation is often a matter of writing the next chapter in the narrative of our common political heritage, clarifying what is meant by values such as liberty and equality, and applying these meanings to the sorts of practical problems that present themselves to courts.[50]

In practice, Wendel posits,

> [a] judge seeking to determine what the Constitution requires or permits in any given case should, on this narrative approach to interpretation, understand him- or herself as part of a historically extended tradition of trying to work out what the words of the text mean not in the dictionary but *in practice*, in the life of the political community. . . . The subjectivity of the interpreter is constrained by the narrative itself, which permits some creativity but always reminds the interpreter that, at root, it is not *his* or *her* story to alter, but only to make a good-faith effort to continue.[51]

There are a number of problems with Wendel's proposed interpretive methodology. First, it is far from clear what "the narrative of our common political heritage" properly references. Was the Supreme Court decision that desegregated public schools, *Brown v. Board of Education*, a natural extension of the American story as a movement toward further equality—as many classical liberals would contend? Or might critical race theorists and white supremacists alike reach the conclusion that *Dred Scott v. Sandford* was a more appropriate extension of the fundamentally racialist American narrative, with *Brown v. Board* as an unusual outlier? Wendel provides no clear normative ground for adjudicating between these narratives. At most, he refers to "the promise of the Constitution to establish a system of democratic self-governance"—but *Dred Scott*, after all, was about the threshold question of who counted as a member of that self-governing polity in the first place.

Second, does not Wendel's willingness to invite judges to "writ[e] the next chapter in the narrative of our common political heritage" stand in deep tension with his commitment to democratic values?[52] Paradoxically, a juristocratic approach that collapses the judicial and legislative functions into a single entity has far more in common with Adrian Vermeule's model of "common-good constitutionalism" than with anything resembling democratic procedure.

Finally, for Wendel to claim that his narrative and nonliteral hermeneutic is a more "Lutheran" approach to interpretation is, at the very least, hard to square with Luther's absolute insistence on the *very* literal significance of the Eucharistic *est* (among other things).[53] To the extent there is an interesting parallel here between the role of the judge and that of the Lutheran preacher (a point Wendel rightly notes, and with which this chapter concurs), the relevant point of comparison is found in the twin binaries of *law/equity* and *Scripture/proclamation*; these binaries emphasize the complementary relationship between text and context. To affirm that the preached "Word of God" is *more than* the written biblical text on the page—because it is always spoken in a particular setting for a particular purpose to particular listeners—is not to affirm that the preached Word is *radically other than* the text, or somehow supplants it. Wendel therefore errs in claiming, in simplistic fashion, that the Word/words distinction can ground an approach to legal interpretation that freely departs from the original intent of the text.

In short, Wendel's proposed alternative to originalism is inert on arrival, and does not follow from Lutheran theological principles. The failure of Wendel's argument, however, is not sufficient in itself to establish that Lutheran jurists ought to be originalists under present conditions. For that, additional work is required.

NOTES TOWARD A "LUTHERAN ORIGINALISM"

On the whole, the Lutheran jurisprudential tradition generally suggests a view of law that is consistent with the essential core of originalist methodology: written law serves to restrain unbridled and dictatorial exercises of power, and (as Eisermann's example of the city walls reflects) this law generally ought to be interpreted consistently with its historical meaning. However, unlike much contemporary originalist scholarship, the Lutheran jurisprudential tradition is unafraid of acknowledging a degree of ambiguity in the application of the law, and does not claim that all legal problems can be solved formalistically. Taking all of this into account, what might a historically informed Lutheran approach to originalist interpretive methodology look like in the modern day?

Such a "Lutheran originalism" would, it seems to me, entail two specific revisions to orthodox legal originalism: (1) a shift away from the standard "original public meaning" formulation and a return to an earlier language of "original intent," and (2) an increased willingness to engage the questions of moral and political order that inevitably press in on the boundaries of originalist practice.

On the first point, texts *as* texts necessarily presume authors, since what distinguishes a written document from a mere scattering of unintelligible scribbles on a page is the presumption that authorial intent underlies the markings on the page. And from a Lutheran standpoint, an affirmation of something akin to classical intentionalism necessarily follows from the aforementioned preaching/judging parallel. Theologically, the meaning of the Scriptures is not contingent upon the existence of a particular public; the meaning of the biblical text is *what God intended that it mean*, even where that intent might unsettle dominant public understandings of the words recounted in Scripture. To adopt the alternative—to reject divine intent as the organizing principle of biblical interpretation and to stress something more like "original public meaning"—is, implicitly, to reject the presumption of the unity of the text itself, since the individual documents comprising the Bible stem from different periods and were addressed to different publics. Put more succinctly, in the context of biblical interpretation, prioritizing original public meaning over original intent vests primary interpretive authority in the initial historical recipients of the text rather than in its originating source—and that move necessarily destabilizes the internal coherence of Scripture, by excluding the possibility that its constituent texts form part of a single *divine* narrative.

And thus the analogy is brought home. Just as the Lutheran preacher is constrained in his range of textual interpretation by the underlying assumption that the biblical text presupposes an intelligent author—and thus he ought to preach in a manner consistent with the perceived intent of that author—the jurist is properly constrained by the knowledge that the legal text presupposes intelligent authorship and an intelligible meaning.[54]

However, that does not quite resolve the question of the *choice between* original intent and original public meaning as methodologies. All originalists would likely agree that the law's scope is limited and that it reflects intent, but might reach different conclusions about the relevant interpretive resources to consult. Does the Lutheran tradition offer any insights into this second-order issue?

At root, the question of intent and public meaning is a question of authority. *With whom does authority lie: with the one or ones from whom the text proceeds, or with those who originally received it?* In the theological context, this question can be answered fairly straightforwardly: authority lies with the God who speaks through the text.

But the Lutheran tradition has extended that claim further: the text is not simply a message from the divine, even a message to be cherished for all time, but rather a *thing through which certain functions are accomplished*, or *through which its Author is still doing things*. For Luther, "the Word is so effective that whenever it is seriously contemplated, heard, and used, it is bound never to be without fruit. It always awakens new understanding, pleasure, and devoutness and produces a pure heart and pure thoughts."[55] And in the *Small Catechism*, Luther stresses that "the Holy Spirit has called me by the Gospel . . . . In the same way he calls, gathers, enlightens, and sanctifies the whole Christian church on earth."[56] In other words, there is a functional, rather than simply communicative or expressive, dimension to Scripture: its "words are not lazy or dead, but are creative, living words."[57] The Word's Author is actively performing functions—calling, gathering, enlightening, sanctifying, and so on—through the text. "Authority" can here be envisioned less as the power of a single sovereign who stands behind the text, and more as the overarching design of the One who intentionally coordinates and draws together His people.[58]

An interesting parallel emerges here. The Constitution—and, for that matter, statutes—are likewise "functional" texts that serve a particular purpose. They lay out the nation's political underpinnings, "constituting" its governing institutions and coordinating its diverse members. And by whom was this organizing work of small-c "constitution," embodied by the large-C Constitution, effected? That work was done by the representatives chosen by and embodying "the People," set apart from the rest to exercise authority on their behalf.

What implications follow from this? If the Constitution is understood as a small-c "constitution" that *does something*, the centrality of intention—or maybe better, purpose—comes to the fore. The Constitution is a document not merely reflecting "intention" in an abstract sense—whatever that might mean—but rather "intention *to do a particular thing*," in this case structuring the nation's foundational institutions.[59] Hence, given the nature of the document itself, the views of the authors of the text regarding its meaning take precedence over those of individuals not themselves seeking to accomplish that end (i.e., its third-party readers). After all, an *identification* of the "particular thing" being done, over against other potential purposes, must be made by someone—and the creator of the text, who is seeking to do something through it, is plainly best situated to do so. A Lutheran conception of the Word's active function helps draw out this point.

Of course, ascertaining intention is never necessarily straightforward.[60] As Wendel rightly points out,

> it can be quite a difficult task to ascertain the intention of the authors of a text, and the difficulty of this task becomes greater with increasing temporal and cultural gaps between the moment of authorship of a document and its interpretation by a reader.[61]

But as Stanley Fish bluntly explains,

> In many cases and for many reasons it may prove impossible to figure out what the intention is, but that does not change the prior fact that figuring out what the

intention is is the interpreter's job, irrespective of whether or not he or she succeeds in doing it. Getting the right answer to the question "what is the meaning of a text?" is no guarantee that you will be able to do what the answer directs you to do.[62]

And it is at this juncture that the second distinctive feature of a "Lutheran originalism" comes to the fore: a willingness to do the work of the application and the contextualization that fall under the classical heading of "equity"—that is, the fleshing-out of the law's generalities, in the service of justice. For example, when considering language as gnomic as the Constitution's Ninth Amendment—"[t]he enumeration in the Constitution, of certain rights, shall not be construed to deny or disparage others retained by the people"[63]—it is no good to follow Robert Bork in dismissing the text as an "inkblot" that cannot be intelligibly applied.[64] The Ninth Amendment is part of the law, and it is part of the judicial function to give it a rational interpretation—even if that means turning to extraconstitutional sources such as the Anglo-American legal tradition.

Taken together, this outline suggests a way in which today's jurists may draw on the Lutheran jurisprudential tradition to shore up contemporary originalism's seeming vulnerabilities. What is incorporated here is not only an intentionalism that allows the most farfetched textual interpretations to be swiftly ruled out, but an awareness of the equity principles that authorize jurists to freely draw on the faculties of practical reasoning integral to the judicial role, such as when they are invited to do so by a text like the Ninth Amendment. And none of this need entail that the historical meaning of the text, when ascertainable, should be subverted or rejected. Thus, the normative values of traditional originalism are still retained. By consistently following such a logic,

> a Lutheran jurist might not approach such a problem in the radically skeptical way that strict judicial constructionists have done, by defining the judicial office over against the other locations of power within government. Rather, the Lutheran position would construct a positive vision of the role of the judge, both in restraining evil and in providing for the nurture of the community.[65]

So, in the end, should a Lutheran jurist be an originalist? Yes—but he or she should be a thoroughly *Lutheran* one, with all that that entails.

NOTES

1. Martin Luther, *Luther's Small Catechism with Explanation*: 307–348 (St. Louis: Concordia Publishing House, 2017), 54–55.

2. Luther, *Luther's Small Catechism*, 53; see also Carl E. Braaten, "A Lutheran Affirmation of the Natural Law," in *Natural Law: A Lutheran Reappraisal*, ed. Robert C. Baker and Roland Cap Ehlke (St. Louis: Concordia Publishing House, 2011), 3–16, 12.

3. See Michael Hanby, "The Birth of Liberal Order and the Death of God: A Reply to Robert Reilly's *America on Trial*," *New Polity* 2, no. 1 (February 2021): 84; see also Patrick J. Deneen, *Why Liberalism Failed* (New Haven, CT: Yale University Press, 2018). For a lengthier exploration of this turn from a Lutheran perspective, see Korey D. Maas, "Luther and Liberalism: A Tale of Two Tales (Or, A Lutheran Showdown Worth Having," *Concordia Theological Quarterly* 83, no. 3 (2019): 229–236.

4. See Hanby, "The Birth of Liberal Order and the Death of God," 82–83.

5. See, e.g., Gunnar Gundersen, "Originalism Has Failed," *The American Mind* (May 6, 2020), https://americanmind.org/features/waiting-for-charlemagne/originalism-has-failed/.

6. Robert H. Bork, *The Tempting of America: The Political Seduction of the Law* (New York: Touchstone, 1990), 12.

7. Confirmation Hearing on the Nomination of Elena Kagan to be an Associate Justice of the Supreme Court of the United States: Hearing Before the Senate Committee on the Judiciary, 111th Congress (2010).

8. On questions left unanswered by *Dobbs*, see Adrian Vermeule, "How to Read Dobbs," *Ius et Iustitium* (June 25, 2022), https://iusetiustitium.com/how-to-read-dobbs/ ("*Dobbs* is rife with ambiguities and silences, and poses as many further questions as it answers . . . . How far does *Dobbs* go, exactly? How far can it be taken?"). On the post-*Dobbs* electoral backlash, see Elizabeth Nash and Isabel Guarnieri, "In the US Midterm Elections, Resounding Victories for Abortion on State Ballot Measures," *Guttmacher Institute* (November 9, 2022), https://www.guttmacher.org/2022/11/us-midterm-elections-resounding-victories-abortion-state-ballot-measures.

9. Adrian Vermeule, "Beyond Originalism," *The Atlantic* (March 31, 2020), https://www.theatlantic.com/ideas/archive/2020/03/common-good-constitutionalism/609037/.

10. Vermeule, "Beyond Originalism."

11. Vermeule, "Beyond Originalism."

12. Vermeule, "Beyond Originalism."

13. Brad S. Gregory, *The Unintended Reformation: How a Religious Revolution Secularized Society* (Cambridge, MA: Harvard University Press, 2012), 145.

14. Gregory, *The Unintended Reformation*, 154, 163.

15. Robert R. Reilly, *America on Trial: A Defense of the Founding* (San Francisco: Ignatius, 2020), 154–156; Andrew Willard Jones, *The Two Cities: A History of Christian Politics* (Steubenville, OH: Emmaus Road Publishing, 2021), 164–169.

16. See Jones, *The Two Cities*, 125.

17. For more on this question, see John Ehrett, "'Common-Good Constitutionalism' and the Oath-Breaking Problem," *Patheos—Between Two Kingdoms* (March 31, 2020), https://www.patheos.com/blogs/betweentwokingdoms/2020/03/common-good-constitutionalism-and-the-oath-breaking-problem/; see also John Ehrett, "The

Oath-Breaking Dilemma," *The American Mind* (May 19, 2020), https://americanmind.org/features/waiting-for-charlemagne/the-oath-breaking-dilemma/.

18. Ken I. Kersch, *Conservatives and the Constitution: Imagining Constitutional Restoration in the Heyday of American Liberalism* (Cambridge: Cambridge University Press, 2019), 81–93.

19. See Kersch, *Conservatives and the Constitution*, 96–100.

20. John O. McGinnis and Michael B. Rappaport, "Original Methods Originalism: A New Theory of Interpretation and the Case Against Construction," *Northwestern University Law Review* 103, no. 2 (2009): 751–802.

21. Randy E. Barnett, *Restoring the Lost Constitution: The Presumption of Liberty* (Princeton: Princeton University Press, 2004), 54, 271.

22. Jack M. Balkin, *Living Originalism* (Cambridge, MA: Harvard University Press, 2011), 9.

23. See Steven G. Calabresi and Hannah M. Begley, "Originalism and Same-Sex Marriage," *University of Miami Law Review* 70, no. 3 (2016): 648–707.

24. See Antonin Scalia and Bryan A. Garner, *Reading Law: The Interpretation of Legal Texts* (St. Paul, MN: Thomson/West, 2012).

25. See Michael Ramsey, "SCOTUSblog on Originalist Amicus Briefs," *The Originalism Blog* (August 24, 2018), https://originalismblog.typepad.com/the-originalism-blog/2018/08/scotusblog-on-originalist-amicus-briefsmichael-ramsey.html.

26. See Bostock v. Clayton County; 590 U.S., 140 S. Ct. 1731 (June 15, 2020).

27. Josh Hawley, "Was It All for This? The Failure of the Conservative Legal Movement," *Public Discourse* (June 16, 2020), https://www.thepublicdiscourse.com/2020/06/65043/.

28. For a lengthier treatment of this debate, see John Ehrett, "The Bork Paradox and the Conservative Legal Movement," *American Affairs* 5, no. 3 (Fall 2021): 86–98.

29. Martha C. Nussbaum, "Equity and Mercy," *Philosophy & Public Affairs* 22, no. 2 (1993): 92–96.

30. Nussbaum, "Equity and Mercy," 92–94.

31. Martin Luther, "On Civil Authority," trans. and ed. W. H. Carruth, *The Open Court* 8 (1917): 492.

32. Note that Philip Melanchthon, however, was more cynical—at least in his early 1521 writings—about the utility of secular law, though his critique is better read as a preference for a "theonomic" social order than an anarchic one. See Philip Melanchthon, "*Loci Communes Theologici*," trans. Lowell J. Satre, in *Melanchthon & Bucer*, ed. Wilhelm Pauck (Louisville, KY: Westminster John Knox Press, 2006), 129 ("It is within the power of Christians either to use the Mosaic judicial codes or not. I should like . . . that the Mosaic laws be received in place of those of the Gentiles, which are often stupid. . . . [M]an ought to prefer the Word of God to human constitutions."). One might even hazard that Melanchthon is a sort of "original intent originalist" who simply prefers to take divine positive law as the founding "constitutional" text, though his remarks here are not specifically directed to the question of interpretive methodology.

33. John Witte, Jr., *Law and Protestantism: The Legal Teachings of the Lutheran Reformation* (Cambridge: Cambridge University Press, 2004), 168.

34. Johannes [Eisermann] Ferrarius, *A vvoorke of Ioannes Ferrarius Montanus, touchynge the good orderynge of a common weale* [*On the Good Ordering of a Commonwealth*], trans. William Bavand (London: Ihon Kingston, 1559), 11. Here, as well as below, I have rendered archaisms in the text into contemporary English for ease of reading.

35. Eisermann, *On the Good Ordering of a Commonwealth*, 65.

36. Eisermann, *On the Good Ordering of a Commonwealth*, 49.

37. Eisermann, *On the Good Ordering of a Commonwealth*, 49–50.

38. Eisermann, *On the Good Ordering of a Commonwealth*, 49.

39. Eisermann, *On the Good Ordering of a Commonwealth*, 49–50.

40. Eisermann, *On the Good Ordering of a Commonwealth*, 50.

41. Eisermann, *On the Good Ordering of a Commonwealth*, 50.

42. Eisermann, *On the Good Ordering of a Commonwealth*, 49–50.

43. Witte, *Law and Protestantism*, 165.

44. Witte, *Law and Protestantism*, 166.

45. From Luther's *Operationes in Psalmos*, in the 5th volume of the Weimar Edition of Luther's works (*WA* 5, page 537); quoted here from A. Skevington Wood, *Captive to the Word: Martin Luther, Doctor of Sacred Scripture* (Grand Rapids: Eerdmans, 1969), 90.

46. From Luther's commentaries, first book of the tenth volume of the Weimar Edition of Luther's works (*WA* 10, i, page 48); quoted here from Wood, *Captive to the Word*, 90.

47. W. Bradley Wendel, "*Nomos* and Narrative in Civil Law and Theological Ethics," in *On Secular Governance: Lutheran Perspectives on Contemporary Legal Issues*, ed. Ronald W. Duty and Marie A. Failinger (Grand Rapids: Eerdmans, 2016), 9–28, 17. See also Matthew Best, "Jesus Was Not an Originalist," *Medium* (March 23, 2021), https://pastormatthewbest.medium.com/jesus-was-not-an-originalist-8753bee097d7; and Paul Nuechterlein, "Time for Serious Conversation About America's Sacred Text," *Girardian Reflections on the Lectionary* (February 2017), http://girardianlectionary.net/blogs/2017-2/time-serious-conversation-americas-sacred-text/.

48. Wendel, "*Nomos* and Narrative in Civil Law and Theological Ethics," 18.

49. Wendel, "*Nomos* and Narrative in Civil Law and Theological Ethics," 11.

50. Wendel, "*Nomos* and Narrative in Civil Law and Theological Ethics," 15.

51. Wendel, "*Nomos* and Narrative in Civil Law and Theological Ethics," 19.

52. Wendel, "*Nomos* and Narrative in Civil Law and Theological Ethics," 15.

53. For Luther and the Lutheran tradition after him, Jesus's words at the Last Supper—"this is my body" (Latin: *hoc est corpus meum*), found at Matt. 26:26, Mark 14:22, and Luke 22:19—underscore the real presence of Christ's body and blood in the Eucharistic elements of bread and wine. To support that interpretation, the Lutheran tradition has placed great weight on the word *est*, or "is," in the clause. See Roland H. Bainton, *Here I Stand: A Life of Martin Luther* (Nashville: Abingdon-Cokesbury Press, 1950), 206.

54. See Marie Failinger, "The Justice Who Wouldn't Be Lutheran: Toward Borrowing the Wisdom of Faith Traditions," *Cleveland State Law Review* 46 (1998): 672 (explaining that "an intentionalist must at least reconstruct a human context and set of ideas specific to historical characters to give evidence for his argument"). In her article, Failinger engages in a lengthy exploration of the jurisprudence of Chief Justice William Rehnquist, a longtime member of a Lutheran congregation, and examines how Rehnquist's view of the relationship between law and religion is largely inconsistent with traditional Lutheran theological thought on the subject.

55. Martin Luther, "*The Large Catechism*," trans. William H. T. Dau and G. Friedrich Bente, in *Concordia: The Lutheran Confessions—A Reader's Edition of the Book of Concord*: 349–440 (St. Louis: Concordia Publishing House, 2007), part I, paragraph 101.

56. Martin Luther, "*The Small Catechism*," trans. William H. T. Dau and G. Friedrich Bente, in *Concordia: The Lutheran Confessions—A Reader's Edition of the Book of Concord* (St. Louis: Concordia Publishing House, 2007), part II, article 3.

57. Luther, *The Large Catechism*, part I, paragraph 101.

58. For more on the theme of authority as coordination, see generally Lee J. Strang, *Originalism's Promise: A Natural Law Account of the American Constitution* (New York: Cambridge University Press, 2019), 226–307. For a more critical treatment of this paradigm, see Steven D. Smith, *Fictions, Lies, and the Authority of Law* (Notre Dame, IN: University of Notre Dame Press, 2021), 13–18, 176–178.

59. Compare Anthony Thiselton, *Why Hermeneutics?: An Appeal Culminating with Ricoeur* (Eugene, OR: Cascade Books, 2019), 60–61, 78–79 (discussing the goal-directed nature of intentionality).

60. It can be difficult, but it is not impossible. See Richard S. Kay, "Original Intention and Public Meaning in Constitutional Interpretation," *Northwestern University Law Review* 103, no. 2 (2009): 725 (explaining, in defense of original intent, that "[i]nterpreters committed to ascertaining the genuine intentions of a collection of real human beings will also sharply disagree. But those disagreements are based on the production and examination of evidence."). Kay points out that on an original-public-meaning view, where rights-claims are concerned, "[i]t will not be difficult to discover a suitable hypothetical reader to take the words in their widest sense;" Kay, "Original Intention and Public Meaning," 723.

61. Wendel, "*Nomos* and Narrative in Civil Law and Theological Ethics," 22.

62. Stanley Fish, "The Intentionalist Thesis Once More," in *The Challenge of Originalism: Essays in Constitutional Theory*, ed. Grant Huscroft and Bradley W. Miller: 99–119 (Cambridge: Cambridge University Press, 2011), 116; see also William S. Blatt, "Interpretive Communities: The Missing Element in Statutory Interpretation," *Northwestern University Law Review* 95, no. 2 (2001): 629–689.

63. United States Constitution, Amendment IX.

64. Confirmation Hearing on the Nomination of Robert H. Bork to be an Associate Justice of the Supreme Court of the United States, Hearing Before the Senate Committee on the Judiciary, 100th Congress (1987).

65. Failinger, "The Justice Who Wouldn't Be Lutheran," 676.

WORKS CITED

Bainton, Roland H. *Here I Stand: A Life of Martin Luther.* Nashville: Abingdon-Cokesbury Press, 1950.

Balkin, Jack M. *Living Originalism.* Cambridge, MA: Harvard University Press, 2011.

Barnett, Randy E. *Restoring the Lost Constitution: The Presumption of Liberty.* Princeton, NJ: Princeton University Press, 2004.

Best, Matthew. "Jesus Was Not an Originalist." *Medium* (March 23, 2021). https://pastormatthewbest.medium.com/jesus-was-not-an-originalist-8753bee097d7.

Blatt, William S. "Interpretive Communities: The Missing Element in Statutory Interpretation." *Northwestern University Law Review* 95, no. 2 (2001): 629–689.

Bork, Robert H. *The Tempting of America: The Political Seduction of the Law.* New York: Touchstone, 1990.

Bostock v. Clayton County. 590 U.S., 140 S. Ct. 1731 (June 15, 2020).

Braaten, Carl E. "A Lutheran Affirmation of the Natural Law." In *Natural Law: A Lutheran Reappraisal*, edited by Robert C. Baker and Roland Cap Ehlke, 3–16. St. Louis: Concordia Publishing House, 2011.

Calabresi, Steven G. and Hannah M. Begley. "Originalism and Same-Sex Marriage." *University of Miami Law Review* 70, no. 3 (2016): 648–707.

Confirmation Hearing on the Nomination of Robert H. Bork to be an Associate Justice of the Supreme Court of the United States, Hearing Before the Senate Committee on the Judiciary, 100th Congress (1987).

Confirmation Hearing on the Nomination of Elena Kagan to be an Associate Justice of the Supreme Court of the United States: Hearing Before the Senate Committee on the Judiciary; 111th Congress (2010).

Deneen, Patrick J. *Why Liberalism Failed.* New Haven, CT: Yale University Press, 2018.

Ehrett, John. "'Common-Good Constitutionalism' and the Oath-Breaking Problem." *Patheos—Between Two Kingdoms* (March 31, 2020). https://www.patheos.com/blogs/betweentwokingdoms/2020/03/common-good-constitutionalism-and-the-oath-breaking-problem/.

———. "The Oath-Breaking Dilemma." *The American Mind* (May 19, 2020). https://americanmind.org/features/waiting-for-charlemagne/the-oath-breaking-dilemma/.Gregory

———. "The Bork Paradox and the Conservative Legal Movement." *American Affairs* 5, no. 3 (Fall 2021): 86–98.

Failinger, Marie. "The Justice Who Wouldn't Be Lutheran: Toward Borrowing the Wisdom of Faith Traditions." *Cleveland State Law Review* 46 (1998): 643–704.

Ferrarius, Johannes [Eisermann]. *A vvoorke of Ioannes Ferrarius Montanus, touchynge the good orderynge of a common weale* [*On the Good Ordering of a Commonwealth*], translated by William Bavand. London: Ihon Kingston, 1559.

Fish, Stanley. "The Intentionalist Thesis Once More." In *The Challenge of Originalism: Essays in Constitutional Theory*, edited by Grant Huscroft and Bradley W. Miller: 99–119. Cambridge: Cambridge University Press, 2011.

Gregory, Brad S. *The Unintended Reformation: How a Religious Revolution Secularized Society*. Cambridge, MA: Harvard University Press, 2012.

Gundersen, Gunnar. "Originalism Has Failed." *The American Mind* (May 6, 2020). https://americanmind.org/features/waiting-for-charlemagne/originalism-has-failed/.

Hanby, Michael. "The Birth of Liberal Order and the Death of God: A Reply to Robert Reilly's *America on Trial*." *New Polity* 2, no. 1 (February 2021): 54–85.

Hawley, Josh. "Was It All for This? The Failure of the Conservative Legal Movement." *Public Discourse* (June 16, 2020). https://www.thepublicdiscourse.com/2020/06/65043/.

Jones, Andrew Willard. *The Two Cities: A History of Christian Politics*. Steubenville, OH: Emmaus Road Publishing, 2021.

Kay, Richard S. "Original Intention and Public Meaning in Constitutional Interpretation." *Northwestern University Law Review* 103, no. 2 (2009): 703–726.

Kersch, Ken I. *Conservatives and the Constitution: Imagining Constitutional Restoration in the Heyday of American Liberalism*. Cambridge: Cambridge University Press, 2019.

Luther, Martin. "On Civil Authority," translated and edited by W. H. Carruth. *The Open Court* 8 (1917): 478–495.

———. "*The Large Catechism*." Translated by William H. T. Dau and G. Friedrich Bente. In *Concordia: The Lutheran Confessions—A Reader's Edition of the Book of Concord*: 349–440. St. Louis: Concordia Publishing House, 2007.

———. "*The Small Catechism*." Translated by William H. T. Dau and G. Friedrich Bente. In *Concordia: The Lutheran Confessions—A Reader's Edition of the Book of Concord*: 307–348. St. Louis: Concordia Publishing House, 2007.

———. *Luther's Small Catechism with Explanation*. St. Louis: Concordia Publishing House, 2017.

Maas, Korey D. "Luther and Liberalism: A Tale of Two Tales (Or, A Lutheran Showdown Worth Having." *Concordia Theological Quarterly* 83, no. 3 (2019): 229–236.

Melanchthon, Philip. "*Loci Communes Theologici*." Translated by Lowell J. Satre. In *Melanchthon & Bucer*, edited by Wilhelm Pauck. Louisville, KY: Westminster John Knox Press, 2006.

McGinnis, John O. and Michael B. Rappaport. "Original Methods Originalism: A New Theory of Interpretation and the Case Against Construction." *Northwestern University Law Review* 103, no. 2 (2009): 751–802.

Nash, Elizabeth and Isabel Guarnieri. "In the US Midterm Elections, Resounding Victories for Abortion on State Ballot Measures." *Guttmacher Institute* (November 9, 2022). https://www.guttmacher.org/2022/11/us-midterm-elections-resounding-victories-abortion-state-ballot-measures.

Nuechterlein, Paul. "Time for Serious Conversation About America's Sacred Text." *Girardian Reflections on the Lectionary* (February 2017). http://girardianlectionary.net/blogs/2017-2/time-serious-conversation-americas-sacred-text/.

Nussbaum, Martha C. "Equity and Mercy." *Philosophy & Public Affairs* 22, no. 2 (1993): 83–125.

Ramsey, Michael. "SCOTUSblog on Originalist Amicus Briefs." *The Originalism Blog* (August 24, 2018). https://originalismblog.typepad.com/the-originalism-blog/2018/08/scotusblog-on-originalist-amicus-briefsmichael-ramsey.html.

Reilly, Robert R. *America on Trial: A Defense of the Founding*. San Francisco, CA: Ignatius, 2020.

Scalia, Antonin and Bryan A. Garner. *Reading Law: The Interpretation of Legal Texts*. St. Paul, MN: Thomson/West, 2012.

Smith, Steven D. *Fictions, Lies, and the Authority of Law*. Notre Dame, IN: University of Notre Dame Press, 2021.

Strang, Lee J. *Originalism's Promise: A Natural Law Account of the American Constitution*. New York: Cambridge University Press, 2019.

Thiselton, Anthony. *Why Hermeneutics?: An Appeal Culminating with Ricoeur*. Eugene, OR: Cascade Books, 2019.

Vermeule, Adrian. "Beyond Originalism." *The Atlantic* (March 31, 2020). https://www.theatlantic.com/ideas/archive/2020/03/common-good-constitutionalism/609037/.

———. "How to Read Dobbs." *Ius et Iustitium* (June 25, 2022). https://iusetiustitium.com/how-to-read-dobbs/.

Wendel, W. Bradley. "*Nomos* and Narrative in Civil Law and Theological Ethics." In *On Secular Governance: Lutheran Perspectives on Contemporary Legal Issues*, edited by Ronald W. Duty and Marie A. Failinger, 9–28. Grand Rapids: Eerdmans, 2016.

Witte, John, Jr. *Law and Protestantism: The Legal Teachings of the Lutheran Reformation*. Cambridge: Cambridge University Press, 2004.

Wood, A. Skevington. *Captive to the Word: Martin Luther, Doctor of Sacred Scripture*. Grand Rapids: Eerdmans, 1969.

Chapter 6

The Originalist Hermeneutic in Biblical and Constitutional Context

Comparing and Contrasting the Notion of Originalism in Two Very Different Fields

Mark A. Snoeberger

The second element of Charles Ryrie's well-worn sine qua non of dispensationalism is a "literal" hermeneutic.[1] This adjective has proven less than satisfactory over the years. The term regularly earns snickers from critics as connoting wooden interpretation that eschews figures of speech (and, to be honest, some dispensationalists have given credence to this criticism by being slow to admit to obvious figures in the Bible). Certain dispensationalists have also abused the principle of literalism variously by minimizing context, discovering meaning chiefly in etymology or strict dictionary definitions, by developing other, rogue hermeneutical principles (e.g., the "law of first mention"), or by being overly skeptical about the evolutionary nature of language.[2]

Because of these abuses, careful dispensationalists have for decades sought diligently for a better label for their hermeneutical approach, but no clear winner has emerged. Some have added adjectives (a *consistently* literal approach); others have multiplied qualifiers such as "normal," "plain," or "ordinary," but these beg the question, and often pejoratively. Others have opted for the more broadly accepted "grammatical-historical" rubric, but since a vastly diverse field of scholars uses this rubric, its value for identifying a distinctively dispensational approach is limited.

Others still have conceded the elusiveness of a trim label and have instead offered a series of descriptive principles that clarify what "literalism" means for them. John Feinberg and Michael Vlach are exemplary in this regard: both argue that (1) the Old Testament must be permitted to speak on its own terms without reinterpretation by the New Testament; that (2) promises made to ethnic Israel must be fulfilled by ethnic Israel (and that no amount of typologism can alter this conclusion); and that (3) while there exist multiple senses of key terms such as "seed" and "Israel," no one sense swallows up the others.[3] Rolland McCune has offered, more abstractly, a series of four "received laws of language" that he defends transcendentally in defining what he means by *literalism,*

- the Univocal Nature of Language Meaning;
- the Jurisdiction of Authorial Intent;
- the Unitary Authorship [and Intention] of Scripture;
- and the Textually Based Locus of Meaning.[4]

Each of these helps to clarify the idea of literalism and allays at least some misunderstanding; still, one longs for a more nimble label to precisely capture the traditional dispensational approach to hermeneutics. Other competing biblical theologies sport concise hermeneutical labels—labels like *mythological*, *anagogical*, *typological*, *Christological* (or *Christotelic*), *complementary*, and *sensus plenior* come to mind—but traditional dispensationalists have been stymied in this regard.

Thankfully, the discipline of secular jurisprudence has recently come through with a more carefully defined and more publicly accepted term that is positioned to compete for the elusive label that dispensationalists are seeking, namely *originalism*. But are biblical literalism and constitutional originalism synonymous concepts? This essay explores the development of constitutional originalism, then compares and contrasts originalism with the "literal" hermeneutic long employed by dispensationalists. While this study falls short of finding synonymy between constitutional and biblical originalism, it finds greater similarity than constitutional originalists have generally conceded.

THE IDEA OF CONSTITUTIONAL ORIGINALISM

Saying that *originalism* is a better-defined and more publicly accepted idea than *literalism* may seem to be a case of faint praise. Originalism (and the subsidiary idea of *textualism*) has been widely misunderstood in modern literature and in the court of public opinion. The newness of this notion[5] and the swift evolution of the concept even among proponents has also rendered settled definition elusive. The idea of originalism may be ancient, but the quest to define the term in modern jurisprudence has proven turbulent.

When Brest defined *originalism* in 1980, he precipitated debate in his definition: "By 'originalism' I mean the familiar approach to constitutional adjudication that accords binding authority to the text of the Constitution or the intention of its adopters." He then moved swiftly to identify two distinct forms of originalism, viz., *strict textualism* (a.k.a., so Brest opines, *strict constructionism*) and *strict intentionalism.*[6] In so doing, Brest was confused, I believe, on three counts: (1) he bifurcated the originalist community into competing camps—strict textualists and strict intentionalists; then he misrepresented (2) the intentionalist camp as operating on the absurd assumption that the whole collective of the framers and ratifiers of the Constitution sported a singular intention whenever they spoke[7] and (3) the textualist camp as arguing nothing more than wooden reconstruction of the Constitution according to its very most basic linguistic units: *words*.

The Specter of Competing Originalisms

The very earliest originalists used as part of their vocabulary the idea of "original intent," a label familiar to biblical hermeneuts.[8] By this phrase they spoke not of an elusive, shared intention of all the framers and ratifiers, but the *individual* intentions of *specific* framers and ratifiers—intentions that frequently were held in common. Edwin Meese is exemplary of this understanding, arguing that the originalist impulse looks, when possible, for "demonstrable consensus among the framers and ratifiers," but in the absence of such consensus settles on an interpretation that does "not contradict the text of the Constitution itself."[9] Supreme Court Justice Antonin Scalia, likewise, argued that originalism is, at its heart, the discovery of the "'objectified' intent" of the framers,[10] noting that "if we were really looking for the subjective intent of the enacting legislature we would more likely find it by paying attention to the text (and legislative intent) of the statute in isolation."[11] Both men agreed that "intention" is discovered principally in texts, but allowed that when a given text is less than perfectly clear, consensus among the framers may be sought. "Intentionalism" and "textualism" were not, at least early on, sparring partners, but friends.

As time has passed, however, a gradual diminution of the "original intent" emphasis has occurred. In part this is because of the misunderstanding and scorn propagated by Brest and others of his ilk, but the driving concern, it seems, was the insidious abuse of "intent" language to reconcile originalism and living constitutionalism. One H. Jefferson Powell, for instance, in a 1985 article, "The Original Understanding of Original Intent," cleverly argued, using originalist principles, that it was not the intent of the framers for moderns to interpret the Constitution according to the principles of originalism.[12] Eventually, originalism itself was threatened by the idea that "We are all Originalists." The idea of original intent needed to be tempered.

Scalia took the lead in proposing changes to originalist vocabulary, pleading in a 1986 address before the Attorney General's Conference of Economic

Liberties for his fellow-originalists to "change the label from the Doctrine of Original Intent to the Doctrine of Original Meaning."[13] Justices Thomas, Alito, Barrett, and Gorsuch all eventually followed Scalia in turning against "original intent." The Constitution, they observed, was (1) cobbled together by men with doctrinal differences, was (2) certainly not inerrant, and (3) surely was not free from internal contradiction (which is to say, *The Constitution is not the Bible!*). Further, the pursuit of original intent apart from the text opened doors to selective originalism. In Keith Whittington's words, "The language of original intent too often encouraged the pursuit down false trails in an effort to locate the preferences of political actors, or buried ideas, or value systems."[14] The idea of "authorial intent," in retrospect, turned out to be a much less helpful category in constitutional studies than it is in biblical studies. This abandonment of "original/authorial intent" language effectively narrowed the notions of originalism/textualism to two objective principles: (1) that a text's meaning is *fixed*, and (2) that the locus of that fixed meaning is in the *original public meaning* of that text.

Most modern originalists now see "original/authorial intent" as having become a hostage of *purposivism*, the principal early sparring partner of originalism. Purposivism argues that modern interpreters should seek the "purpose," "spirit," and "intention" of a given text, then extrapolate from these to updated understandings consistent with the original author's *trajectory of thought*, offering suggestions about what the original author might say today had he survived to see the world as it has become.[15] As time has passed, however, purposivism has proved fleeting—a clever stepping-stone for progressive interpreters to achieve their real goal: discovering, by any means possible, "what the judges currently thought it desirable for it [the text] to mean."[16]

Originalism, Textualism, and Constructionism

We must now take up the question whether Originalism, Textualism, and Constructionism are synonymous or incongruent ideas. We have noted above that critics of Originalism have tended to (1) distinguish originalism from textualism, but to (2) equate textualism and constructionism. I would suggest that the opposite is closer to the truth: originalism and textualism are very nearly synonymous, and the supposed identity of textualism with constructionism is much more strained.

It is commonly believed that textualism is a rogue extrapolation of originalism, an extreme form of originalism that is in many ways incompatible with it. This is not the case. Most originalists use the terms *originalism* and *textualism* interchangeably, using the latter as an alternative to purposivism which points to the location of Constitutional meaning *in the text*. Others view originalism as instead a broad category of which textualism is a part. In the latter approach, *originalism* is an approach to hermeneutics that can accommodate successfully any genre, identifying the original public meaning that intelligent readers would have deduced, at the time of writing, by means of a shared body of syntax/devices/figures/genres,[17] while *textualism*, more narrowly, reflects the application of originalist principles to statutory law—a literary genre that is extremely precise and legally binding, and which allows almost no wiggle-room—not only in interpretation, but even in application. In either case, however, originalism and textualism remain compatible.

In the run-up to the Neil Gorsuch confirmation, one shocking example of the textualist approach circulated widely. In the case *TransAm Trucking v. Administrative Review Board*, for which Gorsuch wrote a minority dissent, a trucker, Alphonse Maddin, lost the function of both his cabin heat and his trailer brakes (though not the brakes on his cab) on a bitterly cold night. Bound by contract to stay with his load, he called his supervisor and requested assistance, but the response was slow. After additional calls and fearing for his life, Maddin unhitched the trailer, abandoned his cargo, and drove his cab to safety—an offense for which he was fired. A majority of judges ruled in favor of Maddin, arguing that he had obeyed the "spirit" of his contract (though not the letter), and that he had assumed reasonably and in good faith that his employer would view his circumstances as extraordinary, releasing him from the stringent demands of the contract between them. Gorsuch demurred, arguing that contracts, being precise legal instruments, are to be read exactly—the trucker had violated his contract and could be fired. Gorsuch's concern was *precedent*: if one trucker was free to impose his own personal ethical standards on, and invent exceptions in, the discharge of a contract, then *any* party to *any* contract might potentially do the same, eventually destroying the very concept of a legal contract entirely.[18] This "textualist" approach to statutory law specifically, while shocking to many, is essential to the successful perpetuation of the rule of law generally.

While textualism does not threaten originalism, however, there *is* a rogue expression of originalism that does threaten the model: *strict constructionism*. A textualist, Scalia notes, *construes* a text neither "strictly" nor "leniently," but "reasonably."[19] The lenient constructionist, he argues, is a "nihilist"—one for whom words have no meaning at all and may be assigned whatever meaning the interpreter wishes.[20] What interests us more is Scalia's assessment of the strict constructionist, whom he also holds in very low regard. A strict constructionist (what some might label a "wooden literalist") is one who construes every text according to the most common denotation of the words used. Scalia's specific example of strict constructionist abuse is a case in which a criminal was liable to a statutorily increased jail term for "using a firearm" in the commission of a crime. The criminal being tried had offered a handgun as trade for illegal drugs. The majority opined that the criminal deserved the longer sentence, but Scalia demurred. Why? Because while the criminal technically "used a firearm," he did not "use a firearm" in the specific sense obviously intended by the statute (i.e., he didn't use it *as a weapon*).[21] Words have a range of meaning, but can never mean all of those meanings in any one context—to do so is to commit what James Barr labeled the "illegitimate totality transfer fallacy."[22] Nor, further, may an interpreter select from that range of meanings a particular meaning that serves his own ends. We select reasonable meanings; to insist on unreasonably strict meanings is to employ, as Scalia describes it, "a degraded form of textualism that brings the whole philosophy into disrepute."[23]

Both Scalia and Supreme Court Justice Amy Coney Barrett reject, interestingly, a favorable comparison of constitutional originalism and biblical literalism based on their understanding that strict constructionism is the cardinal crime of biblical literalism: biblical literalism "strips language of its context" and understands language by "mechanistically consulting dictionary definitions" apart from shared figures of speech and all the lively nuance that make up the social construct of linguistic communication.[24] The question is whether this assessment is correct. We thus turn the corner in our presentation to search for potential points of comparison and contrast between constitutional originalism and biblical literalism.

CONTRASTS BETWEEN CONSTITUTIONAL ORIGINALISM AND DISPENSATIONAL LITERALISM

We have demonstrated in the foregoing that several self-described originalists disclaim association with biblical literalism. However, it seems to me that the two primary reasons they offer for this disassociation are not so significant as they initially appear. The first reason is semantic, viz., the biblical originalist's supposed engagement in the "illegitimate totality transfer fallacy" and other similar semantic fallacies.[25] But here's the thing: the fact that grammatical-historical biblical interpreters such as D. A. Carson *agree* with Scalia and Barrett that these are *fallacies* undermines the latters' criticisms. I submit that Barrett, Scalia, and others tend to extend censorious derogation toward biblical literalism all the while complaining that others do to them the very same thing! In the last analysis, this contrast between constitutional originalism and biblical literalism is not so very great, and might perhaps be turned into a favorable comparison—constitutional originalists and biblical literalists are persistently and uncharitably accused of identical errors by their critics.

But semantic concerns are not the only differences between constitutional originalism and biblical literalism. We have noted above that constitutional originalists, secondly, increasingly hold "original/authorial intent" at arm's length. Modern constitutional originalists understand authorial intent to be not only elusive and distilled (since there are many independent voices), but also irrelevant (since we already have their intent "objectivized" in texts[26]) and destructive (since the individual framers and ratifiers possessed intentions that differed not only from each other, but even from their own writings). The authors may even have inadvertently written something other than they intended. All of these factors have led constitutional originalists to focus on the "original public meaning" of the texts and to abandon their quest for original intent except in the very rarest of instances. This may seem at first blush an insuperable barrier to adopting the term *originalist* to describe dispensational literalism.

I am not sure, however, that this is the case. The reason that constitutional originalism holds "original/authorial intent" at arm's length is not a difference of hermeneutical method, but a difference between their respective literary bodies: the Constitution and the Bible. *Very simply, the Bible is inspired, but the United States Constitution is not.* Because of the miracle of inspiration, original intent and original public meaning are rendered synonymous in a way that is true of no other literary corpus ever conceived. Inspiration, by its very definition, assures us that "there is an identity between [the authors'] words and [God's],"[27] and, further, that there is an identity between the authors' *intentions* and God's. Even more than this, the miracle of inspiration, conducted over fifteen centuries, ascertains that there is no discrepancy between *any* of the words/intentions of dozens of human authors. This extended miracle eliminates nearly all of the constitutional originalist's concerns about original intent: each biblical text has a single meaning; no errors of transmission occurred in the communication of the Bible; and perfect harmony exists between all of its authors. These facts mean that, unlike the constitutional originalist, the biblical literalist has at his disposal robust access to the *analogia scriptura*, whereby he may freely compare Scripture with Scripture to discover additional clues about original *intent* in his quest for original *meaning*. In the last analysis, however, the difference between biblical literalism and constitutional originalism is not one of method, but one of literary corpus. Methodological harmony between the two hermeneutical approaches is not disrupted.

Peter J. Smith and Robert W. Tuttle, whose article "Biblical Literalism and Constitutional Originalism" is currently the most careful comparison/contrast of the two approaches,[28] identify another pair of contrasts between biblical literalism and constitutional originalism. Unlike constitutional originalism, they observe, biblical literalism reads the Bible (1) as an act of faith in (2) a God with universal jurisdiction—God must be obeyed as a matter of absolute moral ought because he is always good, true, and right.[29] Constitutional originalists, no matter how assertive, have never gone so far as this. Smith and Tuttle's observations are unobjectionable and true so far as they go, but do not rise (and I borrow from E. D. Hirsch's overused and sometimes abused categories) to methodological differences in *discovering meaning*, but only in *making application*. The diverse scope of the authority of the Bible vs. the Constitution demands no substantive change to the method for the discovery of meaning in either document. In other words, the difference is again not one of hermeneutical method but of the nature of the literary corpus with which each party deals.

A final contrast between biblical literalism and constitutional originalism generally (and textualism specifically) is the much broader range of genres in the Bible than is found in the United States Constitution. Legal material of any sort makes up only a small percentage of the Bible and statutory law even less. This observed disconnect is mitigated in part, however, by the fact that the covenants, which figure so prominently in biblical-theological discussion, fall into these genre categories. Unlike casual agreements which are easily amended, covenants are precise legal contracts to which parties are bound by oath, and which countenance no changes to their terms or beneficiaries apart from formal emendation (or even a total replacement), complete with new certifications. One may easily make changes to a casual promise,[30] but a covenant is extremely rigid—much like modern marriage covenants or "testamentary" covenants (wills).[31] Traditional dispensationalists argue that God's exclusive covenants with ethnic Israel operate the same way—and, furthermore, that there is no legal provision in the divine legal system *ever* to amend the parties or terms of these covenants, because these covenants specify, in their own terms, their own eternal and inalterable nature.[32]

I conclude, preliminarily, that, on close review, none of the most commonly observed differences between constitutional originalism and dispensational literalism amount to substantive differences of method.

FAVORABLE COMPARISONS BETWEEN CONSTITUTIONAL ORIGINALISM AND DISPENSATIONAL LITERALISM

In addition to the contrasts detailed above, Smith and Tuttle also identify four key similarities between biblical literalism and constitutional originalism: "commitment to the text," "reaction and restoration," a "populist impulse" (i.e., the idea that ordinary people can understand old texts), and the "idea of the faithful interpreter."[33]

The first of these comparisons (commitment to the text) is notable, but ultimately irrelevant, I would argue, to our study. Constitutional originalists and biblical literalists are both deeply committed to their respective documents, but this says little about their quest for *meaning*. It simply says that, once meaning is discovered, both parties hold their discoveries in high regard.

The second comparison (reading as restoration), however, is a key point of comparison. Both constitutional originalists and dispensational literalists are committed to "construing" meaning principally from an analysis of the text itself. Both groups are disinclined to impose upon the plain meaning of the text anachronisms such as new cultural norms, new legislative factions (creeds?), the assured results of science, later revelation, new definitions of words, and hermeneutical devices unknown to the original readers. And while it is surely true that some dispensationalists have erred in making constructions that are too strict, damaging the credibility of the biblical literalism (much as Scalia lamented, above, the degradation of constitutional originalism in the hands of strict constructionists[34]), this does not give credence to what Scalia calls "lenient constructions." The task of the interpreter is to reconstrue *original* meaning using principally the text in hand.

Smith and Tuttle's third comparison (a populist impulse) is also crucial to both approaches. The development of technical hermeneutical approaches that render meaning the property principally of scholars—those who have insights that exceed that of the common reader—is a concern for both. I speak here of the proliferation of critical hermeneutics (e.g., literary approaches such as rhetorical criticism, form criticism, genre criticism, source/redaction criticism, canonical criticism; paleo-orthodox/denominational/theological approaches; and provincial/cultural approaches such as feminist criticism, post-colonial criticism, liberation criticism, etc.), and closer at hand, the evangelical explosion of what Mike Horton has incisively denominated "type-aholism."[35] This is not to say that all of these approaches are equally troubling (indeed, several of these offer helpful insights for the hermeneutical task); still, to the degree that any of these approaches places the plain meaning of a text hopelessly out of reach for the ordinary reader, their value is overwrought. The constitutional originalist and the dispensational literalist agree that if the plain sense makes sense, we should seek no other sense.

The fourth concern (the idea of a faithful interpreter) is also a key similarity between constitutional originalism and biblical literalism. Both approaches agree that there is a fixed meaning in every text that does not evolve with the many progressive "movements" that dot our age. It is the task of the faithful interpreter to discover and to hold tenaciously to the original meaning of their respective documents if their cherished ideas (Western Civilization and Christianity, respectively) are to survive.

CONCLUSION

While it is surely impossible to posit strict synonymy between constitutional originalism and dispensational literalism, I believe that the *methods* employed both by constitutional originalists and by dispensationalist literalists have significant continuity. The label *originalist* as a descriptor of the traditional dispensational hermeneutical approach may not be a perfect one, but it brings us much closer to an accurately descriptive label for the dispensational hermeneutic than any other label has managed to do.

NOTES

1. Charles C. Ryrie, *Dispensationalism*, rev. and expanded ed. (Chicago: Moody Press, 1995), 40. Portions of this chapter were previously published in the 2022 issue of the *Detroit Baptist Seminary Journal*; Mark A. Snoeberger, "Refining Dispensational Discourse: Reconsidering Four Common Expressions," *Detroit Baptist Seminary Journal* 27 (2022): 15–30; used with permission.

2. During my first year of seminary, one of my professors, a dispensationalist, encouraged me to read Vern Poythress's *Understanding Dispensationalists*, 2nd ed. (Phillipsburg, NJ: Presbyterian & Reformed, 1993). Nestled among some of Poythress's less-than-fully-convincing criticisms of dispensationalism, my professor told me, were some valid criticisms of hermeneutical fallacies occasionally committed by dispensationalists under the banner of "literalism." This volume, together with D. A. Carson's iconic *Exegetical Fallacies* (Grand Rapids: Baker, 1984), supplied me with correctives that refined my conception of *literalism* away from some of its historical abuses.

3. John S. Feinberg, "Systems of Discontinuity," in *Continuity and Discontinuity: Perspectives on the Relationship Between the Old and New Testaments*, ed. John S. Feinberg (Wheaton: Crossway, 1988), 63–85; Michael J. Vlach, *Dispensationalism: Essential Beliefs and Common Myths*, rev. and updated ed. (Los Angeles: Theological Studies Press, 2017), 30–50.

4. Rolland D. McCune, "The Hermeneutics of Dispensationalism, or, What Is Literal Interpretation?" Presentation at the Mid-America Conference on Preaching; Inter-City Baptist Church, Allen Park, MI (March 11, 1994), 39–44. By a "transcendental" defense, I mean that that McCune argues these principles to be presuppositional to linguistic discourse: One must assume these principles in order even to discuss their legitimacy.

5. The term *originalism* first appears, pejoratively, in Paul Brest's critique of the conservative impulse then threatening the long-standing liberal control of the Supreme Court; Paul Brest, "The Misconceived Quest for the Original Understanding," *Boston University Law Review* 60 (1980): 204–238.

6. Brest, "The Misconceived Quest," 204.

7. Brest, "The Misconceived Quest," 204. He reiterates that strict originalists imagine that there is a single intention shared by all of "the [Constitution's] framers and the people who adopted it." This, he suggests, is a laughably impossible idea.

8. Robert Bork speaks of the "framers' intent" in his early work, "Neutral Principles and Some First Amendment Problems," *Indiana Law Journal* 47 (Fall, 1971): 13. This article is sometimes regarded as the earliest formal expression of modern originalism. See also Raoul Berger's terminology throughout *Government by the Judiciary: The Transformation of the Fourteenth Amendment* (Cambridge, MA: Harvard University Press, 1977).

9. Edwin Meese, "Speech to the D.C. Federalist Society Lawyers Division on a Jurisprudence of Original Intention," Delivered November 15, 1985, Washington, DC. Available online at American Rhetoric Online Speech Bank, www.americanrhetoric.com/speeches/edwinmeeseDCfederalistsociety.htm.

10. Antonin Scalia, *A Matter of Interpretation: Federal Courts and the Law*, ed. Amy Guttmann (Princeton, NJ: Princeton University Press, 1997), 17.

11. Scalia, *A Matter of Interpretation*, 17.

12. H. Jefferson Powell, "The Original Understanding of Original Intent," *Harvard Law Review* 98, no. 5 (1984): 885–948. See also and especially Jack Balkin's concept of "Framework Originalism" (also called "Living Originalism"), a syncretistic idea that the framers established a "framework" to be filled in not only by legislators, but also by judges who would need to "engage in considerable constitutional construction as well as the elaboration and application of previous constructions"; Jack M. Balkin, "Framework Originalism and the Living Constitution," *Northwestern University Law Review* 103, no. 2 (2009): 551.

13. Antonin Scalia, "Address by Justice Antonin Scalia before the Attorney General's Conference on Economic Liberties in Washington, DC," in *Original Meaning Jurisprudence: A Sourcebook* (Washington, DC: Office of Legal Policy, U. S. Dept. of Justice, 1987), 101–106, 106.

14. Keith Whittington, "Originalism: A Critical Introduction," *Fordham Law Review* 82, no. 2 (2013): 381.

15. Amy Coney Barrett, "Assorted Canards of Contemporary Legal Analysis: Redux," *Case Western Reserve Law Review* 70, no. 4 (2020): 856–857.

16. Antonin Scalia, "Originalism: The Lesser Evil," address delivered at the William Howard Taft Constitutional Law Lecture, Cincinnati (September 16, 1988).

17. Note that by involving the reader in the process, I am not suggesting that originalism reduces to a reader-response approach to interpretation. I am simply suggesting that the meaning of texts is known to the reader because words have meanings that the transmitter and the receiver must share if real communication is to occur. To use McCune's categories, above, originalism elevates the "Textually Based Locus of Meaning" very nearly to the exclusion of the "Jurisdiction of Authorial Intent."

18. For further detail, see TransAm Trucking, Inc. v. Administrative Review Board, United States Department of Labor, Case 15-9504, 10th Circuit Court of Appeals; filed August 8, 2016, https://law.justia.com/cases/federal/appellate-courts/ca10/15-9504/15-9504-2016-07-15-0.html.

19. Scalia, *A Matter of Interpretation*, 23. The term *construe*—to "analyze the arrangement and connection of words"; "construe," Merriam-Webster; https://www.merriam-webster.com/dictionary/construe—is the root that undergirds the term *constructionism*. These terms are neutral apart from a modifier.

20. See above, note 16.

21. Scalia, *A Matter of Interpretation*, 24.

22. James Barr, The Semantics of Biblical Language (Oxford: Oxford University Press, 1961), 218.

23. Scalia, A Matter of Interpretation, 218.

24. Barrett, "Assorted Canards," 857; see also Barr, The Semantics of Biblical Language, 24. Their concern is also reflected in Elizabeth-Jane McGuire and Steven F. McQuire, "Originalism Isn't the Judicial Version of Biblical Fundamentalism," *Church Life Journal* (12 October 2020), https://churchlifejournal.nd.edu/articles/originalism-isnt-the-judicial-version-of-biblical-fundamentalism/.

25. Among these Scalia and Barret identify as endemic to biblical literalism what D. A. Carson labels the "root fallacy," "semantic anachronism," "semantic obsolescence," and "selective and prejudicial use of evidence" (Carson, *Exegetical Fallacies*, 26–40, 54–55).

26. Scalia, *A Matter of Interpretation*, 17.

27. John M. Frame, *Systematic Theology: An Introduction to Christian Belief* (Phillipsburg, NJ: P&R Publishing, 2013), 562.

28. Peter J. Smith and Robert W. Tuttle, "Biblical Literalism and Constitutional Originalism," *Notre Dame Law Review* 86, no. 2 (2011): 693–763. Another incisive set of comparisons and contrasts may be discovered in Frank S. Ravitch, "Interpreting Scripture/Interpreting Law," in *Hermeneutics and the Authority of Scripture*, ed. Alan Cadwallader (Adelaide: ATF Press, 2011), 11–19. The latter is quite favorable to synonymy between constitutional and biblical literalism, but treats both rather negatively.

29. Smith and Tuttle denominate these as differences of (1) "the scope of and jurisdiction of the text" and of (2) "the duty of the interpreter"; Smith and Tuttle, "Biblical Literalism and Constitutional Originalism," 750–754.

30. Were I to make a casual arrangement to watch a ballgame on TV with one of my sons, I could later include another son and make it a family event. I could even improve the original plan by buying tickets and taking all my sons to the game. No party would complain that I had violated any hermeneutical standards, because the genre is flexible—not infinitely so (I can't leave the original promisee home and take someone else entirely), but generously so. The "complementary hermeneutic" and "references plenior" model are viable options.

31. If, in my duly signed and notarized "last will and covenant," I leave everything to my oldest son, no judge can decide after my demise to share my estate with other "referents" of his choosing, based, say, on his beliefs about my unstated intentions. The only way anyone else could inherit a part of my estate is to unearth a more recent "last will and covenant," also duly signed and notarized, that expressly annuls the first one.

Likewise, if I sign a marriage contract of exclusive fidelity to one woman "until death do us part," I cannot informally add another "referent" at a later time. To do so would not be viewed as a matter of "complementary" magnanimity, but a terrible miscarriage of justice and a crime (not to mention an act of evil). If, indeed, this is how biblical covenants work, then one's biblical theology must adjust accordingly.

32. This rigidity is established, I believe, in the literature, and is crucial to the traditional dispensational approach. As Roy Beacham notes, "Only the stated, contracting parties partook directly of the covenant responsibilities and benefits. To be named in the legal instrument as an enacting party to the instrument was to incur, legally, its responsibilities, advantages, and/or penalties. By nature and design, covenants were exclusive: they established an absolute and unique relationship of fealty between the contracting parties"; Roy Beacham, "The Church Has No Legal Relationship to or Participation in the New Covenant," update of presentation at the Council on Dispensational Hermeneutics, Baptist Bible Seminary, Clarks Summit, PA (September 23, 2009), 7, https://dispensationalcouncil.org/wp-content/uploads/2018/07/09_Roy_Beacham_ANE-Covenants-and-NC.pdf. Moshe Weinfeld draws further attention to the marital language incorporated into the new covenant as uniquely designed to emphasize *exclusivity*. Both parties (the Suzerain and his vassals) are narrowly and deliberately named so as to prohibit expansion or emendation; Moshe Weinfeld, "בְּרִית, *berîth*," *Theological Dictionary of the Old Testament*, Vol. 2, ed. G. J. Botterweck and H. Ringgren (Grand Rapids: Eerdmans, 1975), 253–278, 278.

33. Smith and Tuttle, "Biblical Literalism and Constitutional Originalism," 721–750.

34. Scalia, *A Matter of Interpretation*, 23.

35. Michael Horton, "A Covenant Theology Response," in *Covenantal and Dispensational Theologies: Four Views on the Continuity of Scripture*, ed. Brent E. Parker and Richard J. Lucas (Downers Grove, IL: InterVarsity Press, 2022), 183–200, 183.

WORKS CITED

Balkin, Jack M. "Framework Originalism and the Living Constitution." *Northwestern University Law Review* 103, no. 2 (2009): 549–614.

Barr, James. *The Semantics of Biblical Language*. Oxford: Oxford University Press, 1961.

Barrett, Amy Coney. "Assorted Canards of Contemporary Legal Analysis: Redux." *Case Western Reserve Law Review* 70, no. 4 (2020): 855–869.

Beacham, Roy. "The Church Has No Legal Relationship to or Participation in the New Covenant." Update of presentation at the Council on Dispensational Hermeneutics, Baptist Bible Seminary, Clarks Summit, PA (September 23, 2009). https://dispensationalcouncil.org/wp-content/uploads/2018/07/09_Roy_Beacham_ANE-Covenants-and-NC.pdf 11.

Berger, Raoul. *Government by the Judiciary: The Transformation of the Fourteenth Amendment*. Cambridge, MA: Harvard University Press, 1977.

Bork, Robert. "Neutral Principles and Some First Amendment Problems." *Indiana Law Journal* 47, no. 1 (Fall, 1971): 1–35.

Brest, Paul. "The Misconceived Quest for the Original Understanding." *Boston University Law Review* 60 (1980): 204–238.

Carson, D. A. *Exegetical Fallacies*. Grand Rapids: Baker, 1984.

"construe." *Merriam-Webster.* https://www.merriam-webster.com/dictionary/construe.

Feinberg, John S. "Systems of Discontinuity." In *Continuity and Discontinuity: Perspectives on the Relationship Between the Old and New Testaments*, edited by John S. Feinberg, 63–85. Wheaton: Crossway, 1988.

Frame, John M. *Systematic Theology: An Introduction to Christian Belief.* Phillipsburg, NJ: P&R Publishing, 2013.

Horton, Michael. "A Covenant Theology Response." In *Covenantal and Dispensational Theologies: Four Views on the Continuity of Scripture*; edited by Brent E. Parker and Richard J. Lucas, 183–200. Downers Grove, IL: InterVarsity Press, 2022.

McCune, Rolland D. "The Hermeneutics of Dispensationalism, or, What Is Literal Interpretation?" Presented at the Mid-America Conference on Preaching. Inter-City Baptist Church, Allen Park, MI (March 11, 1994).

McGuire, Elizabeth-Jane and Steven F. McQuire. "Originalism Isn't the Judicial Version of Biblical Fundamentalism." *Church Life Journal* (12 October 2020). https://churchlifejournal.nd.edu/articles/originalism-isnt-the-judicial-version-of-biblical-fundamentalism/.

Meese, Edwin. "Speech to the D.C. Federalist Society Lawyers Division on a Jurisprudence of Original Intention." Delivered November 15, 1985, Washington, DC. Available online at American Rhetoric Online Speech Bank. www.americanrhetoric.com/speeches/edwinmeeseDCfederalistsociety.htm.

Powell, H. Jefferson. "The Original Understanding of Original Intent." *Harvard Law Review* 98, no. 5 (1984): 885–948.

Poythress, Vern. *Understanding Dispensationalists*, 2nd ed. Phillipsburg, NJ: P&R Publishing, 1994.

Ravitch, Frank S. "Interpreting Scripture/Interpreting Law." In *Hermeneutics and the Authority of Scripture*, edited by Alan Cadwallader, 11–19 (Adelaide: ATF Press, 2011).

Ryrie, Charles C. *Dispensationalism*, revised and expanded ed. Chicago: Moody Press, 1995.

Scalia, Antonin. "Address by Justice Antonin Scalia before the Attorney General's Conference on Economic Liberties in Washington, D.C." In *Original Meaning Jurisprudence: A Sourcebook*, 101–106. Washington, DC: Office of Legal Policy, U. S. Dept. of Justice, 1987.

———. *A Matter of Interpretation: Federal Courts and the Law*, edited by Amy Guttmann. Princeton, NJ: Princeton University Press, 1997.

———. "Originalism: The Lesser Evil." Address delivered at the William Howard Taft Constitutional Law Lecture, Cincinnati (September 16, 1988).

Smith, Peter J. and Robert W. Tuttle. "Biblical Literalism and Constitutional Originalism." *Notre Dame Law Review* 86, no. 2 (2011): 693–763.

TransAm Trucking, Inc. v. Administrative Review Board, United States Department of Labor. Case 15-9504. 10th Circuit Court of Appeals. Filed August 8, 2016. https://law.justia.com/cases/federal/appellate-courts/ca10/15-9504/15-9504-2016-07-15-0.html.

Vlach, Michael J. *Dispensationalism: Essential Beliefs and Common Myths*, revised and updated ed. Los Angeles: Theological Studies Press, 2017.
Weinfeld, Moshe. "בְּרִית, *b*[e]*rîth*." In *Theological Dictionary of the Old Testament*; vol. 2, edited by G. J. Botterweck and H. Ringgren, 253–278. Grand Rapids: Eerdmans, 1975.
Whittington, Keith. "Originalism: A Critical Introduction." *Fordham Law Review* 82, no. 2 (2013): 375–409.

Chapter 7

Originalism and the Sources of Authority

Mark J. Boone

Originalism in Christian theology claims that the meaning of the Bible should be sought in the intent of its original human authors. This theology has roots at least as deep as Augustine, but is prominent more recently in evangelical theology such as that expressed in the Chicago Statement on Biblical Inerrancy. Originalism in the study of American law, by contrast, usually claims that the meaning of the Constitution is in the text of the Constitution, rather than in the mind of its authors. This theory has been aptly expressed by scholars such as Michael Paulsen and Gary Lawson. So theological originalism is an *intentionalism*, meaning that it locates original meaning in the intention of the biblical authors. But legal originalism is a *textualism*, meaning that it locates original meaning in the text.

This is no coincidence. A theory of textual meaning ought to fit the text concerned. A difference in the source of a text's authority makes a difference in where we look for its meaning. Contemporary theories of biblical and legal originalism reflect this. The nature of an authoritative text and of its authority determines what version of originalism is applied to the text. The source of the Bible's authority is God's own authority, mediated through the office of the apostle or prophet; so the author's intent must be the proximate source of that authoritative meaning. The immediate source of the Constitution's legal authority is the people, and so the location of its meaning is not the minds of the authors, but that to which the people have unmediated access—the text. (Note that I say the "immediate" source—the *ultimate* source may be a higher authority, "the laws of nature and of nature's God," but that is a theoretical question outside the scope of this essay. However, Mark Eckel addresses that topic in his second essay in this volume.)

Despite the considerable interest in each originalism and the occasional connection made between the two, this point is often glossed over or neglected entirely.[1] For example, theologian Albert Mohler connects originalism in theology and law and says that they have essentially the same hermeneutic, treating both as intentionalisms.[2]

In what follows I will first give a short overview of the sort of philosophy of language that motivates originalism. Then I will consider originalism in Christian theology before turning to originalism in law.

WHY ORIGINALISM?

A short overview of some reasons for originalism would be in order, not directly to support my thesis so much as to clarify the originalist theories to follow. (However, I am an originalist myself, and these are some of my reasons for being one.)

Why would anyone be an originalist? There may be interesting reasons for or against originalism in a particular field, but the basic idea may be understood in general and common-sensical terms. Originalism begins with a simple idea: written texts are ways of communicating, and sometimes they succeed at their job.

This is the theory I call *textual realism*: there is a text, and it has an original meaning, which normally has something to do with its author and which is oftentimes to some significant degree accessible to us. There are limitations, of course: you can't understand the Bible without the help of translations unless you know some Hebrew or Greek, it's difficult for the best of us to understand much of Hegel, and so on.

All the same, it is perfectly normal for a written text to convey information from author to reader. My wife texts me, saying, "Please pick up bananas when you go to the store," and I understand her. I read Aristotle's *Nichomachean Ethics* and learn a little bit about his moral theory. You log onto a news site and read to learn something about what's going on in Ukraine. You are reading this text right now. Hopefully you are understanding most or all of it. (If not, you may need to try again later, or work harder; alternatively, you might be able to blame me for not writing clearly.) Assuming you can understand a good bit of what you are reading, you could agree or disagree. You could even write down your agreement or disagreement and email it to me. If you write clearly and if I read carefully, I would then be able to read and understand your objection.

Say we take a strongly skeptical theory toward textual meaning: textual meaning is always and entirely in the eye of the beholder. Now let's say that you were to take that as an objection to originalism. Say, further, that you were to write that objection down in an email or an academic paper. Say that you then try to share your objection to textual realism with someone else.

Would you want to take any *credit* for your work, or would you expect your readers to end up with at least some of the same evidence against originalism which *you* have? If so, then you have contradicted your own theory.[3]

In short, textual realism has something interesting going for it: It is not even possible to object to it without contradicting yourself—not, that is, as long as your objection is in writing and you expect your reader to credit you with your own ideas. In fact, textual realism is so common-sensical that it's virtually impossible to doubt it consistently. Consider Aristotle's definition of happiness as "an activity of soul in accordance with perfect virtue." Aristotle's *Nichomachean Ethics* is a text based on lecture notes taken by his students. Technically, Aristotle did not write it himself. Even if he had, the original manuscripts are long lost, and they were in Greek.

But can a philosopher comment on Aristotle's definition of happiness—can he agree with it, object to it, and so on? Of course. Similarly, we can read Homer's *Odyssey* or the Confucian *Analects* and say that it is beautiful, insightful, and so on. That's just common sense. If we want to get technical we can always point out that the meaning of Aristotle, Homer, and other ancients is not quite 100 percent available to us; we deal in approximations of their meaning given the elapsed time, the cultural differences, the translation issues, the history of the textual transmission, and so forth. But we can still talk about Aristotle's philosophy—not just the philosophy we might refer to as "Aristotle's," but what is actually *Aristotle's philosophy*. Textual realism is this common-sense.

Textual realism is a form of what the philosophers call "critical realism." The realities of textual meaning are never *fully* knowable to us, but only knowable in approximation. So are the thoughts of other minds, and so of course are the meanings of the words with which we communicate. That's life. We always see through a glass—sometimes more darkly, sometimes pretty clearly.

In acknowledging textual realism, one is, of course, disagreeing with the influential academic theory that original meaning is unknowable, mythical, or otherwise irrelevant. According to Jacques Derrida, "*There is nothing outside of the text*."[4] In other words, no understanding or account of anything is exhaustive, correct in every detail, and accessible to the attentive reader. Everything is interpreted; more precisely, every account of anything is *an interpretation*. We do not pass beyond a text in order to know the mind of its author. According to Roland Barthes, the author is, in fact, dead.[5] Similarly, reader-response theory teaches that the meaning of a text is in its reading. Stanley Fish explains that the *community* of readers determines the reading of a text.[6] The theory of the living Constitution has it that the meaning of the Constitution includes things in the minds of neither the authors nor the original readers. Hence Justice Anthony Kennedy's words:

> The generations that wrote and ratified the Bill of Rights and the Fourteenth Amendment did not presume to know the extent of freedom in all of its dimensions, and so they entrusted to future generations a charter protecting the right of all persons to enjoy liberty as we learn its meaning.[7]

Nevertheless, a quick perusal of the citations in my last paragraph reminds us of the curious truth that we still hold out the commonsense notions that authors should be credited for their words and ideas, which readers still have some hope of understanding to at least some extent.

More could be said on behalf of textual realism, but a short look is enough. The idea here was merely to introduce one important motive for originalist thinking. The common-sense position of textual realism entails that a text's meaning is, or at least includes, its original meaning. For the very meaning with which textual realism is concerned was present in the beginning, when first the text was written.

ORIGINALISM IN CHRISTIAN THEOLOGY

A study of Christian biblical originalism shows a strong emphasis on the human authors of the Bible and their intentions in writing. This emphasis corresponds to the doctrine in Christian theology that the Bible is the inspired word of God because it is the product of human authors who were inspired by God.

Christian theology of the Bible is, of course, a vast area of study. We only have time for a quick survey of some notable sources which are originalist or at least related to originalism. Let us consider first biblical originalism and then the corresponding doctrine of the Bible's inspiration and authorship.

Biblical Originalism

Most versions of orthodox Christian theology are committed to the doctrine that the sense of the Bible intended by its human authors is without error. This entails at least a *weak* originalism: the Bible's divine meaning includes, and is consistent with, the original meaning of the text. After a quick look at Augustine, Aquinas, Jean-Luc Marion, and Vatican II, I will turn to contemporary evangelical inerrancy, which tends more strongly toward *strong* originalism, meaning that all biblical meanings are original ones.[8] Although the contemporary evangelical inerrantist tradition does not quite say this (and even denies it), it does come close through its strong emphasis on the method of seeking biblical meaning in its original sense.

Augustine[9] is an inerrantist on the intent of the authors of the Bible. When considering how to interpret Genesis in the *Confessions*, he strongly condemns any suggestion that Moses's ideas while writing Genesis were mistaken.[10] In *On Christian Teaching* he further affirms that God uses the authors of the Bible to speak to us[11] and affirms the Bible's authority.[12]

Augustine also famously claims that a biblical text may have multiple meanings. Other meanings may come in when the original meaning is obscure.[13] Indeed, Augustine suggests that Moses himself may have had multiple meanings in mind and would welcome all true meanings discerned by readers in his text.[14] Multiple meanings are welcome within certain parameters; in the *Confessions*, Augustine mentions that any proposed alternative readings should be true ones, and that we must not accuse a biblical author of intending any false meaning.[15] In *Teaching Christianity* he emphasizes that the test of the truth of the interpretation of an ambiguous passage is that whatever it says be taught clearly elsewhere in the Bible.[16] Augustine himself goes in search of non-original meaning when he proposes figurative interpretations. In the *Confessions*, for example, he engages in a lengthy exposition of the creation story in Genesis 1, interpreting it as the story of sin, salvation, redemption, and the church.[17] In his *Expositions on the Psalms*, Augustine seeks Christological ecclesiological interpretations, for example, reading the tree in Psalm 1 as Christ and its fruit as the church (*Exposition* on Psalm 1, section 3).

This is a limited departure from strong originalism. Any meaning in the Bible which does not fall within the scope of the human authorial intent is still intended by God.[18] In other words, Augustine remains a strong divine originalist. Moreover, he retains a strong sense of the importance of the original meaning intended by the human authors of the Bible.[19] Every meaning of every biblical passage *anywhere* is taught as the straightforward original intention of a human author of the Bible *somewhere*. In language resembling that of Craig Carter, we can say that in Augustine's hermeneutics the original (human) meaning of the Bible controls all other meanings.[20] Perhaps Augustine could be characterized as a strong originalist with respect to the Bible as a whole, but a weak originalist with respect to some of its parts.

Similarly, Thomas Aquinas begins his magnificent *Summa Theologica*[21] by explaining that divine revelation was necessary to give us knowledge beyond what reason alone can achieve. This revelation, written in the Bible, includes everything meant by its human authors but also much else, encompassing everything intended by God. (Aquinas specifically cites Augustine on the subject.)

The same emphasis on the importance of original authorial intent is also found in contemporary Roman Catholic sources, such as Vatican II:

> Therefore, since everything asserted by the inspired authors or sacred writers must be held to be asserted by the Holy Spirit, it follows that the books of Scripture must be acknowledged as teaching solidly, faithfully and without error that truth which God wanted put into sacred writings for the sake of salvation.[22]

Echoing what many Protestant theologians have also said, the text continues:

> For the correct understanding of what the sacred author wanted to assert, due attention must be paid to the customary and characteristic styles of feeling, speaking and narrating which prevailed at the time of the sacred writer, and to the patterns men normally employed at that period in their everyday dealings with one another.[23]

We may briefly take note of a fascinating work in continental philosophy of religion drawing from postmodern philosophy. Catholic philosopher Jean-Luc Marion's *God Without Being* draws from the likes of Nietzsche and Heidegger to argue against any attempt to make God fit within the bounds of human reason, which would effectively make an idol in place of the true God. God is beyond reason. Marion further urges that we recognize the Bible as a book whose meaning likewise will not fit within the narrow limits of our rationality, or be circumscribed within the minds of its human authors. Biblical meaning is controlled only by God.[24] This is a powerful reminder that Christian theology often resists strong human originalism, although Marion is consistent with weak human originalism and is also a divine originalist.

Let us now turn to contemporary evangelical inerrancy, whose central text is the Chicago Statement on Biblical Inerrancy.[25] The Chicago Statement claims that the Bible is inerrant according to the original meaning intended by its authors in the autographs. This description of the location of biblical meaning calls for a number of qualifications—for example, that we do not, technically, have those autographs and that "hyperbole and metaphor [must be treated as] hyperbole and metaphor, generalization and approximation as what they are, and so forth."[26] This has led to some attention on these qualifications—as if they made inerrancy some sort of unusual, newly invented, or highly technical doctrine. This is a misunderstanding. Chicago Statement inerrancy is a textual (and authorial) realism coupled with a doctrine of biblical authority and inspiration.[27] The bulk of these qualifications are merely in interest of stating textual realism precisely. Inerrancy's critics, when faced with our quote from Aristotle earlier, would presume that we can get to Aristotle's meaning—albeit with the help of textual critics and translators, and with certain limitations. If ever it should become needful to articulate and systematically explain these limitations, it would look a lot like the Chicago Statement's collection of qualifications and distinctions—with relevant differences since Aristotle is one man to the Bible's diverse crew of writers, since the autographs in his case came from his students' notes, and so on.

Chicago Statement inerrancy, being a variant of textual realism, strongly emphasizes original intent as the locus of biblical meaning. That pushes biblical inerrancy a long way toward strong intentionalist originalism: "Scripture is inerrant, not in the sense of being absolutely precise by modern standards, but in the sense of making good its claims and achieving that measure of focused truth at which its authors aimed."[28] The Bible's meaning is without error, and to find it we look to the intentions of its human authors. We know these intentions by studying the text as a human text—with attention to original languages, historical circumstances, cultural idioms, geographical context, and so on. These are very much the characteristics of a strong intentionalist originalism: textual meaning is original authorial meaning, and the business of textual interpretation is to find these authorial intentions in their original context.[29]

Contemporary evangelical inerrancy also has a non-originalist aspect. The Chicago Statement on Biblical *Hermeneutics*, a sequel document, denies in its Article XVIII "that the writers of Scripture always understood the full implications of their own words."[30] This, at first glance, appears to be a restriction on human intentionalist originalism. At least respecting certain Old Testament prophecies, biblical meaning is not limited to authorial intentions.[31] Evangelical inerrancy nods to the Augustinian tradition and cannot *quite* be called a strong intentionalist *human* originalism. But perhaps it is something near enough—an approximation of intentionalist human originalism, with some exceptions for God's intentions.

Appearances, however, can be deceiving, and we need to take a closer look.

The same Statement affirms "that the meaning expressed in each biblical text is single, definite and fixed."[32] As Geisler explains, the point of this Article is that "What a passage means is fixed by the author and is not subject to change by readers."[33] Article XVIII actually "builds on Article VII, and the challenge in writing Article XVIII is that "evangelical scholars are divided" on "whether God intended more by a passage of Scripture than the human author did," although they agree that the meaning of the passage is a unity.[34] Evangelical inerrancy as represented in these sources concurs that each biblical passage has a "single meaning," that this single meaning is intended by the human author, and that some of these passages have multiple "implications" and "applications."[35] Moreover, it is normal within this tradition to reference divine *intentions* exceeding those of the human author. Accordingly, this sort of inerrancy claims to be a strong intentionalist human originalism, but only on the technicality that applications, implications, and even divine intentions not be classified under the term "meaning." In short, although the terminology is somewhat complicated, evangelical inerrantists are at least somewhat closer to the likes of Augustine and Aquinas than is usually appreciated.[36]

The Nature of the Bible

Why all this emphasis in Christian theology on the intentions of human biblical authors? According to orthodox Christian theology the Bible is the word of God and divinely inspired. Using Pauline language (2 Tim. 3:16), God breathed out this book. The Bible's words are composed by God. Yet God did not inscribe the Bible on stone tablets (well, not *most* of it), nor dictate it to human scribes (again, not *most* of it). The Bible is of largely human composition. In biblical inspiration, God guides human writers to write his message for us, protecting them from error in the process. "Men spoke," and they "spoke from God as they were carried along by the Holy Spirit" (2 Pet. 1:21 ESV). Which men? Those chosen by God for the job, those appointed to give God's verbal message to his people. Although it would be difficult to state thoroughly and precisely who is and who is not such a person, the prophet and the apostle at least are easy enough to name (Eph. 2:20). The prophet (in, for example, Deuteronomy 18 and Jeremiah 1) is appointed by God to speak his message, he speaks all that God commands him to speak, and he speaks the very words of God—God's words are in his mouth. The apostle (in, for example, Paul's letter to the Galatians) is appointed to testify to Jesus the Messiah and Son of God, to teach Jesus's message with Jesus's own authority. Between them, at least according to Christian tradition, apostles and prophets are responsible for writing most of the Bible—at least the entirety of the Torah, much of the Psalms, the books of Isaiah and Jeremiah and the other major and minor prophetic books, two of the Gospels, the letters of Paul and Peter and John, and Revelation. Much else in the Bible either closely concerns prophets or apostles or is written as an extension of their ministry (as the Gospel of Mark is commonly understood as being rooted in the apostolic ministry of Peter, and the Gospel of Luke in that of Paul and other apostles he apparently interviewed; see Luke 1:1–4).[37]

Now this traditional account may still be a bit oversimplified. Perhaps, even within a particular book of the Bible, someone else in addition to the prophet or apostle had a hand in authorship. Silas, as Peter's amanuensis, may have changed a few words for clarity of expression in Greek. A later scribe seemingly added to the Torah some observations on the death of Moses. The Bible may be more of a cooperative effort than we usually think, and inspiration of the Bible may extend to *groups* of people who collectively wrote some of its texts. If this is correct, then a prophetic or apostolic *origin* of Scripture is the relevant concept here. The revelation comes through them, and the

Bible's meaning comes through the minds of those faithful writers who helped to convey their message, as well as through the minds of the prophets and apostles themselves.

In short, Christian theology considers the Bible, like Jesus Christ himself, to have both a divine and a human aspect. God works through the human to get his message across. The source of biblical authority is God, but the means of conveying his truth to us is a human author, who in most cases is not merely receiving dictation but actually *writing*. The first Chicago Statement: The Bible is "God's own Word, written by men prepared and superintended by His Spirit."[38] Its authority comes from God, running through the author. It is *their* original intentions in composing the sacred text which *God* intended to be written there, and so it is *these* intentions we must seek. Biblical *authority* is well named, for it is the *author*'s. Accordingly, originalism in Christian theology pertains to their authorship. The writings are inspired because of what God did in the writers.[39]

ORIGINALISM IN LAW

Things are a bit different in law. A study of American legal originalism shows a strong emphasis on the original text as a means of understanding the law known to the original readers. This emphasis corresponds to the American governing principle that the people are sovereign and that their will is the source of legitimate government.[40]

As we did with the Bible, so with the Constitution: we will first consider the very idea and the structure of constitutional originalism and then consider the nature of this particular authoritative text.

Constitutional Originalism

A brief look at originalism in either law or theology is necessarily an exercise in selectivity; there is much written on this topic, and what one chooses to cover is likely to be influenced to some extent by background, personal preferences, and past reading choices. As my personal interests and knowledge in theology lean toward Chicago Statement inerrancy and Augustine, in law they lean toward law scholar Michael Paulsen as well as a few great historical interpreters of the Constitution such as James Madison, Thomas Jefferson, and Abraham Lincoln. Let us consider these matters in the form of, first, a parable, followed by some objections and responses, and then by an analysis of the theory of legal originalism. Then, finally, we will take an extended look at who exactly has the right and responsibility to interpret the Constitution.[41]

What Is Originalism in Law?

Suppose that, one fine Monday morning, I say to you,

> Here is a wonderful document. It establishes a republic having a federal government with checks and balances for the purpose of protecting our natural rights and securing the blessings of liberty. It is a living document, and it explains how we can update it if we need to.

And you say, "This is a good document."

On Tuesday I say, "The document has some new sentences. Now it also says we should end slavery." And you say, "That is also good."

On Wednesday, however, I say, "Now the document says there are some other rights that overrule some of the old ones." And you say, "Can I read the new sentences?" I reply: "There are no new sentences, only a new meaning." You ask, "Where did the old meaning go, and how did you squeeze the new meaning into the old sentences?"

On Thursday I say,

> Now the document says we have the right to marry any way we like. Today two men can marry each other, and tomorrow they can marry five men or five women; after that, perhaps they can marry their siblings if they really want to.

You ask when the document began to mean this, and I answer "Just this morning." You ask when I updated the words to include this new meaning and I say, "The words have not changed since Tuesday."

Originalism in law is the theory that the meaning of the Constitution does not change except when the text changes. That is, every change in constitutional *meaning* is accompanied by a change in the *words*.

Some objections to originalism may help to clarify.

Objection 1: The original meaning of the Constitution is outdated.

Originalism means looking to the original meaning of *all* the relevant parts of the constitution *when they were written and adopted*.[42] An originalist looks primarily to the meaning of the Constitution at the time of the nation's founding not because the original version is more important than later amendments, but because that is when most of the text was first made law. When interpreting the 14th Amendment he looks to the 1850s and 1860s. For the twenty-sixth, he looks to the 1970s! Originalism recognizes that *any* part of the Constitution can be updated as needed through the amendment process. In fact, in a sense, all citizens are potentially indirect authors of the Constitution; they choose the federal and state representatives who select the original meaning of the *next* addition to the Constitution.

Objection 2: It is too hard to know what was in the minds of the authors.

The original meaning of nearly any text can take some work to understand. (And, if it is ever unclear in any very problematic way, perhaps we can clarify by adding an amendment.) Moreover, this objection applies only to the usefulness of the claim that meaning is located here or there, but does not affect its *truth*. It is hard for me to know what sort of rocks are a mile under my home, but that does not render the sentence "There are granite rocks a mile under my home" either true or false.

In addition, Originalism does *not* depend on the minds of the authors as such; it depends on the meaning of the words at the time—on which more shortly!

Objection 3: The Founders envisioned the laws applying in different ways than we now know to be necessary.

If these applications are part of the meaning of the text, then this is Objection 1 again. If these applications are not part of the meaning, then this is not an objection to originalism, but just some advice on how to apply it (and perhaps very good advice at that).

Objection 4: The Constitution is about law and ethics, and these things do not allow for clear and precise language of the sort that originalism requires.

I rather doubt whether language about ethics or law is necessarily less clear and precise than language about physics, history, food, football, and so on. Even so, this is no case against originalism. If it refers to the vagueness and ambiguity of application, then it is a retread of Objection 3. If it refers to the difficulty of understanding original meaning, it is a retread of Objection 2. If it refers to some lack of stable reality with which ethics and law are concerned, then this is a more serious concern, but a matter for metaphysics (that branch of philosophy concerned with the study of reality). Still, for my part, I think it would be appropriate for moral relativists to not try and impose their relativism on the rest of us.

Objection 5: Language never has any fixed meaning anyway.

Fixed or not, if language can communicate such an objection from a critic to an originalist, then it should be a workable enough tool for, for example, James Madison to communicate to us a restriction on the federal government's powers.

What these objections and responses show is that originalism is based in plain old common sense, indicating that the burden of proof lies with its detractors. As Carson Holloway puts it, this is "the ordinary way that we would seek to understand the meaning of any written document—and indeed any communication at all."[43] Normally when people with some facility for reading read things written with at least a modicum of clarity, the way written language works is the way presumed by originalism. Language is a vehicle for communication, and the meaning of written language follows its communicative function; what it *means* is what the original reader can understand. As a default setting, we should presume that originalism is true of any text, although it is possible to give reasons for originalism as a theory in American law specifically.[44]

Attention to the particularities of American law also helps us understand originalism in law. But first we need to make a distinction between *textualism* and *intentionalism*.

Is original meaning *in the text* or *in the mind of the author*? Sticking to authorial intent alone is problematic. Consider Professor Dumbledore in the Harry Potter series, whom author J. K. Rowling announced is homosexual *after* the series wrapped up. The text contains no support for this. If authorial intent is all there is to meaning, then Dumbledore has *always* been gay; but if Rowling should change her mind later, then he will *never* have been gay; so it will be true *and* false that he was gay yesterday.

We need a subtler theory for a situation like this. Originalist *textualism* will do the job: the meaning is *in* the text, although it is shaped by the author. We should seek for meaning in the text itself, informed by our knowledge of the author's mind.

But when we are talking about the Constitution, the authors are not the only ones to consider. Madison points out that the Constitution is given its authority *by the people*:

> [The Constitution] was nothing more than the draft of a plan, nothing but a dead letter, until life and validity were breathed into it by the voice of the people, speaking through the several State Conventions.[45]

Madison also tells us the interpretation of the Constitution is only "legitimate" in "the sense in which the Constitution was accepted and ratified by the nation."[46] The people are the immediate source of the Constitution's authority, so *their* understanding is more important than the authors'. Contemporary originalism underwent a shift toward considering the adopters as well as the authors of the Constitution. Contemporary originalism began with Judge Bork, who emphasized the original intent in writing on the part of the constitutional authors. Originalists later shifted to emphasize the original understanding in approving by the constitutional adopters.[47]

But they did not stop there. What matters most is neither authorial intent nor what the adopters thought, but *what the text itself means*. That is the real significance of Madison's sense-in-which-it-was-accepted. There is little need to ask "What was so-and-so thinking in year such-and-such?" The bigger question is "What did these words mean in year such-and-such?" So contemporary originalists have shifted again: to an emphasis on the original *meaning* in *reading* by *reasonable and informed readers*. The story of these shifts in originalist legal theory has been told by Paulsen, Kesavan, Delahunty, and Yoo.[48]

So, besides the presumption from common sense, an originalist may find support for originalism in law from the nature of the American experiment in self-government. What, after all, is the point of the American system of government without a written Constitution operating as the one supreme law? Or the point of a written Constitution whose meaning was duly adopted as law only to be changed later by a meaning adopted in some other way? Or the point of a written Constitution whose meaning changes when the writing stays the same?

Of course, such a document still calls for interpretation and for application to new circumstances. But who gets to interpret the Constitution?

Who Can Interpret the Constitution?

Most seem to think that the Supreme Court's interpretations of the Constitution are final. Some go so far as to say that *only* the Supreme Court has any business interpreting the Constitution. We must distinguish two theories here:

- *Judicial Supremacy*: Interpretations of the Constitution by the Supreme Court overrule all other interpretations.
- *Judicial Exclusivity*: Only the Supreme Court actually has the right to interpret the Constitution.

There are three possible positions on these theories. One could reject both, accept both, or accept Judicial Supremacy but not Judicial Exclusivity. Great interpreters of the Constitution have considered this question, turning up some powerful arguments against Judicial Supremacy and, especially, Exclusivity. We will go over these classic arguments in some detail before considering their significance.

We begin with the Constitutional Convention and the first Congress.

On July 21, 1787, the Constitutional Convention debated the idea that the federal Judiciary should share with the Executive branch "the Revisionary power" (which from the text of the debate looks to me more like the presidential line-item veto than like any power the President actually has now).[49]

Mr. Madison is in favor of the Revisionary power. *Mr. Gerry* is against it, explaining that Congress is for writing laws, and the federal Courts for explaining them: this provision would make "the Expositors of the Laws, [into] the Legislators which ought never to be done." *Mr. Strong* agrees "that the power of making ought to be kept distinct from that of expounding, the laws. No maxim was better established. . . . Federal Judges have the supremacy in interpreting lesser laws." This suggests a strong belief at least in Judicial Supremacy, possibly Judicial Exclusivity.

Two years later, a debate occurred in the First Federal Congress, on June, 16, 1789, over whether the Senate's consent is needed in *firing* as well as in *hiring* presidential appointees.[50]

Mr. Smith initially says only that the Judiciary has the job of interpreting the Constitution: The matter they are debating should be "left to the decision of the judiciary." *Madison* disagrees. He says that constitutional interpretation "may come with as much propriety from the legislature as any other department of government." The legislative branch is the proper place to disambiguate the Constitution: if "the constitution is undecided" on a question, "it is likely that it is submitted to the discretion of the legislature." So Madison clearly opposes Judicial Exclusivity.

Mr. White states a preference for judicial over congressional disambiguation of the Constitution: "I would rather the judiciary should decide the point than us, because it is more properly within their department." White eloquently supports Judicial Supremacy (if not Exclusivity): "Let us then leave the constitution to a free operation, and . . . if any one supposes himself injured by their determination, let them have recourse to the law, and its decision will establish the true construction of the constitution."

After this, Smith explicitly endorses Judicial *Exclusivity*: merely "to give a legislative construction of the constitution" would be "an infringement on the powers of the judiciary." A line from Smith is a fine summary: "Sir, it is the duty of the legislature to make laws, your judges are to expound them."

Finally, *Mr. Ames* gives us a clear statement of Judicial Supremacy but *not* Exclusivity. Congress can and should interpret the Constitution, but the Judiciary can and will correct their interpretation if necessary: "If we declare justly on this point it will serve for a rule of conduct to the executive magistrate; if we declare improperly the judiciary will revise our decision."

Let's turn to James Madison and Thomas Jefferson.

In response to the Alien and Sedition Acts (1798), Virginia and Kentucky passed the famous Virginia and Kentucky Resolutions, written respectively by Madison and Jefferson, which condemned the Acts as unconstitutional and urged opposition from other states. Madison tells us that the Constitution is a compact among the states, who, as parties to the agreement, "have the right, and are in duty bound, to interpose for arresting the progress of the evil" of unconstitutional federal acts.[51]

There are two Kentucky Resolutions; the second was written in response to the resolutions of some other states objecting to the first. Jefferson tells us that the Constitution is a compact among the states, which remain parties to the agreement. As such, each state has a right to interpret the Constitution for itself: "each party [to the compact] has an equal right to judge for itself."[52] The federal government (judiciary included) is not supreme in constitutional interpretation. He gives once in each Resolution what we could call *the Tyranny Argument*:

> The government created by this compact was not made the exclusive or final judge of the extent of the powers delegated to itself; since that would have made its discretion, and not the Constitution, the measure of its powers.[53]
>
> [The principle] that the general government is the exclusive judge of the extent of the powers delegated to it, stop[s] nothing short of despotism; since the discretion of those who administer the government, and not the constitution, would be the measure of their powers.[54]

The states' right to constitutional interpretation is equal to the federal government's. However, their power to *enact* their interpretations is much less than their right to *interpret*. Kentucky deems the Alien and Sedition Acts unconstitutional, but the authority to remove them lies elsewhere. The states should work toward a Congressional repeal. Meanwhile, they must "bow to the laws of the Union." They may only fight federal misinterpretation of the Constitution in a constitutional manner. You cannot kill the Constitution in order to save it. State power to correct federal misinterpretation is limited by the Constitution itself, and largely consists of sending wiser people to Congress to make better laws.

Although Jefferson uses the word "nullification," he does not have in mind the usual sense that term carries of a right of states to unilaterally nullify federal law within their own borders. It is not unilateral: Jefferson appeals to "the several states." Nor is it not about defying federal law, which he explicitly says must be obeyed. It is about returning federal law to constitutional norms. That notion of unilateral nullification was a big deal later on, and mistakenly took inspiration from Madison and Jefferson. Fritz gives us a good overview of Madison on the subject, recommending the word "interposition" rather than "nullification." Interposition is "public opinion, protests, petitions, and legitimate actions of state legislatures" which would "[focus] attention on whether the government was acting in conformity with the Constitution."[55]

That is a striking rejection of Judicial Exclusivity; it also "could involve individual citizens,"[56] who themselves have a right to interpret the Constitution!

Now let's look at some Presidential commentary on the subject of who can interpret the Constitution.

In 1815 President Madison vetoes the national bank bill:

> Waiving the question of the constitutional authority of the Legislature to establish an incorporated bank as being precluded in my judgment by repeated recognitions under varied circumstances of the validity of such an institution

in acts of the legislative, executive, and judicial branches of the Government, accompanied by indications, in different modes, of a concurrence of the general will of the nation, the proposed bank does not appear to be calculated to answer the purposes [that would justify this bill].[57]

Madison goes on to explain that he is vetoing the national bank on *policy* grounds, although he has been persuaded of its constitutionality. Why has he been thus persuaded? Because *the people* have interpreted the Constitution in favor of allowing the bank. They did so via the actions of *all three* branches of government. Here is a clear rejection of Judicial *Exclusivity*: Congress and the president have the business of interpreting the Constitution. So do the People through "different modes," such as sending people with their views to the White House and the Capitol.

Andrew Jackson, vetoing the national bank, says that all branches of the federal government, and also the states, have an equal right to interpret the Constitution.[58] He further claims that the federal judiciary's interpretations do not overrule the interpretations of other government officials.

Jackson also employs *the Oath Argument*, which will come up again and goes something like this:

> Every official who swears an oath to affirm the Constitution is obligated to defy, within the limits of his own powers as defined by the law, any interpretations of the Constitution which he believes to be contrary to it. Judicial interpretations of the Constitution may be contrary to the Constitution. So every official who swears an oath is obligated to defy, within the limits of his own powers as defined by the law, judicial interpretations of the Constitution which he believes to be contrary to the Constitution.

Jackson further says:

> The Congress, the Executive, and the Court must each for itself be guided by its own opinion of the Constitution. Each public officer who takes an oath to support the Constitution swears that he will support it as he understands it, and not as it is understood by others. It is as much the duty of the House of Representatives, of the Senate, and of the President to decide upon the constitutionality of any bill or resolution which may be presented to them for passage or approval as it is of the supreme judges when it may be brought before them for judicial decision. The opinion of the judges has no more authority over Congress than the opinion of Congress has over the judges, and on that point the President is independent of both.

Finally, we have Abraham Lincoln. In his 1861 First Inaugural Address Lincoln rejects both Judicial Supremacy and Exclusivity.[59] He acknowledges that federal judicial decisions as such are "binding in any case upon the parties to a suit as to the object of that suit, while they are also entitled to very high respect and consideration in all parallel cases by all other departments of the Government." However, he goes on to level the Tyranny Argument against Judicial Supremacy:

> If the policy of the Government upon vital questions affecting the whole people is to be irrevocably fixed by decisions of the Supreme Court, the instant they are made in ordinary litigation between parties in personal actions the people will have ceased to be their own rulers, having to that extent practically resigned their Government into the hands of that eminent tribunal. Nor is there in this view any assault upon the court or the judges.

Next, let's take a look at the analysis of the the great Senator Daniel Webster (of Massachusetts). Webster has a famous response to Jackson's veto message.[60] Webster firmly endorses Judicial Supremacy without Exclusivity, claiming that (prior to Jackson) this has been the dominant theory:

> Hitherto it has been thought that the final decision of constitutional questions belonged to the supreme judicial tribunal. The very nature of free government, it has been supposed, enjoins this; and our Constitution, more-over, has been understood so to provide, clearly and expressly. . . . After a law has passed through all the requisite forms; after it has received the requisite legislative sanction and the executive approval, the question of its constitutionality then becomes a judicial question, and a judicial question alone.

He gives a superb argument against Judicial Exclusivity, more explicit and thorough than Ames and Madison had been in the First Congress: Congress has the right and responsibility,

> in the exercise of its functions, to consider the constitutionality of a law proposed to be passed. . . . neither branch can be compelled to pass any law, or do any other act, which it deems to be beyond the reach of its constitutional power.

The same is true of the president when it comes to executing a law. One cannot responsibly write or sign a law without considering its constitutionality, which requires interpreting the Constitution.

In Webster's Second Reply to Hayne,[61] part of a series of debates between Webster and Senator Hayne of South Carolina, he makes an impressive case for Judicial Supremacy. He says Judicial Supremacy is taught *in the Constitution itself.* He repeatedly argues for this based on the facts that the Constitution makes federal law supreme over state law[62] and that it gives the Supreme Court power over "all cases arising under the Constitution."[63] Since cases requiring constitutional interpretation are cases arising under the Constitution, they fall under the Supreme Court's jurisdiction.

However, Webster makes a mistake. His premise is that the Constitution gives the Supreme Court jurisdiction over all cases concerning constitutional interpretation arising under the Constitution. The conclusion which is supposed to follow from that is that the Supreme Court's interpretations of the Constitution overrule all other interpretations. However, what follows is only that the Supreme Court has supremacy in interpretations of the Constitution *as it relates to standing law. Those* are the cases arising in the courts under the Constitution. The Court lacks jurisdiction to rule on a merely possible law, and also when Congress considers *eliminating* some standing law. Webster's argument does not actually apply to what Jefferson, Madison, Jackson, and Lincoln were talking about. Webster is debating with Hayne whether we must comply with *standing* law. The argument *thus applied* is good, important, and, apparently, consistent with Madison, Jefferson, Jackson, and Lincoln. Hayne thought his state could nullify a federal law, which is contrary to the teachings of Jefferson, who permits only constitutional means of defying errant interpretations of the Constitution. But when it comes to making changes in the standing law, Webster's argument for Judicial Supremacy has no weight.

Let's look at the Supreme Court on the question of who can interpret the Constitution.

In footnote 7 of *United States vs. Morrison* (2000),[64] the Supreme Court, citing some earlier cases, both affirms Judicial Supremacy and makes the same argument against Judicial Exclusivity as Webster:

> It is thus a "'permanent and indispensable feature of our constitutional system'" that "'the federal judiciary is supreme in the exposition of the law of the Constitution.'" *Miller* v. *Johnson*, 515 U.S. 900, 922—923 (1995) (quoting *Cooper* v. *Aaron*, 358 U.S. 1, 18 (1958)). No doubt the political branches have a role in interpreting and applying the Constitution, but ever since *Marbury* this Court has remained the ultimate expositor of the constitutional text. As we emphasized in *United States* v. *Nixon*, 418 U.S. 683 (1974), "[I]n the performance of assigned constitutional duties each branch of the Government must initially interpret the Constitution, and the interpretation of its powers by any branch is due great respect from the others.

Let's turn to law scholar Michael Paulsen, who rejects Judicial Supremacy and Exclusivity. His argument against the authority of precedent also functions nicely as an argument against Judicial Supremacy.[65] If the Supreme Court's decisions are not binding constitutional interpretations even *on courts*, then they certainly are not binding on anyone else. Here is my reconstruction of his argument:

1. Either a judicial precedent is consistent with the Constitution, or it is not.
2. If it is consistent with the Constitution, then it adds no support to later decisions because the Constitution is enough.
3. If it is not consistent, then it is unconstitutional.
4. If a judicial precedent either adds no support to later decisions or is unconstitutional, then judges do not need to adhere to it.
5. Therefore, there are no judicial precedents to which judges need to adhere.

In Paulsen's article on *Marbury vs. Madison*, he explains that the reasoning in that famous case supports what he calls *Constitutional* Supremacy, not Judicial Supremacy.[66] The same logic leads to the conclusion that the executive and legislative branches, as well as the states, are equally qualified to interpret the Constitution. The separation of powers in the constitutional system includes *a separation of the power to interpret the Constitution.* Note that, according to Paulsen, *Marbury*'s logic includes the Oath Argument—twenty-nine years before Jackson's veto message.

What are some of the alternatives to Judicial Supremacy? I distinguish three possible versions of what Paulsen characterizes as Constitutional Supremacy; these are the alternatives to Judicial Supremacy:

- *Weak Constitutional Supremacy*: The three branches of government have an equal power to interpret the Constitution. Congress and the President may *not* violate Supreme Court orders.
- *Moderate Constitutional Supremacy*: The three branches of government have an equal power to interpret the Constitution. Congress and the President may violate Supreme Court orders that are contrary to the Constitution. Each branch must do what is Constitutionally *required*, no matter what the other branches say.
- *Extreme Constitutional Supremacy*: The three branches of government have an equal power to interpret the Constitution. Congress and the President may violate Supreme Court orders that are not supported by the Constitution. Each branch may do what is Constitutionally *permitted*, no matter what the other branches say.

Where do our foes of Judicial Supremacy stand on this question? Here's my sense of where their positions would lead them:

- Paulsen himself would go with Moderate Constitutional Supremacy. (His use of the oath argument would seem to rule out the Weak view.)
- The logic of *Marbury vs. Madison*, assuming that Paulsen explains it correctly, would also support the Moderate view.

- Jefferson's stand for the rule of *even unconstitutional* law in the Kentucky Resolutions would rule out both the Moderate and the Extreme views.
- Jackson's principles in the veto message take us only as far as Weak Constitutional Supremacy (although his actions in the Trail of Tears may go as far as the Extreme view).
- Lincoln's principles in the Inaugural Address would seem to rule out both Extreme and Moderate Constitutional Supremacy.

Steven Calabresi wrote:[67]

> Presidents and Congresses have traditionally challenged the Supreme Court in this country by insisting on their textually granted co-equal powers as constitutional interpreters. Jefferson did this in challenging the Alien and Sedition Acts, Jackson did it in challenging the constitutionality of the Bank of the United States, Lincoln did it in challenging the constitutionality of *Dred Scott*, Franklin Roosevelt did it in challenging the nine old men, and Ronald Reagan did it in challenging *Roe v. Wade*. There may be a tradition in ordinary times of deferring to the Supreme Court on many constitutional issues like the meaning of the First Amendment, but there is also a tradition, on big occasions, of the political branches reasserting their roles as constitutional interpreters.

These interpreters overwhelmingly reject Judicial Exclusivity, but are divided over Judicial Supremacy. We have seen some interesting arguments against Judicial Supremacy and Exclusivity, and Webster's argument for Judicial Supremacy. Having explained my concern with Webster's argument, it seems to me that Judicial Supremacy doesn't have much room to stand on—outside of cases pertaining to standing law.

So I reject Judicial Supremacy. I also reject (with our interpreters) Extreme Constitutional Supremacy. What about Moderate versus Weak Constitutional Supremacy? That is a difficult question. Since the Supreme Court can get the Constitution dreadfully wrong and since (as Paulsen would say), we must adhere to the Constitution as supreme law, it must be possible (albeit unusual) for a government official to interpret the Constitution correctly in defiance of the Supreme Court's interpretation. There might, moreover, be circumstances when *not* defying the Court's interpretation would force you to violate the Constitution yourself; what else can you do but resign or defy the Court? That speaks in favor of Moderate Constitutional Supremacy.

But Webster's argument is important when it comes to standing law, and this rules out both Moderate and Extreme Constitutional Supremacy. Jefferson's salutary doctrines likewise support Weak Constitutional Supremacy, which permits resignation in extreme circumstances, and allows for *other* means of fighting bad federal Court interpretations (such as, most obviously, putting *new* people on the Court).

And that speaks in favor of Weak Constitutional Supremacy. As for the Oath Argument, it only applies within the scope of an official's power and, when it comes to a standing law upheld by federal courts, Webster's argument can be taken as showing the limitations of that power. This would prevent most or all situations in which *not* defying the Court's interpretation would force a public official to violate the Constitution; such a defiance is not part of such an official's powers within the scope of the Oath Argument.

The testimony of these great Constitutional interpreters, and more importantly their arguments, rule out Extreme Constitutional Supremacy and, as far as I can tell, Moderate as well. Weak Constitutional Supremacy seems to me to be the strongest position. Webster, I deem, is correct that the Court's authority in "all cases arising" would, if exercised to approve a standing law, render the Court's ruling inviolable as long as both it and that judicial judgment stand.

All the same, the arguments are quite clear on one thing: both Judicial Supremacy and Judicial Exclusivity are wrong.

The Nature of the Constitution

These lengthy considerations lead us to a simple but very important conclusion concerning the nature of originalism in law. We have seen how contemporary originalist legal theory has shifted from a consideration of authorial intent to, ultimately, the idea that the meaning of the Constitution is located where the people can access it—namely, the text. We have seen the grounds for a similar conclusion regarding who has the right and responsibility to interpret the Constitution—primarily the people, and secondarily the whole range of governmental branches and offices which represent them. Assuming I understand them rightly, two luminaries in particular, one historical and one contemporary, teach an important doctrine. Madison and Paulsen show that the Constitution belongs to "We, the people." Its authority derives from *them*,[68] its meaning is where *they* may find it, and it is *theirs* to interpret.

And indeed it is "We, the people," whom the Constitution itself in its preamble identifies as the source of its authority. The same people are given authority over their government in the structure of government set up by the Constitution. This is a working out of the doctrine proclaimed in the Declaration of Independence that legitimate governments "derive their just powers from the consent of the governed."

Such a law will require a hermeneutics appropriate to it. The essential characteristic of this particular law is the sovereign authority of the people. The appropriate hermeneutics will privilege this authority. Accordingly, an originalism for the Constitution ought to be one which recognizes that the source of the Constitution's authority is the people.

In short, it is no accident that originalism in law has crystallized as a textualism rather than an intentionalism. Originalism for the Constitution fits the Constitution. It fits the nature of the authority of the text. The authority of the Constitution has for its immediate source the people, not the authors; therefore, its meaning must be in the text, where the people have access to it, not in the authors' minds. Put differently, a text is a means of communication, usually between author and reader, and hence authorial intentionalism is usually a good bet for being the right kind of originalism. However, the Constitution is an act of communication conveying instructions from the people of the United States of America to their central government. So it can't be an authorial intentionalism. The authors are not, in their capacity as authors, parties to this particular act of communication. The text's meaning must be an act of the people, making textualism a stronger candidate for being the correct version of constitutional originalism.

CONCLUSION

Although we have encountered various perspectives in Christian theology, we have seen that there is a strong originalist streak in orthodox Christianity from church fathers up to the recent evangelical articulation of inerrancy. Although theoretical reflection on the American Constitution is multifaceted, diverse, and subtle, originalism's roots run as deep as the founders while its branches stretch from several places on the Supreme Court to some very fine contemporary scholarship. Two salient characteristics of originalism emerge: that the Christian theological variety is an intentionalism and that the American legal variety is a textualism. Moreover, there is a difference in the sources of authority acknowledged by these theories; one looks to God's authority mediated through the apostolic or prophetic authors of the Bible, another to the sovereign people of the United States who are the immediate source of the authority of American law. And the differences match. Biblical authority runs through the biblical authors, and they are the source of its meaning. Constitutional authority runs through the people, so constitutional meaning must derive from that to which they all have access, the text.

In short, the source of a text's authority is relevant to the locus of its meaning. Originalism in theology and law may have a lot in common, but there is one major difference. In law, originalism fits the nature of the Constitution, a document whose source of authority requires that its meaning be in the text. In biblical theology, originalism fits the nature of the Bible, a document whose source of authority requires that its meaning be under the control of its human authors.

NOTES

1. For an introduction to the literature on connections between biblical and legal hermeneutics, see Peter Smith and Robert Tuttle, "Biblical Literalism and Constitutional Originalism," *Notre Dame Law Review* 86, no. 2 (2011): 693–764. Smith and Tuttle correctly point out that originalism in law is not committed to the propriety of the Constitution or to the view that it is *morally* as well as legally correct—a distinction between legal originalism and the hermeneutics of evangelical Bible believers. Note that Smith and Tuttle focus what they call biblical *literalism*, not necessarily originalism.

2. "The original meaning of the original authors should determine the interpretive framework. That's simply to say that the one who authors a text has the first and most important right to say what it means"; Albert Mohler, "Wednesday, August 1, 2018," *The Briefing* (August 1, 2018). AlbertMohler.com, https://albertmohler.com/2018/08/01/briefing-08-01-18/ . However, Mohler does at times link originalism in theology and law in ways suggesting textualism somewhat more than intentionalism. For example, according to originalist textualism "the truth resides in the text; the text is a matter of language, letters, sentences; it is a matter of propositional statements with an intention that is reflected by the author at the time"; Albert Mohler, "Thursday, September 6, 2018," *The Briefing* (September 6, 2018). AlbertMohler.com, https://albertmohler.com/2018/09/06/briefing-9-6-18/. Mohler has also discussed the difference between textualism and originalism with Stanley Fish; see Albert Mohler, "Is There a Truth in This Class? A Conversation with Stanley Fish," *Thinking in Public* (March 28, 2016). AlbertMohler.com, https://albertmohler.com/2016/03/28/thinking-in-public-stanley-fish. Topically related to all this conversation, Jeffrey Kendall connects Judge Scalia's originalism to Catholic biblical interpretation; Kendall, "Scalia, Originalism and the Bible," *MuleSense* (February 18, 2016), https://www.mulesense.net/scalia-originalism-and-the-bible/.

3. I go over this in more detail in "Is There Life in This Author? The Living Author and the Business and Importance of the Humanities in South Asia," in *Transcultural Humanities in South Asia: Critical Essays on Literature and Culture*, ed. Waseem Anwar and Nosheen Yousaf: 83–94 (London: Taylor & Francis, 2022).

4. Jacques Derrida, *Of Grammatology*; trans. Gayatri Chakravorty Spivak (Baltimore: Johns Hopkins University Press, 1974), 158.

5. Roland Barthes, "The Death of the Author;" in *Image-Music-Text*, trans. Stephen Heath: 142–148 (London: Fantana, 1977).

6. Stanley Fish, *Is There a Text in This Class?: The Authority of Interpretive Communities* (Cambridge, MA: Harvard University Press, 1982). Please note, however, that Fish's own account is subtle; that this particular book is written largely in the context of the interpretation of *literature*; and that Fish himself is more of an intentionalist originalist when it comes to the Constitution. For an introduction to Fish's legal originalism, the interested reader might consult Stanley Fish, "Intention Is all There Is: A Critical Analysis of Aharon Barak's Purposive Interpretation in Law," Cardozo Law Review, 29, no. 3 (2008): 1109–1146 or Mohler, "Is There a Truth in This Class?"

7. Associate Justice Anthony Kennedy, Majority Opinion in *Obergefell et al v. Hodges, Director, Ohio Department of Health, et al.* 576 U. S. (June 26, 2015).

8. On the terms "weak" and "strong originalism," and other related working definitions, see the introduction to this volume.

9. For a handy overview of Augustine's hermeneutics, see Frederick Van Fleteren, "Principles of Augustine's Hermeneutic: An Overview," in *Augustine: Biblical Exegete*, ed. Frederick Van Fleteren and Joseph C. Schnaubelt (New York: Peter Lang, 2001), 1–32. Also recommended is Michael Cameron, *Christ Meets Me Everywhere: Augustine's Early Figurative Exegesis* (Oxford: Oxford University Press, 2012), Introduction and Chapter 1.

10. Augustine, *Confessions*, 12.18.

11. Augustine, *De Doctrina Christiana*, 2.5.6.

12. Augustine, *De Doctrina Christiana*, 2.37.41.

13. Augustine, *Confessions*, 12.18 and 12.23–25.

14. Augustine, *Confessions*,12.26 and 12.31.

15. Augustine, *Confessions*, 12.13.

16. Augustine, *Teaching Christianity*, 3.27.38.

17. Augustine, *Confessions*, 13.12–34.

18. See Augustine, *Teaching Christianity*, 3.27.38. Michael Fiedrowicz is helpful here; see General Introduction to *Expositions of the Psalms: 1–32*, trans. and notes by Mariah Boulding, in The Works of Saint Augustine: A Translation for the 21st Century, Part III, Vol. 15, ed. John E. Rotelle, introduction by Michael Fiedrowicz (Hyde Park: New City Press, 2005), 24–26.

19. See Mark Ellingsen, *The Richness of Augustine: His Contextual and Pastoral Theology* (Louisville: Westminster John Knox, 2005), chapter 2.

20. Craig A. Carter, *Interpreting Scripture with the Great Tradition: Recovering the Genius of Premodern Exegesis* (Grand Rapids: Baker, 2018), chapter 6.

21. Aquinas, *Summa Theologica*, First Part, Question 1.

22. Documents of the Second Vatican Council, *Dei Verbum*, Chapter III.

23. Documents of the Second Vatican Council, *Dei Verbum*, Chapter III.

24. Jean-Luc Marion, *God Without Being*, trans. Thomas A. Carlson (Chicago: University of Chicago Press, 1991), 156.

25. The International Council on Biblical Inerrancy, The Chicago Statement on Biblical Inerrancy (Chicago, 1978).

26. The International Council on Biblical Inerrancy, Chicago Statement on Biblical Inerrancy, Exposition, section on Infallibility, Inerrancy, Interpretation.

27. I find unconvincing Pelikan's concerns with biblical originalism as in "constant danger of substituting pedantry for living experience" and also in "danger of absolutizing the wrong original." Textual (and authorial) realism, by definition, only does these things when it is *not* done well. Jaroslav Pelikan, *Interpreting the Bible and the Constitution* (New Haven: Yale University Press, 2004), 98.

28. The International Council on Biblical Inerrancy, Chicago Statement on Biblical Inerrancy, Exposition, section on Infallibility, Inerrancy, Interpretation.

29. Two useful sources on this notion are the Chicago Statement on Biblical Inerrancy; Exposition; Infallibility, Inerrancy, and Interpretation and The International Council on Biblical Inerrancy, The Chicago Statement on Biblical Hermeneutics (Chicago, 1982), Articles X–XVII.

30. The International Council on Biblical Inerrancy, Chicago Statement on Biblical Hermeneutics, Article XVIII.

31. Pelikan explores this challenge for originalism in *Interpreting the Bible and the Constitution*, 100.

32. The International Council on Biblical Inerrancy, Chicago Statement on Biblical Hermeneutics, Article VII.

33. Norman Geisler, Commentary on The Chicago Statement on Biblical Hermeneutics; http://www.bible-researcher.com/chicago2.html.

34. Geisler, Commentary on The Chicago Statement on Biblical Hermeneutics.

35. Geisler, Commentary on The Chicago Statement on Biblical Hermeneutics.

36. Aquinas also emphasizes that the plurality of biblical meanings are a unity rooted in the intent of the author, appealing as usual to Augustine; Aquinas, *Summa Theologica*, First Part, Question 1, Article 10, Reply to Objection 1.

37. For a better understanding of this way of thinking about the New Testament, I recommend Michael J. Kruger, *The Question of Canon: Challenging the Status Quo in the New Testament Debate* (Downers Grove: InterVarsity Press, 2013).

38. Chicago Statement on Biblical Inerrancy, A Short Statement, 2.

39. One influential recent theory of biblical meaning, that of Vanhoozer, considers the Bible in light of speech-act theory from philosophy of language: Biblical meaning is an action by the author which commands a response on the part of the reader. This I would classify as a variation of originalism. However, it is not an *intentionalism* so much as a *textualism* with a strong intentionalist aspect; roughly, the Bible's meaning is in the text and is shaped or perhaps controlled by authorial intent. See Kevin J. Vanhoozer, *Is There a Meaning in This Text?* (Grand Rapids: Zondervan, 1998).

40. Ronald R. Garet suggests that a weakness of originalism is that it pays "insufficient attention" to the sources of constitutional authority; Garet, "Comparative Normative Hermeneutics: Scripture, Literature, Constitution," *Southern California Law Review* 35 (1985): 117–119. Garet: "The failings of originalism stem from its inability to explain what it is about the original understanding that is authoritative"; Garet, "Comparative Normative Hermeneutics," 117. Again, "If originalism is to succeed as a component of constitutional hermeneutics, it must explain why the 'original understanding' conveys authority in the constitutional hermeneutical context when it does not convey authority in other hermeneutical contexts"; Garet, "Comparative Normative Hermeneutics," 118. I think this is insightful yet not entirely correct, as the following discussion shows. To be precise, Garet is correct that originalist thought in law has often neglected this topic; however, it has not been ignored entirely, and a clear enough answer is available by looking at originalist theory.

41. I have been discussing these matters on Ricochet.com since 2015 using the screen name "Saint Augustine." A good bit of what follows is modified from posts written there.

42. Originalism does not teach that the Constitution "must be interpreted to mean exactly what it meant at the time it was ratified"; Cass Sunstein, *Radicals in Robes: Why Extreme Right-Wing Courts Are Wrong for America* (New York: Basic Books, 2005), xiii.

43. Carson Holloway, "In Defense of Originalism," *Public Discourse* (April 3, 2018), https://www.thepublicdiscourse.com/2018/04/21097/. For a more detailed development of some of these ideas, I recommend Gary Lawson, "No History, No Certainty, No Legitimacy . . . No Problem: Originalism and the Limits of Legal Theory," *Florida Law Review* 64, no. 6 (2012): 1551–1571.

44. Holloway goes over some in his article; Paulsen gives one in Michael Stokes Paulsen, "Does the Constitution Prescribe Rules for its Own Interpretation?" *Northwestern University Law Review* 103, no. 2 (2009): 857–921. Another is in Robert J. Delahunty and John Yoo, "Saving Originalism," *Michigan Law Review* 113, no. 6 (2015): 1081–1113.

45. James Madison, Speech in the 4th Congress on the Jay Treaty, April 6, 1796.

46. James Madison, Letter to Henry Lee (June 25, 1824).

47. An understanding of this development and the reasons behind it seems absent from Pelikan's look at problems with originalism in *Interpreting the Bible and the Constitution*, 98–99. Pelikan apparently takes difficulties with legal intentionalism as problematic for originalism as such.

48. Delahunty and Yoo, "Saving Originalism," 1088–1097; Vasan Kesavan and Michael Stokes Paulsen, "The Interpretive Force of the Constitution's Secret Drafting History," *Georgetown Law Journal* 91 (2003): 1113–1214.

49. James Madison, *Notes on the Debates in the Federal Convention*, July 21, 1787.

50. First Federal Congress, the Congressional Register, June 16, 1789.

51. James Madison, *Virginia Resolution of 1789*.

52. Thomas Jefferson, the Kentucky Resolutions of 1798.

53. Jefferson, Kentucky Resolutions of 1798.

54. Thomas Jefferson, Kentucky Resolution of 1799.

55. Christian G. Fritz, "Interposition and the Heresy of Nullification: James Madison and the Exercise of Sovereign Constitutional Powers," *First Principles* 41 (February 21, 2012): 1.

56. Fritz, "Interposition and the Heresy of Nullification," 2.

57. James Madison, Veto Message on the National Bank; January 30, 1815.

58. Andrew Jackson, Veto Message on the National Bank; 10 July, 1832.

59. Abraham Lincoln, First Inaugural Address; March 4, 1861.

60. Daniel Webster, Speech on the Presidential Veto of the Bank Bill; July 11, 1832.

61. Daniel Webster, Second Speech on Foot's Resolution; United States Senate, January 26–27, 1830.

62. In the Constitution's Supremacy Clause: Article VI, Clause 2.

63. In Article III, Section 2, Clause 1.

64. Chief Justice John Rehnquist, Majority Opinion in *United States v. Morrison*; 529 U.S.; 120 S. Ct. (May 15, 2000).

65. See, for example, Michael Stokes Paulsen, "The Irrepressible Myth of *Marbury*," *Michigan Law Review* 101, no. 8 (August 2003): 2706–2743; and "Everything You Need to Know about Constitutional Law," *Public Discourse* (May 19, 2015), https://www.thepublicdiscourse.com/2015/05/15013/.

66. Paulsen, "The Irrepressible Myth."

67. Steven Calabresi, "Text, Precedent, and the Constitution: Some Originalist and Normative Arguments for Overruling *Planned Parenthood of Southeastern Pennsylvania v. Casey*," *Constitutional Commentary* 22 (2005): 345.

68. A helpful source on the human sources of the Constitution according to originalist theory, although not explicitly drawing out the contrast from biblical originalism, is Steven Smith, "Reply to Koppelman: Originalism and the (Merely) Human Constitution," *Constitutional Commentary* 27 (2010): 189–199. This difference has implications for the Constitution's accuracy. Smith and Tuttle, for example, claim that according to legal originalism it does not even make sense to describe the Constitution as true; its meaning is legal; its sentences define the law rather than describe an external reality. However, Paulsen suggests that the meaning of the Constitution, while by definition correct as law, can nonetheless be absurd; his favorite example is the fact that "the vice president would preside at his own impeachment trial"; "The Text, the Whole Text, and Nothing but the Text, So Help Me God: Un-Writing Amar's Unwritten Constitution," *The University of Chicago Law Review* 81, no. 3 (2014): 1414 n. 56 and 1431–1432.

WORKS CITED

Aquinas. *Summa Theologica.*

Augustine. *Confessions.*

———. *De Doctrina Christiana.*

Barthes, Roland. "The Death of the Author." In *Image-Music-Text*; translated by Stephen Heath: 142–148. London: Fantana, 1977/

Boone, Mark J. "Is There Life in This Author? The Living Author and the Business and Importance of the Humanities in South Asia." In *Transcultural Humanities in South Asia: Critical Essays on Literature and Culture*, edited by Waseem Anwar and Nosheen Yousaf: 83–94. London: Taylor & Francis, 2022.

Calabresi, Steven. "Text, Precedent, and the Constitution: Some Originalist and Normative Arguments for Overruling *Planned Parenthood of Southeastern Pennsylvania v. Casey*." *Constitutional Commentary* 22 (2005): 311–348.

Cameron, Michael. *Christ Meets Me Everywhere: Augustine's Early Figurative Exegesis*. Oxford: Oxford University Press, 2012.

Carter, Craig A. *Interpreting Scripture with the Great Tradition: Recovering the Genius of Premodern Exegesis*. Grand Rapids: Baker, 2018.

Delahunty, Robert J. and John Yoo. "Saving Originalism." *Michigan Law Review* 113, no. 6 (2015): 1081–1113.

Derrida, Jacques. *Of Grammatology*, translated by Gayatri Chakravorty Spivak. Baltimore: Johns Hopkins University Press, 1974.

Documents of the Second Vatican Council.

Ellingsen, Mark. *The Richness of Augustine: His Contextual and Pastoral Theology*. Louisville: Westminster John Knox, 2005.

Fiedrowicz, Michael. General Introduction to *Expositions of the Psalms: 1–32*, translation and notes by Mariah Boulding. In The Works of Saint Augustine: A

Translation for the 21st Century, Part III, Vol. 15, edited by John E. Rotelle, introduction by Michael Fiedrowicz, 13–66. Hyde Park: New City Press, 2005.

First Federal Congress. The Congressional Register.

Fish, Stanley. *Is There a Text in This Class?: The Authority of Interpretive Communities*. Cambridge, MA: Harvard University Press, 1982.

———. "Intention Is all There Is: A Critical Analysis of Aharon Barak's Purposive Interpretation in Law." *Cardozo Law Review*, 29, no. 3 (2008): 1109–1146.

Fritz, Christian G. "Interposition and the Heresy of Nullification: James Madison and the Exercise of Sovereign Constitutional Powers." *First Principles* 41 (February 21, 2012): 1–17.

Garet, Ronald R. "Comparative Normative Hermeneutics: Scripture, Literature, Constitution." *Southern California Law Review* 35 (1985): 35–134.

Geisler, Norman. Commentary on The Chicago Statement on Biblical Hermeneutics. http://www.bible-researcher.com/chicago2.html.

Holloway, Carson. "In Defense of Originalism." *Public Discourse* (April 3, 2018). https://www.thepublicdiscourse.com/2018/04/21097/.

The International Council on Biblical Inerrancy. *The Chicago Statement on Biblical Inerrancy*. Chicago, 1978.

The International Council on Biblical Inerrancy. *The Chicago Statement on Biblical Hermeneutics*. Chicago, 1982.

Jackson, Andrew. *Veto Message on the National Bank*. July 10, 1832.

Jefferson, Thomas. *The Kentucky Resolutions of 1798*.

———. *Kentucky Resolution of 1799*.

Kendall, Jeffrey. "Scalia, Originalism and the Bible." *MuleSense* (February 18, 2016). https://www.mulesense.net/scalia-originalism-and-the-bible/.

Kennedy, Associate Justice Anthony. Majority Opinion in *Obergefell et al v. Hodges, Director, Ohio Department of Health, et al*. 576 U. S. June 26, 2015.

Kesavan, Vasan, and Michael Stokes Paulsen. "The Interpretive Force of the Constitution's Secret Drafting History." *Georgetown Law Journal* 91 (2003): 1113–1214.

Kruger, Michael J. *The Question of Canon: Challenging the Status Quo in the New Testament Debate*. Downers Grove: InterVarsity Press, 2013.

Lawson, Gary. "No History, No Certainty, No Legitimacy . . . No Problem: Originalism and the Limits of Legal Theory." *Florida Law Review* 64, no. 6 (2012): 1551–1571.

Lincoln, Abraham. *First Inaugural Address*. March 4, 1861.

Madison, James. Letter to Henry Lee. June 25, 1824.

———. *Notes on the Debates in the Federal Convention*.

———. Speech in the 4th Congress on the Jay Treaty. April 6, 1796.

———. *Veto Message on the National Bank*. January 30, 1815.

———. *Virginia Resolution of 1789*.

Marion, Jean-Luc. *God Without Being*, translated by Thomas A. Carlson. Chicago: University of Chicago Press, 1991.

Mohler, Albert. "Is There a Truth in This Class? A Conversation with Stanley Fish." *Thinking in Public* (March 28, 2016). AlbertMohler.com. https://albertmohler.com/2016/03/28/thinking-in-public-stanley-fish.

———. "Wednesday, August 1, 2018." *The Briefing* (August 1, 2018). AlbertMohler.com. https://albertmohler.com/2018/08/01/briefing-08-01-18/.

———. "Thursday, September 6, 2018." *The Briefing* (September 6, 2018). AlbertMohler.com. https://albertmohler.com/2018/09/06/briefing-9-6-18/.

Paulsen, Michael Stokes. "The Irrepressible Myth of *Marbury*." *Michigan Law Review* 101, no. 8 (August 2003): 2706–2743.

———. "Does the Constitution Prescribe Rules for its Own Interpretation?" *Northwestern University Law Review* 103, no. 2 (2009): 857–921.

———. "The Text, the Whole Text, and Nothing but the Text, So Help Me God: Un-Writing Amar's Unwritten Constitution." *The University of Chicago Law Review* 81, no. 3 (2014): 1385–1441.

———. "Everything You Need to Know about Constitutional Law." *Public Discourse* (May 19, 2015). https://www.thepublicdiscourse.com/2015/05/15013/.

Pelikan, Jaroslav. *Interpreting the Bible and the Constitution.* New Haven: Yale University Press, 2004.

Rehnquist, Chief Justice John. Majority Opinion in *United States v. Morrison.* 529 U.S. 120 S. Ct. (May 15, 2000).

Smith, Peter and Robert Tuttle. "Biblical Literalism and Constitutional Originalism." *Notre Dame Law Review* 86, no. 2 (2011): 693–764.

Smith, Steven. "Reply to Koppelman: Originalism and the (Merely) Human Constitution." *Constitutional Commentary* 27 (2010): 189–199.

Van Fleteren, Frederick. "Principles of Augustine's Hermeneutic: An Overview." In *Augustine: Biblical Exegete*, edited by Frederick Van Fleteren and Joseph C. Schnaubelt, 1–32. New York: Peter Lang, 2001.

Vanhoozer, Kevin J. *Is There a Meaning in This Text?* Grand Rapids: Zondervan, 1998.

Webster, Daniel. Second Speech on Foot's Resolution. United States Senate. January 26–27, 1830.

———. Speech on the Presidential Veto of the Bank Bill. July 11, 1832.

Chapter 8

A Difference between Biblical and Constitutional Originalism

Menashe C. Roberts

The Talmud relates the story of an individual seeking to convert to Judaism on the supposition that he only be instructed in the written law, the written text of the Torah, and not on the oral law, the oral tradition that is said to explain the written text.[1] The individual approached the two leading sages of his era, Hillel and Shammai.[2] First, the individual asked Shammai, "How many Torahs do you have?" to which Shammai responded, "Two: the Written Torah and the Oral Torah." The petitioner requested of Shammai, "Convert me on the condition that you only teach me the Written Torah because I do not believe you about the Oral Torah." Shammai promptly dismissed him.

The petitioner then approached Hillel and posed the same proposition, that Hillel convert him and solely instruct him on the Written Text of the Torah and not the Oral Torah. Hillel converted the individual and immediately began instructing the proselyte, teaching him the letters of the Written Torah, the letters of the Hebrew alphabet. Hillel began "Aleph, Bet, Gimmel, Daled . . ." and then ended the lesson, bidding his eager student return the next day. When the next day came the acolyte returned and Hillel began with a review of the previous day's lesson, but this time he reversed the order and told him that the first Hebrew letter was Tav and not Aleph. The student stopped Hillel and said, "But yesterday you told me the opposite of what you are telling me today," to which Hillel responded "If you relied upon me telling you what the letters were yesterday, then you should rely on what I teach you regarding the Oral Torah."

This vignette encapsulates the idea that there can be no reading of the Torah's text without some sort of oral component in addition to the text's written word.[3] The entire meaning of any given section of the Pentateuch cannot be ascertained from the words of the text alone; there is, inextricably linked to the text of the Written Torah, an Oral Torah.[4] While the exact relation between the Written Torah and the Oral Torah is not the focus of this chapter, the idea of the necessity of the Oral Torah for a proper understanding of the meaning of the Written Torah appears to negate a certain type of theory that one might use to ascertain the meaning present in the written Pentateuch, namely the hermeneutic of textualism.

One theory of constitutional interpretation is known as originalism. This theory posits that the "object of constitutional interpretation should . . . remain fixed by factors like original public understandings or authorial intentions."[5] This definition also sets up two of the classic ways that one can arrive at the "original" meaning of a text. These sub-theories are known as textualism and intentionalism. Textualism is the position that the original meaning of a text is contained within the text and, therefore, is whatever the text would have meant to a reasonable person at the time of the text's authorship.[6] Intentionalism is the view that the original meaning of the text is inextricably linked to the intention of the authors.[7]

For the most part, both forms of Originalism have found their respective supporters in the scholarly works of theology and legal theory. Textualism, as a method of legal interpretation, was made popular by the late Supreme Court justice Antonin Scalia.[8] This method is popular for interpreters of the US Constitution as well as judges who interpret their own legal and civil codes. Intentionalism tends to be popular among theologians who view the meaning of the biblical text as linked to the intentions of the authors. (The discussion of who "the authors" of the biblical texts are is an orthogonal issue not germane to this essay.)

One potential motivation for thinking that it is generally appropriate to use textualism to interpret legal codes, such as the Constitution of the United States or the Bible, is because both of these textual domains are often very similar. Regarding the Pentateuch, for example, Jewish theologians have maintained that there are 613 individual commandments.[9] Thus, it may be proper to interpret the portion of the Pentateuch that concerns the legal code in a manner similar to that in which we interpret other legal codes. For example, when the Pentateuch states, "You shall sanctify my sabbaths," it is commanding individuals to behave in a certain way (Ex. 31:13).[10] Similarly, when the Bill of Rights says, "Congress shall make no law" the text is commanding the legislature to behave in a certain way (US Constitution, Amendment I). Thus, if it is correct to interpret one body of laws using the textualist method, then perhaps it would be appropriate to apply the same method in the interpretation of another body of laws. There does not, at least at first glance, seem to be a compelling reason why textualism about the US Constitution should be any different from textualism about the legal portions of the Pentateuch. If textualism is an appropriate method to interpret one body of laws, it ought to be appropriate for interpreting other bodies of law as well.

What follows is a demonstration of how and why employing a textualist interpretation of the legal portions of the Pentateuch is wrongheaded. However appropriate it may be for Scalia and other textualists to use a textualist methodology to interpret the US Constitution, this method simply will not work for the Torah. I will explain that the textual domains of the US Constitution and the Torah's legal code are dissimilar such that applying textualism to the text of the Torah is impossible. I will focus on one dissimilarity in particular which concerns the very foundational formation of the Torah's legal code, the Hebrew language. Semitic languages, of which the Hebrew language is a member, are structured differently than Indo-European languages like English. Vowels are not endemic to many Semitic languages; the consonants that comprise the languages' "alphabetical" system can have radically different meanings depending on their vocalization. Hence, "What would this text have meant to a reasonable person at the time?" is not a well-formed question. The text is meaningless without vocalization.[11] I will explain how we have the vocalizations that we do have. I will also tackle the issue of translation from an unvocalized language to a vocalized one, demonstrating that translations of texts are not the "original" meaning, at least not original in the relevant ways that would support a textualist framework.

I will first consider how one might attempt to apply textualism in reading the Torah. Then, I will explain the significance of the absence of vowels in the original writing of the Torah and show how this situation renders many words in the Torah ambiguous. I will also explain why other words in the Torah are vague. Next, I will explain why translating the Torah into a different, vocalized language does not remove the difficulty. When words in the written Torah are ambiguous due to their lack of vowels, the only solution is to clarify them by vocalizing them with vowels, a process which must derive some information from tradition and not from the written text. My concluding remarks will be a recount of the interpretive benefits that one can employ when textualism about the Pentateuch is abandoned.

TEXTUALISM AND THE PENTATEUCH

Scalia describes how textualists ought to treat the meaning of legal documents: "in their full context, words mean what they conveyed to reasonable people at the time they were written," which is to say that a given written word in any legal code means whatever it would have meant at the time of a statute's adoption or dissemination.[12]

Thus the textualist aims to investigate the meaning of written words at the time of a legal text's creation. For example, when the Bill of Rights declares "Congress shall make no law" it is incumbent upon the textualist to investigate what the words "Congress" and "law" meant to reasonable people at the time the Bill of Rights was written (US Constitution, Amendment I). Scalia and Garner note that this process won't necessarily be an easy task, nor should we expect it to be; they lay out what is required to properly engage in a textualist interpretation. "The endeavor requires aptitude in language, sound judgement, the suppression of personal preferences regarding the outcome, and, with older texts, historical linguistic research."[13] By analogy, we ought to investigate what various biblical injunctions would have meant to a reasonable person at the time of the Bible's dissemination.[14]

While translational issues of biblical texts can generally be very complicated and have indeed garnered their own section later in this chapter, let us for the moment assume that the translation I am about to present is fair and accurate. With this in mind, we will examine a number of the Pentateuch's injunctions to consider how a textualist ought to interpret them.

When we come across the injunction, "Do not cook a kid in its mother's milk" we must identify all the key terms in this injunction and ascertain what they would have meant to reasonable Israelites at the time of the Torah's dissemination (Ex. 23:10).[15] Determining which animal (or animals) the Israelites classified as "a kid," what they considered to be "cooking," which animal bore the relationship "mother" to the "kid" in question, and what constituted that animal's milk is required aptly to lay out a textual reading of this verse. When a different verse asserts that if a woman "gives birth to a female she shall be impure for two weeks," it is incumbent upon the textualist to ascertain what exactly "two weeks," "a female," and "impure" would have meant to a reasonable Israelite at the time (Lev. 12:5). The textualist must also ascertain what "vicinity" means when the Israelites were told that "no man may leave his vicinity" on the Sabbath (Ex. 16:29). Likewise, the textualist must ask what "work" would have meant to a reasonable Israelite at the time of the injunction "You shall do no work" (Lev. 23:3), and so on.

At first glance, the textualist program appears reasonable. A simple investigation into what these verses would have meant to a reasonable person at the time of their dissemination certainly seems like an attainable goal. If a textualist must ascertain what "vehicle" would have meant to a reasonable person at the time when an injunction is given that "no vehicle may enter the park," then it stands to reason that they should have no problem ascertaining what "work" means to a reasonable person at the time the injunction "you shall do no work" (Lev. 23:3) is given.[16] The same goes for the permissions, prohibitions, and prescriptions contained within the Pentateuch.

I will now introduce another level of difficulty to the job of our intrepid textualist by looking at injunctions that contain homographs. A homograph refers to two words that are spelled the same but mean different things. Breaking it down further, a single morpheme (the smallest unit of language) can express two different definitions. The word "bank," when used as a noun, is a homograph; it can either mean "the rising ground bordering a lake, river, or sea or forming the edge of a cut or hollow" or it could mean "an establishment for the custody, loan, exchange, or issue of money, for the extension of credit, and for facilitating the transmission of funds."[17] So the word "bank" is *ambiguous*; it has two possible meanings, and it is the job of the textualist to disambiguate this word. Scalia defines ambiguity in this context, explaining that "A word or phrase is ambiguous when the question is which of two or more meanings applies."[18] This contrasts with his definition of vagueness; vagueness for Scalia is "when [a word's] unquestionable meaning has uncertain application to various factual situations."[19]

Suppose a city has a local ordinance which states, "The bank must close at two thirty p.m." It is a reasonable question to ask whether the ordinance refers to a local topographical feature or a local financial institution, as we have established that the homograph "bank" is ambiguous. Textualism does have methods for parsing or disambiguating the meaning of homographs. The textualist, for instance, can appeal to the legal context that surrounds this individual law. If the ordinance is found in a codex of collected laws about our city's parks and recreation facilities, then we are entitled to assume that "bank" means the bank of a river and not a financial institution. This application of legal context is what Scalia calls the "whole-text canon" which is "to consider the entire text, in view of its structure and of the physical and logical relation of its many parts."[20]

The Pentateuch contains various ordinances that are both vague and ambiguous. Vagueness is present as, for example, the text never directly specifies what specific instances of "work" are prohibited on the Sabbath, making the ordinance vague. The same applies when the Israelites are injuncted not to leave their "place" on the Sabbath. Ambiguity is present, as I will show, when a word such as "milk" can have multiple possible meanings without any built-in way of distinguishing between the two. Due to the alphabetical structure of biblical Hebrew many of its nouns are inherently ambiguous.

THE CASE OF THE TWO ALPHABETS

Colloquially, the term "alphabet" is used to describe any system that translates speech into a written format. However, linguistically, this is not the proper use of the term "alphabet." An alphabet specifically is a system of characters that contains both vowels and consonants.[21] Not all systems of writing have this feature of both vowels and consonants endemic to the language. That is, not all writing systems have graphemes (letters) that form both vowels and consonants. Alphabets have graphemes for both consonants and vowels (B, C, D, A, E, I) while Hebrew only has graphemes for consonants. Both Greek and Latin are alphabets, containing graphemes for consonants and vowels. For writers and readers of English, the Latin alphabet, which nearly all of this chapter is written in, contains both vowels and consonants. Semitic languages, such as Hebrew, are more properly termed *abjads* (pronounced "ab-djad") rather than *alphabets* because these writing systems do not contain vowels in the same way that alphabets do.[22]

In the Latin alphabet morphemes (potential words) are formed by combining graphemes (written symbols) for consonants and graphemes for vowels. For instance, the consonant "C," the Vowel "A," and the consonant "T" combined together form the morpheme CAT. There is no possible reading of the morpheme CAT other than "cat." For the Latin alphabet, there is no *morpheme-ambiguity* about this, no ambiguity inherent in the word as to whether or not the morpheme CAT could correspond to the word "cat" or the word "dog."

Hebrew's graphemes, however, only function as consonants; thus its morphemes are often ambiguous. A text in biblical Hebrew requires vocalization, that is adding vowels in by reading, in order to disambiguate its morphemes. For instance, the Hebrew consonants "Aleph (א)" and "Lamed (ל)," when combined, form the morpheme "AL (אל)."[23] Since I have not provided the vocalization for this morpheme, it could be vocalized as "God," or it could be vocalized as a preposition roughly meaning "too" or "on." The morpheme "AL (אל)" is ambiguous. The meaning of "AL (אל)," unvocalized, could be either of two homographs, one which carries the meaning for the word "God" and another which carries the meaning for a preposition.[24] This is why, in linguistics, Semitic writing systems are often called *abjads* as opposed to *alphabets*.[25] Alphabets contain graphemes for both vowels and consonants and their morphemes are largely unambiguous, while abjads contain graphemes solely for consonants and its graphemes are often ambiguous.

This does not mean that biblical Hebrew contains no sounds that comprise vowels. Indeed, there do exist vowels in Hebrew orthography which, among other things, assist in disambiguating morphemes. However, these vowels are never present in the "original" texts of biblical Hebrew literature.[26] Further, for Hebrew, a system of characters that represent vowels would not be standardized until the tenth century CE.[27] Before this, vocalizing a text was a matter of instances. In each reading of a particular text, the reader would vocalize aloud either to an audience or just himself. Thus, the disambiguation of homographs would occur at an instance of vocalization and repeated instances of the same vocalization would become a tradition of vocalization. Eventually this tradition of vocalization would become standardized in the forms of the diacritic characters that represent vowel pronunciations that were placed alongside and then eventually inside the Hebrew text. This program was done by a group known as the Masoretes, and the earliest text we have that contains both consonants and vowels would become the Masoretic Text. Collectively, the system of diacritic symbols they left us is known as the nikud system. It is no accident that the terms "Masoretic" and "Masorete" are diminutive forms of the Hebrew word "Masorah," which means tradition, for the Masoretes standardized and preserved for subsequent generations a tradition of Torah vocalizations.[28]

No instance of vocalization or of a vocalized tradition is present within Torah scrolls that are in religious use today, just as they were not present in previous Torah scrolls before the advent of the nikud system. Given the relative recentness of biblical Hebrew's systemization of vowel characters, which exist as an overlay to the text and therefore not necessarily a part of the text, we can assume that no reasonable person at the time of the Pentateuch's dissemination employed the diacritic characters that we use as vowels today. Thus, disambiguating homographs was an extratextual affair, and the only way to garner meaning from the Pentateuch was to rely on either an instance, or a tradition, of the text's vocalization.[29]

Even though vowels are not endemic to the original biblical Hebrew text, this does not leave us at a total loss for disambiguating homographical morphemes based on original texts; sometimes we can rely on the context in surrounding verses, or even in the same verse in which the morpheme is present. For instance, the Hebrew morpheme חלב (HLV) can be vocalized either as חָלָב (HLV^1) or as חֵלֶב (HLV^2) where HLV^1 means "milk" and HLV^2 means "fat." Context can help disambiguate this morpheme for animal sacrifices in which a male animal is mentioned in conjunction with HLV; we can know that the HLV, in this instance, is fat since male animals do not produce milk. This is exemplified in the verse, "Take all the HLV that covers the entrails, the protuberance on the liver, and the two kidneys with the HLV on them and turn them into smoke on the altar" (Ex. 29:13) Since the animal parts being discussed in this verse belong to a "bull" (as stated in 29:11), the injunction here is not ambiguous, similar to how ordinances about a "bank" are not ambiguous based on the relevant legal canon they are found in.

However, not all instances of the morpheme HLV are this easily disambiguated; in some instances context does not indicate how we ought to disambiguate between two homographs. These cases of strong ambiguity can only be disambiguated by an instance of a text's vocalization, as I will show in the next section. Thus, in order to ascertain what these words would have meant "to a reasonable person at the time," one would need to appeal to a tradition of vocalization not contained within, but outside of, the given text.

AMBIGUITY AND VAGUENESS IN THE PENTATEUCH

The verse in Exodus enjoins the hearer, "You shall not cook a kid in its mother's HLV (חלב)" (Ex. 23:19). In the 12th chapter of Leviticus, a woman who bears a daughter "shall be impure SHVAYM (שבעים) like her separation" (Lev. 12:5). Another verse in Exodus enjoins the hearer, "whoever does *work* on it [the Sabbath] shall be cut off from his kin" (31:14). Again, concerning the Sabbath, Exodus instructs the listener, "Let everyone remain in *place*: let no one leave the *vicinity* on the seventh day" (italics added; 16:27–30). Each of these verses represents an instance of vagueness or ambiguity in the Pentateuch. The first two verses have their ambiguous elements left untranslated and unvocalized, while the second two have their vague elements italicized. There are many more such instances of ambiguity within the text of the Pentateuch, but I would like to use these four verses as an example as to why the type of textualism employed in modern legal theories does not work here.

For biblical injunctions which are ambiguous we are left, as I have stated, with two possible meanings for a given homograph and there is no indication from the rest of the text to disambiguate them. For instance, there is no indication in Exodus 23:12 whether one ought to disambiguate HLV to mean HLV^1—milk—or as HLV^2—fat. Thus, what would the injunction have meant to a reasonable person at the time?

One could play a sort of guessing game and attempt to make inferences based on other biblical prohibitions, but the results from such an enterprise would prove fruitless as there is no clear way to determine which inference is better. For instance, one might argue that it was a common practice at the time to boil young animals in their mother's milk, that specific reference to a female in the animal's mother and not a father would indicate milk over fat, and that in many other instances the Torah prohibits killing animals with their young as in Lev. 22:28 and Deut. 22:6–7. However, one could just as easily argue that in many instances the Pentateuch forbids the consumption of fat from certain animals as well as the fat of sacrifices, which should lead us to believe that the verse in question discusses fat rather than milk and that a reasonable person at the time would have known this since, given the commandment's juxtaposition to a discussion of first fruits (in the earlier part of the verse), this commandment is clearly talking about offerings and not general consumptive practice.

Another example of this type of investigation could be run with Lev. 12:3 where the morpheme SHVAYM (שבעים) could either be disambiguated as שְׁבֻעַיִם—two weeks ($SHVAYM^1$)—or as שִׁבְעִים—seventy days ($SHVAYM^2$). One could argue that the following word in the verse "as her separation" indicates that this verse is referencing two weeks, since in other places where the word "her separation" is mentioned she is unclean for seven days. Again, someone might retort that in other instances of the mentioning of "separation" seven days are mentioned as opposed to one week. The odd use of "two weeks" as opposed to "fourteen days" in this verse most likely means that this verse is mentioning seventy days, or else it would have said "fourteen days" in parity with the other verses. Thus a reasonable person at the time would have thought that a woman in this instance would be impure for seventy days.

For instances of vagueness, the aforementioned verse "you shall do no work" never actually describes what work is, despite declaring that performing this work engenders the death penalty. Thus, the term "work" could apply to any number of factual situations with no clear indication of what these factual situations are. How, then, are we to ascertain what "work" would have meant to a reasonable person at the time of the Pentateuch's dissemination? The text does mention not kindling a flame (Ex. 35:3) and ceasing plowing and reaping (34:21), but then again the book of Numbers mentions an instance of someone being put to death for gathering sticks which is neither kindling a flame, plowing, nor reaping (Num. 15:32–36). One might argue that gathering sticks implies an intention to kindle a flame or that the semantic range of "kindle" implies preparation to kindle. However, the verse does not prohibit intention; it only prohibits action, and the semantic range of "kindle" applies more generally to destruction as in Ex. 22:5 rather than preparation. Additionally, later on in the biblical canon Jeremiah reprimands the Judahites for transferring objects and engaging in commerce on the Sabbath; none of these things are expressly forbidden by the plain meaning of the Pentateuch (Jer. 17:21–22).

Further, the injunctions that on the Sabbath day "everyone remain in his place" and "let no man leave his vicinity" are entirely vague as "his place" and "his vicinity" are never defined anywhere in the rest of the Pentateuch. Ought we to assume that "place" refers to the dwelling of one's tent, or should it refer to the entire camp? Since it is juxtaposed with the gathering of manna and the Israelites are enjoined not to gather manna on the Sabbath, should we then assume place is anywhere manna does not fall? The text does not clarify which position is correct; the terms "place" and "vicinity" are left inexplicably vague.

Of course, the Pentateuch remarks repeatedly that its laws are unambiguous and not vague. The Torah's commandments, as far as an individual can practice them, are exoteric. The Pentateuch enjoins the reader (hearer?), "Be careful to heed all these commandments that I enjoin upon you" and "These are the laws and rules that you must carefully observe" (Deut. 12:1, 8). It seems nonsensical for any legal code to command its practitioners to carefully follow ambiguous or vague laws. Additionally, the Pentateuch requires one to "teach them [the commandments] to your children, reciting them when you stay at home and when you are away, when you lie down and when you get up" (Deut. 11:18). I do not suspect that the Israelites were commanded to teach their children about commandments that they themselves thought were vague or ambiguous. Shortly before Moses dies, he informs the Israelites that the Torah "is not too baffling for you, . . . nor is it beyond reach. It is not in the heavens, . . . neither is it beyond the sea, . . . no, the thing is very close to you, in your mouth and in your heart, to observe it" (Deut. 30:11–14). This final exhortation by Moses describes the Torah's commandments as clear, unambiguous, and capable of being observed.

It should be clear, though, that for verses such as we have been considering which, due to their ambiguity and vagueness which cannot be clarified by other strictly textual means, we cannot, with any degree of certainty, assess, based on the text alone, what they would have meant to a "reasonable person at the time." The type of textualism that one would apply to interpreting documents such as the Constitution of the United States cannot be applied to at least certain legal injunctions in the Pentateuch. The text presents itself as clear, but its clarity is not fully self-contained.

One may argue that, as far as ambiguity is concerned, homographs can be disambiguated by their vocalization scheme. Indeed, this is the position that Rabbinic Jews take concerning Ex. 23:19. They would state that the proper vocalization of HLV is HLV^1 (חָלָב) and not HLV^2 (חֵלֶב) and thus the verse is rendered, "Thou shalt not cook a kid in its mother's milk."

Now this is based upon a subscription to a tradition of vocalization and is not based upon a textualist standard. This is an appeal to a specific vocalization scheme—in fact, to a tradition of vocalization that is passed down from the original instance of vocalization (Moses) to the eventual "fixing" of the text into the Masoretic Text with diacritic characters. This is not an appeal to information arising from the text itself, as a textualist would do. While it may be the case that a reasonable person at the time would have heard the proper vocalization scheme for vocalizing the Pentateuch, neither that reader nor we are learning that vocalization from the text itself. We learn nothing from an investigation into what a reasonable hearer of the Pentateuch at the time would have heard, but rather from an appeal to tradition.

Textualists are concerned with what a document, in and of itself, would have meant to a reasonable person at the time of the document's enactment. The Rabbinic method of interpretation is concerned with what the original vocalization scheme was. It may very well be that both approaches are concerned with a kind of originalism about their respective textual domains, but according to the definition of the textualist project that I have laid out, Rabbinic disambiguation methods do not meet that definition of textualism. Textualists who attempt to interpret the United States Constitution and people who subscribe to the Rabbinic method of interpretation "are just doing a different thing."[30] Textualists are concerned with what a document, in and of itself, would have meant to a reasonable person at the time of the document's enactment. This Rabbinic method of interpretation is concerned with what the original vocalization scheme was. It may very well be that both approaches are concerned with a kind of originalism about their respective textual domains, but according to the definition of the textualist project that I have laid out, traditional disambiguation methods do not meet that definition of textualism.

Since the Rabbinic method of interpretation assumes that, concurrent with the biblical text, there is an additional interpretive schema, including the traditional vocalization of the text, it is also perfectly apt for clarifying the vague injunctions present in the Pentateuch. The manner in which these meanings are clarified is not textualist. To parse out the definition of "work" and "place," the Rabbinic method assumes that these words mean specific and highly technical things. "Work" is parsed as performing "any one of the 39 categories of primary labors in the building or function of the Tabernacle."[31] "Place" and "vicinity" are defined to include "2000 cubits beyond the Halachic borders[32] of the city. If one was not in a city at the eve of Shabbos [*sic*] he has 2000 cubits beyond the home or [if he is not in a home outside a city] the four cubits that he occupies."[33] There is no conceivable way that the text of the Pentateuch alone informs one of these definitions based solely on what the meaning of the text would be to a reasonable person at the time. This is why these definitions are all contained in what was considered the "Oral Torah communicated to Moses at Mount Sinai together with the written Torah and subsequently transmitted by oral tradition."[34]

The textualist standard cannot be invoked for disambiguating and clarifying ambiguous and vague verses within the Pentateuch. As I have shown, to do so, it would need to first ascertain which of the many possible vocalization schemata would have been used by a "reasonable person." As an additional—a lesser, but still a very real—problem, it would also have to clarify ultimately vague injunctions that have no definitive referent anywhere else in the text.

TRADUTTORE, TRADITORE

One might be tempted to think that there is a simple solution to interpreting the original meaning of unvocalized texts: Simply translate the unvocalized texts into a vocalized language. Since we have established that biblical Hebrew is an unvocalized language which contains ambiguous homographs, a simple translation from biblical Hebrew into a vocalized language ought to rectify our problem. Then we can turn to this "original translation" for the various ambiguous homographs that we find in the Pentateuch's legal code. The question of which cooking substance is proscribed would disappear as we would simply translate the unvocalized Hebrew word, which could either mean milk or fat, into a vocalized language such as English and settle on the word "milk." Once we vocalize the substance in which it is inappropriate to cook a kid, we can simply fall back to our "original translation" and preserve a textualist's desire for a document's original meaning. I think this idea fails for two reasons. First, the translated information does not fall under something that "a reasonable person at the time" could have understood. Second, while translating a language might be helpful at disambiguating certain homographs, it does so at the cost of sacrificing meaning.

If we assume the Pentateuch's claims about its own chronology in terms of when it was disseminated, the years given are sometime between 1,312 BCE and 1,272 BCE.[35] No reasonable person at this time would have understood any modern language. It's possible that in addition to Hebrew some Israelites may have understood Egyptian, but translating one language with as many obscurities as biblical Hebrew into another obscure language such as Ancient Egyptian[36] would not yield a net positive as far as clarification is concerned. Thus, in actuality, there is no viable language into which to translate the Pentateuch which would satisfy a textualist standard of what a reasonable person at the time would have understood from the text alone. A translation is never the original, no matter how disambiguated the translation is. A translation can never be what a text "would have meant to a reasonable person at the time" because at the time the document was written the meaning would be captured by the original language and not a translation.

There is a wonderful phrase that comes from the Italian language, "*Traduttore, Traditore*." It means either that the translator has betrayed, or that translation is betrayal, or that to translate is to betray. While it is true that translation from one language to another can preserve meaning, it is not true that translation from one language to another *always* preserves original meaning. This is especially the case for translating languages which are unvocalized to languages which are vocalized. Certainly, we can say that the English phrase "I have water" can be translated into the German phrase "Ich habe Wasser," or "Habe Wasser" and the relative meaning is preserved. However, this meaning preservation breaks down when we examine translations from an unvocalized language into a vocalized one. The Hebrew phrase "I want חלב" can either be translated into English as "I want milk" or I want fat" due to the nature of the unvocalized and ambiguous morpheme. Choosing whether the speaker means to request milk or fat is a matter of vocalizing the text, or subscribing to a traditional way in which the text has been vocalized which is not the same thing as ascertaining from the text itself what it would have meant to a reasonable person at the time of dissemination.

All translation requires interpretation; translators are constantly making choices in their translation. In order to get the untranslated data into its translated format, the translators must make choices that they can only hope will preserve the text's original meaning. These translation choices amount to preferences where translators attempt to preserve as much originality as possible, such as focusing on a more literal translation. But this attempt to preserve as much originality as possible is a far cry from what the text would have meant to a reasonable person at a text's dissemination. Rather, a translation is a product of the choices that a reasonable translator made at the time of translation. Further, a translator cannot simply look at a text and ascertain what the various ambiguous homographs would have meant to a reasonable person at the time of the text's dissemination because it is an open possibility what the words could mean. Instead, a translator must rely on a tradition of instances of that text being vocalized and hope that this tradition is the original.

Much ink has been spilt over the legend of the first recorded translation of the Pentateuch from an unvocalized biblical Hebrew to a vocalized Greek. So famous was this first translation known as *the Septuagint* that it would later become the genericized word to describe any translation of any of the books of the Hebrew Bible into Greek.[37] The term "Septuagint" derives from the Greek word for seventy, relating to the seventy elders who were involved in this monumental translation project. While many biblical scholars believe that the origin story of the first Septuagint is legendary or mythical, recounting it is a good way to display some of the issues of translation.

According to the Talmud,

> There was an incident involving King Ptolemy of Egypt, who assembled seventy-two Elders from the Sages of Israel, and put them into seventy-two separate rooms, and did not reveal to them for what purpose he assembled them, so that they would not coordinate their responses. He entered and approached each and every one, and said to each of them: Write for me a translation of the Torah of Moses your teacher. The Holy One, Blessed be He, placed wisdom in the heart of each and every one, and they all agreed to one common understanding. (Meg. 9a[38])

Fascinatingly, the Talmud then proceeds to describe all the errata that the Septuagint's translators placed into their translation:

> And they wrote for him: God created in the beginning [*bereshit*], reversing the order of the words in the first phrase in the Torah . . . . They did so to negate those who believe in the preexistence of the world and those who maintain that there are two powers in the world . . . . And they wrote: I shall make man in image and in likeness, rather than: "Let us make man in our image and in our likeness" (Genesis 1:26), as from there too one could mistakenly conclude that there are multiple powers and that God has human form. Instead of: "Come, let us go down, and there confound their language" (Genesis 11:7), which indicates

> multiple authorities, they wrote in the singular: Come, let me go down . . . . And in the list of unclean animals they wrote for him: The short-legged beast [*tze'irat haraglayim*]. And they did not write for him: "And the hare [*arnevet*]" (Leviticus 11:6), since the name of Ptolemy's wife was Arnevet, so that he would not say: The Jews have mocked me and inserted my wife's name in the Torah. (Meg. 9a–9b[39])

From the perspective of the Talmud, God moves the hands of the translators to produce a translation that contains what appear to be errors. Thus, theoretically, anyone who is familiar with Ptolemaic Greek and familiar with biblical Hebrew would be able to discern that the documents are not identical.

This "first Septuagint," if it existed, is considered a tragedy in Rabbinic literature, as the Mishnah states "and that day was as ominous for Israel as the day on which the golden calf was made, since the Torah could not be accurately translated" (Sof. 1[40]). The comparison to the golden calf is apt because now the fixed referent of the translation would be seen as a standard for people who were unfamiliar with the Hebrew language, which destroys the depth of variable meaning available to an unvocalized text. Just as the golden calf was a graven image humans made of God, so too this Septuagint was like an image of the Torah crafted by humans. Once any given morpheme's possible meaning is fixed by a translation, the variability of the morpheme is lost. As I will clarify in the final section, this variability is part of what gives the Torah its meaning.

In short, there is no getting rid of the challenge of unclear morphemes in the written Torah by translation or by any other means. The right way—and, as it seems to me, the *only* way—is to clarify these morphemes using specific Hebrew vocalizations.

But which vocalizations ought we to use to disambiguate an unclear morpheme in the Torah? We can receive acceptable answers to this question from tradition, but we cannot mine the text of the written Torah for them. This is one difference between originalism as it approaches the Torah and originalism as it approaches laws written in a language that uses an alphabet like the American Constitution: perhaps the Constitution can be interpreted using the toolset of textualist originalism, but the Torah definitely cannot be interpreted using that toolset.

CONCLUSION

There is a famous story told about an applicant to a prestigious law firm, somewhere in New York. As the hiring manager peruses the applicant's documents, she is astonished to see that the applicant attended Harvard Law School. However, she finds it suspicious that the applicant did not also submit a transcript from Harvard. During the interview the hiring manager commends the applicant on their stunning portfolio and asks the applicant why he did not submit the transcript with the rest of his application materials. "Well you see," said the applicant,

> I did complete Harvard Law School but I was never accepted so I did not attend any of the classes there. The course material is the same whether or not you attend any of the lectures or are admitted into the program. I received the course materials from friends of mine who had attended and simply read all the textbooks.

The hiring manager promptly thanked the applicant for his time and sent him on his way.

The Hebrew word תורה—*Torah*—is properly translated as teaching, or instruction. It shares a root with another word מורה—*moreh*—which means "to teach" as in "Who teaches (מורה) like Him?" (Job. 36:22). Both teaching and instruction are multifaceted and rarely limited solely to textual domains. Teaching or instructing happens concurrent with texts but is not solely comprised of texts. The story previously presented attempts to capture this point. A degree from Harvard (or any other prestigious institution) is not reducible to the textual information that one learns during their courses. Rather, concurrent with the texts one studies, a degree shows that one has learned from capable teachers, participated in classes, shown a degree of competence in instruction, and performed a myriad of other non-textual endeavors required to complete the degree. Just as we need not expect instruction from premier educational institutions to be solely textual, so too we need not expect to be able to comprehend the various laws and inunctions in the Torah solely from its text. This is the crux of Hillel's message to his student which I recounted in my introduction.

Indeed, this is perhaps why much of the Pentateuch is inscrutable without some form of interpretive aid. From the ambiguity present in the text's lack of vowels to the vagueness of many of its commandments, there is a whole swath of information that is simply absent. This, however, is not a problem with the text, but is rather the text's intended function. It is not a "bug" but a "feature" of the text that its proper interpretation requires instruction beyond the text's surface meaning.

One upshot of requiring this instruction because of the text's seeming incompleteness is that, within each verse of the text, more than one complementary concept can exist. Thus more information can be contained in a smaller vessel. A single verse can produce not just its plain meaning assigned by a given vocal tradition but complementary readings based on different vocalizations. Take for instance the verse in Exodus which states, "And the tablets were the work of God and the writing was the writing of

God, graven (חָרוּת) upon the tablets" (Ex. 32:16). Now there is another vocalization for the morpheme חרות such that we can generate HRUT^1 and HRUT^2. However, this time, instead of the possible vocalizations being contradictory, they are complementary. The Mishnah in tractate Avot suggests that one might render the morpheme חרות as "not Harut [graven—חָרוּת—HRUT^1] but Herut [freedom— חֵרוּת—HRUT^2]. For there is no free man but one that occupies himself with the study of the Torah" (Pirkei Avot 6:2[41]). Within a single verse that appears in its plain meaning to describe a fact about the tablets that contained the ten commandments, if properly instructed, one can glean a philosophical-theological lesson by switching a single vowel.

Interpreting legal documents such as the US Constitution does not admit of exegesis based on vocalization. In fact, vocalization of words is not even in discussion when one examines the US Constitution because English is a vocalized language. It would be absurd to engage in the type of interpretive framework that exploits different vocalizations to garner different results of something like the US Constitution. There is no debate over which morphemes in the US Constitution correspond to which words in the English language because the whole system of unvocalized morphemes is not something that the Constitution admits of. By parity of reasoning, then, one must assume that you cannot interpret the Pentateuch in a textualist framework. Just as in the case of the US Constitution we cannot engage in exposition based on vocalization because there is only one vocalization, so too one cannot interpret what the Pentateuch means based on a textualist framework.

The Pentateuch and the United States legal canons both share in the identity of "legal code." This does not mean that they are similar in all other respects. What I have shown is that, given the structure of biblical Hebrew as an abjad and not an alphabet, one cannot employ a textualist framework to interpret the Pentateuch. The essential investigative question for the textualist is, "What would this text [in and of itself] have meant to a reasonable person at the time?" Applying this question to the Pentateuch is a category error for one reason and impossible to ascertain for another. The textualist framework as applied to the Pentateuch is a category error because the Pentateuch's meaning is incomplete without a given vocalization scheme, and the text itself does not indicate to us which vocalization scheme is the correct one. It is impossible to ascertain the meaning of many of the Pentateuch's injunctions without appealing to something outside of the text. Both in order to understand which words, that is which vocalized morphemes, the text is using and in order to ascertain to what, if anything, these vocalized morphemes refer, one must appeal to a body of knowledge outside of the text. The same is true for the Torah's vague words, which also require extratextual information to clarify them.

Proper interpretation of the Pentateuch and legal documents such as the US Constitution need not admit of the same methods. One can apply one method, such as textualism, to one legal body and another method to the other legal body. What I have shown is a reason for thinking that one cannot apply the methods of textualism to the Pentateuch. In doing this I have also shown that one cannot "translate" their way out of this by attempting to switch the textual domain from an unvocalized language to a vocalized one. Doing this would undermine the very principles of textualism with which one is seeking to interpret the Pentateuch. Proper interpretation of the Pentateuch requires something other than the methods textualism can provide. If Hillel is to believed, proper interpretation of the Pentateuch requires not only a fluency with the language in which the Pentateuch is written but also a measure of trust in the instructor, and in the oral tradition they convey.

NOTES

1. I would like to acknowledge the assistance of this volume's editors, Dr. Mark J. Boone and Dr. Mark Eckel, for their patience and erudite explanations of originalism. Additionally, and in no particular order, Aaron Graham, Sam Lebens, and Steven C. Skultety for their contributions to this chapter's content. My friend Timothy Eshing provided invaluable editorial assistance. Finally, Devorah Stein, whose insistence on always interpreting my work as a textualist led me to pen this contribution.

2. This entire story can be found in the Babylonian Talmud tractate Shabbat 31a. I have paraphrased from *The William Davidson Talmud* published by Koren and translated by Steinsaltz. I have also weaved insights from the commentary of Rabbi Shlomo Yitzchaki (Rashi), a great medieval Rabbi and commentator on the Hebrew Bible, into the narrative. All citations of the Talmud come from this edition. See the William Davidson Edition of the Koren Noé Talmud, with commentary by Rabbi Addin Even-Israel Stensaltz. *Koren Talmud Bavli* (Koren Publishers Jerusalem Ltd. and The Steinsaltz Center; Sefaria: A Living Library of Jewish Texts Online). https://www.sefaria.org/texts/Talmud.

3. I use "the Torah" and "Pentateuch" interchangeably to refer to the five books of Moses or Genesis, Exodus, Leviticus, Numbers, and Deuteronomy.

4. In Rabbinic literature these two components are called תורה שבכתב (Torah She'b'ksav, the Written Torah) and תורה שבעל פה (Torah She'baal Peh, the Oral Torah).

5. Wil Waluchow and Dimitrios Kyritsis, "Constitutionalism"; *The Stanford Encyclopedia of Philosophy* (2023). https://plato.stanford.edu/entries/constitutionalism/.

6. Antonin Scalia and Bryan A. Garner, *Reading Law: The Interpretation of Legal Texts* (St. Paul, MN: Thomson/West, 2012), 16.

7. Waluchow and Kyritsis, "Constitutionalism."

8. Among other works, Scalia and Garner, *Reading Law*.

9. See: Maimonides' *Sefer HaMitzvot* or *Sefer HaChinuch* for a detailed list of these commandments.

10. All translations of the Pentateuch come from the Contemporary Torah by the Jewish Publication Society, 2006, unless otherwise noted.

11. I use "vocalized" to mean a text that contains both vowels and consonants; thus its meaning would be more discernible to the reader in contrast to an unvocalized text that does not contain vowels and whose possible meanings only become "fixed" once vocalized.

12. Scalia and Garner, *Reading Law*, 16.

13. Scalia and Garner, *Reading Law*, 33.

14. Whether or not there was a particular time when the Pentateuch was disseminated is up to considerable historic debate. However, I take what I think to be the standard Rabbinic approach that the text of the Torah was completed sometime around 1,272 BCE. See also the next note.

15. When exactly this law would have been disseminated to the Israelites is a matter of much historical debate. Since this project is one of applying legal theories, I (perhaps naively) assume that the laws in the Pentateuch were revealed to the Israelite community over the course of a relatively short period, perhaps during their desert wanderings as described in the Book of Numbers.

16. Scalia and Garner discuss such rules about vehicles in *Reading Law*, 36.

17. "Bank," *Merriam Webster*, https://www.merriam-webster.com/dictionary/bank.

18. Scalia and Garner, *Reading Law*, 32.

19. Scalia and Garner, *Reading Law*, 32.

20. Scalia and Garner, *Reading Law*, 167.

21. Peter T. Daniels, "Fundamentals of Grammatology," *Journal of the American Oriental Society* 110, no. 4 (1990): 729.

22. Daniels, "Fundamentals of Grammatology," 729–730.

23. Keep in mind that Hebrew script reads right-to-left, not left-to-right like English.

24. Disambiguating the morpheme might require context, which is why I stressed "by itself."

25. See, again, Daniels, "Fundamentals of Grammatology," 729–730.

26. In addition, most literature in modern Hebrew does not contain vowels past a certain early stage of education.

27. Yehudah HaLevi, *The Kuzari: In Defense of the Despised Faith*, trans. N. Daniel Korobkin (Jerusalem: Feldheim Publishers, 2013), 321.

28. Joshua Blau, *Phonology and Morphology of Biblical Hebrew* (Winona Lake, IN: Eisenbrauns, 2010), 7.

29. I discuss this issue at length in my 2022 MA Dissertation at the University of Mississippi, "Karaites and Reformers: Two Failed Cases of Coherent Interpretation."

30. These are the words Dr. Aaron Graham, Assistant Professor of Philosophy at the University of Mississippi, used in personal conversation with me (July 24, 2022).

31. Dovid Ribiat, *The 39 Melochos: An Elucidation of the 39 Melochos from Concept to Practical Application*, vol. 1 (Monsey, NY: Misrad Hasefer, 1999), 35.

32. Meaning the Jewish legal borders.

33. Ribiat, *The 39 Melochos*, Vol. 1, 26.

34. Ribiat, *The 39 Melochos*, Vol. 1, 26.

35. The Exodus would have occurred in 1,312 BCE or 2,448 AM. 40 years of wandering in the desert gives us 1,272 BCE or 2,488 AM.

36. Our own knowledge of ancient Egyptian comes largely in part from translation projects such as the Rosetta Stone which involved back-translating ancient Egyptian from the known language of Greek. See: "Everything You Ever Wanted to Know About the Rosetta Stone," *The British Museum* (July 14, 2017), https://www.britishmuseum.org/blog/everything-you-ever-wanted-know-about-rosetta-stone.

37. Ryan Reeves, "What Is the Septuagint?" *The Gospel Coalition* (August 12, 2018), https://www.thegospelcoalition.org/article/what-is-the-septuagint.

38. That is, Tractate Megillah in the Babylonian Talmud, Chapter 1, folio 9a. Taken from the William Davidson Talmud.

39. Tractate Megillah in the Babylonian Talmud, Chapter 1, folio 9a–b. Taken from the William Davidson Talmud.

40. That is, Tractate Soferim in the Babylonian Talmud, Chapter 1. Taken from the William Davidson Talmud.

41. That is, chapter 6 in Tractate Pirkei Avot in the Mishnah. I translated this Mishnah myself.

WORKS CITED

"Bank." *Merriam Webster*. https://www.merriam-webster.com/dictionary/bank.

Blau, Joshua. *Phonology and Morphology of Biblical Hebrew*. Winona Lake, IN: Eisenbrauns, 2010.

Daniels, Peter T. "Fundamentals of Grammatology." *Journal of the American Oriental Society* 110, no. 4 (1990): 727–731.

"Everything You Ever Wanted to Know About the Rosetta Stone." *The British Museum* (July 14, 2017). https://www.britishmuseum.org/blog/everything-you-ever-wanted-know-about-rosetta-stone.

HaLevi, Yehudah. *The Kuzari: In Defense of the Despised Faith*, translated by N. Daniel Korobkin. Jerusalem: Feldheim Publishers, 2013.

Reeves, Ryan. "What Is the Septuagint?" *The Gospel Coalition* (August 12, 2018). https://www.thegospelcoalition.org/article/what-is-the-septuagint.

Ribiat, Dovid. *The 39 Melochos: An Elucidation of the 39 Melochos from Concept to Practical Application*, Vol. 1. Monsey, NY: Misrad Hasefer, 1999.

Scalia, Antonin and Bryan A. Garner. *Reading Law: The Interpretation of Legal Texts*. St. Paul, MN: Thomson/West, 2012.

Waluchow, Wil and Dimitrios Kyritsis. "Constitutionalism." *The Stanford Encyclopedia of Philosophy* (2023). https://plato.stanford.edu/entries/constitutionalism/.

William Davidson Edition of the Koren Noé Talmud; with commentary by Rabbi Addin Even-Israel Stensaltz. *Koren Talmud Bavli*. Koren Publishers Jerusalem Ltd. and The Steinsaltz Center. Sefaria: A Living Library of Jewish Texts Online. https://www.sefaria.org/texts/Talmud.

Chapter 9

First Theology and Last Things

Mark D. Eckel

THE TWIN PILLARS OF AUTHORITY AND HUMANITY FOR ALL STUDIES

In dialogue with a colleague at the public university where I teach, we were discussing common ground for agreement.[1] My fellow professor begins his assumption about The Almighty as an agnostic. He does not believe in Divine revelation nor in any holy books that impose their dictates on others. In his view all authority for life comes from humanity. His point of view expounds the judgment that the American Constitution is a living, breathing, malleable document. Recounting all our major agreements—essential ideals of justice, truth, kindness, or compassion—I noted our commitment to the same outcomes. "It strikes me," I began toward the conclusion of our conversation, "That we want the same ends, but it is our beginnings, the origin of our authority, where we differ." He agreed, noting the obvious distinctive, my friend beginning with a human calculus and I starting from a Divine source. As we had up to that point, we agreed to continue our collegial commitments toward what many would call "the common good," while we made it clear that our causal assumptions formed the basis for any disagreement.

In a separate conversation with another colleague, we discussed the problem of our ideals, those already mentioned (truth, justice, kindness), the problem being what humanities professors call "the human condition." My friend argues that he "had hope" in humanity, that our species would "get better and better," and the ultimate end would be the perfection of our race. I asked if he thought such a utopian world had been tried and if any attempts had been successful. "Yes to the first question, but no to the second." My follow-up question was, "If over multiple millennia a utopian world has been tried and found wanting, does the hope of such a paradise by the same race of people seem possible?" His simple answer: "That is the hope." Against his hope, I suggested that humanity was in its corruptible "condition" as a permanent problem unless there was an authority outside our own that not only set the standard but provided the solution: salvation through sacrifice leading to human perfectibility through a savior.

Both conversations address the two-fold concern across all disciplines: What is the origin of authority and what is the nature of humanity? Theological beliefs about both will organize a professor's perspective on law, not to mention science, literature, history, or any other subject of study. If there is a transcendent God who has designed the universe, He not only dictates the laws established in His world, but He has also made His world to operate in a certain way. An outside authority suggests intention, indeed *authorial* intention. Humanity, then, receives a disclosure from this God, a special revelation communicating His Word to the world. So how will humanity respond to God's revelation? Human persons live with the tension in themselves of dignity and depravity. Created in God's image, humanity has worth, value, and dignity. At the same time, the Genesis 3 account shows the origin of our inherent corruption. How humans respond to their sinfulness either recognizes their need for an outside authority to solve the problem of their inherent corruption or constitutes a rebellion against Divine authority.

In the university setting, questions of authority and humanity establish the worldview direction any institution or department may take. The Hebraic-Christian view of special revelation leading to the teaching of authorial intent may be countered in the modern university with a belief that all authority begins and ends with humans. Instead of an author's intention being important in any study, it is the reader's response which becomes authoritative. In like manner, the Hebraic-Christian view of creational revelation tells humans that God's laws, His natural laws, are embedded in the world, necessary for corrupt humanity to obey. But in modern universities, humans re-create themselves and the world, becoming a law unto themselves. The distinction between worldviews is clear. Either authority comes from God or from man. The result of either gives the basis for natural law or law fashioned by human culture, in whatever time or place. The intersection with law is the difference between the US Constitution being interpreted as the intention of the authors or it being a living, breathing document, necessarily changing with cultural powers.

In short, our origin determines our direction, meaning both our ultimate purpose and the way we take to get there. A Hebraic-Christian worldview is very different from those secular worldviews on which there is no higher authority than humanity itself. On the former, God's authority, design, and instructions are the parameters which determine our purpose and the lives we live toward that purpose. In this worldview, authority structures make sense, and the Constitution as a legal authority is grounded in the natural law set by nature's God. But on a worldview in which we ourselves are the highest authority, not only does the original meaning of the law lose its claim to authority, but every other authority does as well.

In this chapter I will explore the conclusion that not only does originalism matter for the law's foundation but that the human condition also makes originalism in law necessary. We, in virtue of our creation, can only live and think within universal parameters set up by God. We need intentional authority structures set up to curb the deleterious effects of our own sinfulness. General guidelines from a biblical view of humanity and the world are applied both in the Bible and in law. In this essay I will explain these things, considering how these principles are applied in both Mosaic and American law.

ORIGINALISM IN AUTHORITY, FOR HUMANITY

Originalism is one way of resisting one of the basic human flaws which threads its way through our race: the thought that we know best. Our current time and place are further advanced, more knowledgeable, more suffused in expanding data, and greater in total information than all other time periods put together. In our current moment, and any that may follow, our intellectual hubris will continue to mark the scarlet letter "A," for we are the final "Authority." Certainly, it is conceivable that our human-only advance comes from a primordial state, full of chance and chaotic change. However, in practical terms, our world seems to exist on a much firmer foundation. We prize our own intentions yet balk at the prospect that our intention has an origin. We elevate artistic, engineering designs but cannot fathom a designed universe. We depend on order and certainty in chemistry or agriculture, sidestepping the possibility that their arrangements may be embedded in a world we were born into. We structure business on mathematical accounting processes whose exacting measures appear to conform to a set of universal rules. The common, ordinary, everyday processes of life over millennia, experienced anywhere in the world, depend on an unseen yet purposeful order that demands our attention. Two questions introduce my conclusion: "Why does it matter if there is an authorial Lawgiver who had an original intention for creation and all of life's processes?" and "What made the original need for human law necessary?"

THREE ORIGIN SUBJECTS, ONE ORIGIN AUTHORITY

Let's return to a discussion part of which is summarized in chapter 1 of this book. The conversation was anything but typical. The studies represented there were cytotechnology, forensic linguistics, and finite math. The first student to enter the discussion had to type out cytotechnology on my cell phone. I had not heard of it before even though I had seen its effects in medical research.

"Does your professor ever talk about origins, where things come from in your study?" I began.

"No," she shook her head, "We don't discuss ideas such as creation or evolution. Evolution is a given."

"Let me ask a different question. Does your professor ever use the words 'awe,' 'beauty,' 'wonder,' or 'amazement' when talking about human cell structure?"

"Oh, yes! All the time! He would say things like, 'If the molecular structure changed a fraction or the cell structure shifted ever so slightly in this or that direction the immune system would not work'."

She paused. Then she said, "You know, now that I think about it, my professor assumes design all the time! He will use the word and I will think to myself, 'How can you use that word if you believe in evolution?'"

"And there it is!" I declared, looking around the table. "No one—Christian or non-Christian—can operate in their respective fields of study without depending on concepts that come from outside themselves."

I looked at the young mathematician sitting across from me. "I bet your math courses suggest that one of the ways a math proof is identified as true is if the equation is beautiful."

He agreed, shaking his head up and down, saying, "Mathematical computation depends on beauty."

The student who has fallen in love with forensic linguistics concurred, "We depend on the framework of logic as we investigate law. We assume logic as the basis for our study."

"Do you see?!" I exclaimed, "The Christian worldview provides the presuppositions for everything! Humans assume beauty, logic, and wonder as results of any investigation without giving a thought about where those ideas originate."

Our discussions around the lunch table continued over a myriad of topics. But we were all reminded again that our scholastic lives are governed by the transcendent God who designs, sustains, and enjoys all things in His creation. At the same time, God is immanent with His creatures, being close to and caring for humans in the creation He made. I left five questions and accordant principles with the students at the discussion's end. I maintained that all teachers and students must assume at least five footers when they construct their foundations for curricula in law or anything else.

An origin for our study makes us ask, "Where is the origin of our subject of study?" The cause of an idea establishes not only the assumptions of the study but the very direction the research will follow. Knowing the source of information allows the researcher to critique not only the evidence but the source of the evidence. Is the source reliable, credible, and trustworthy? Does bias exist? Does the source benefit in some way from the evidence being given? In a court of law, what statutes are missing from an argument that may bring into question the problem of a source? Are all the records taken into account or are some left out of the courtroom proceedings? Who benefits when two parties are negotiating an outcome if lawyers are beholden to an outside benefactor? Revelation in the First Testament was first given to prophets, then priests, then judges, and finally to kings (Deut. 17–18), setting apart the responsibilities of legislation received, judicial oversight needed, and executive action to put the law into effect. The authority of the executive branch meant the kings received God's words and rules last and were responsible to copy the law by hand as a reminder that their leadership came from a source of authority outside themselves. The first three articles of the US Constitution separate the executive from the one who legislates from the one who interprets the law. Separation of powers placing limitations upon each branch are echoes of God's original governmental order.

Boundaries for our schoolwork cause us to question, "Why are limitations built into the world?" Living boundary-less lives is impossible. From street signs to highway lines, from property perimeters to bank accounts, from secure online shopping to in-home security systems, from boarding a plane to applying for a license, from institutional directives to governmental laws, from biological designs to creational orders, from international date lines to national borders, from cradle to grave, boundaries give both definition and freedom. Definition creates systematic understanding of any subject, while freedom allows exploration in any study. If we live authority-less lives, then we are in danger of living boundary-less lives. Freedom of the individual must be based upon inalienable rights, the source of which is the transcendent Creator of the universe. Impartiality is established in the natural law of creation.[2] Justice for all people should be paramount. However, equal opportunity is not the same as equality of outcome. Distribution of resources fails to account for a fallen world with inevitable inequities and personal irresponsibility (Lev. 19:36; Deut. 16:18; 32:4; Ps. 89:14).

Exploration in our field of research suggests, "What else is there to learn?" Original sources provide the opportunity for a treasure trove of deeper research into problems and solutions. The existence of multiple volumes in a law library shows the depth of case law originating from one or more basic principles; the source of any law may have multiple applications across any number of cases. First Testament teaching mandates to protect the poor (Deut. 15:7–11; Prov. 14:21, 31) can be employed in multiple circumstances. Mosaic law sought to protect the poor with provisions for food (the gleaning principle in Lev. 19:9–10), financial help (Deut. 26:12), and equality in courts of law (Ex. 23:6) with warnings against exploitation (Ex. 22:22) and based on pleadings for mercy (Ex. 22:25–27). Human finite, fallen natures display a need for repetition and correction from a Heavenly source of law. Precursor to the US Constitution is the Declaration of Independence which clearly defines the line between "the powers of earth" and "laws of Nature and Nature's God."

Delighted, we pursue creative alternatives thinking, "How can I make this better?" Progress toward good, benefiting people, is an important outcome from the rule of law. Aggrieved parties can find restitution for wrongs committed against them. In economic concerns, for example, precision in measurement (with tools) and calculation (with numbers) produces accuracy. God's accounting of human action, concern for commercial compensation, and ethical, eternal standards for restitution are mirrored in commercial exactitude (Lev. 19:35–37; Deut. 25:13–15; Isa. 59:1–15; Rom. 2:1–11; 2 Thes. 1:5–10). The standard for justice is righteousness. Natural law sets precedence for fairness and equity. Good can be rewarded and evil punished because the Transcendent Source of Truth exists. Justice in human relations should eschew bribery and favoritism while encouraging consistency, mercy, and protection of the poor, weak, and defenseless (Ex. 22:22–24; Prov. 31:1–9; Isa. 1:17; Zech. 7:10; 1 Tim. 5:8, 16; James 1:27). The very nature of betterment ("to form a more perfect union") arises in the opening lines of the US Constitution. Further, the "We the people" clause seeks to "establish Justice" and "promote the general welfare," priorities that have been written in Hebrew and Christian Scriptures.

A lack of fulfillment in our discoveries can occur unless we can answer, "When will I be satisfied?" The biblical perspective looks towards satisfaction through the restoration of all things to God's original intention (Acts 3:21), which the prophets promised, mentioning specific fulfillments (such as the gospel going to the Gentiles) known by God beforehand (Acts 15:18). The Bible presents itself as God's revelatory truth written for those who have witnessed the fulfillment (Greek *telos*) of the ages (1 Cor. 10:11). Now the church proclaims the accomplishment by Jesus of God's eternal plan for setting creation right (Eph. 3:10–11). Jesus's power now works within the church for His glory (Eph. 3:20–21). Christians should focus on the eternal, unseen realities of what Jesus has accomplished (2 Cor. 4:17–18, 5:1), serving "the living God" (Heb. 9:14, English Standard Version) who enables them to do His will (Heb. 13:20–21). The Christian teaching is that those who have benefited from Jesus's mighty works of redemption must now join in the work. In a sense, all has already been fulfilled by his incarnation, death, and resurrection; in another sense, redemption is not yet complete, and working out the results of what Jesus has done is the church's responsibility. They now have "eternal comfort and good hope" enabling them for all the work (2 Thes. 2:16–17), taking hold now of the life of the renewed creation. The good concern of the Declaration of Independence, while less cosmic in scope, still aims at a satisfaction and fulfillment partially informed by theology as an end for which government is suited as a means. The Declaration is concerned for the "Safety and Happiness" of the governed which is the "duty" of the people, while "appealing to the Supreme Judge of the world." Good deeds "are excellent and profitable for everyone" (Tit. 3:8) now, but the ultimate satisfaction and fulfillment of life's opportunities may not be complete until eternity.

One college student in our group told of a conversation she had overheard in her department. "You can hear everything from where I sit in the office," she explained, then continued, "Two accomplished PhD professors were musing aloud saying things like, 'After all our accomplishments, publications, and credits, is *this* all there is?'" "I wish I could have had the liberty to engage in that conversation. Maybe they should talk with us over lunch." And then she added, "I had no idea that the subject of origins gave every discipline not only its authority but, finally, a sense of satisfaction."

Authoritative Structural Concepts Established in Gen. 1:1–2:3 Theology

Fulfillment in one's studies is an affective result of creational law. For years I have been helping K–12 through PhD students think Christianly about their studies. In my own high school classes I asked students to simply observe Genesis 1, collecting their observations. We would then apply the ideas of those observations to many subjects of study to which students might be drawn, including art, self-worth, artificial intelligence, or music. The list is endless. The God of the Bible, both transcendent and immanent at once (Neh. 9:6; Col. 1:17; Heb. 1:3), creates the foundation of natural law on which all other law is built. Incorporating observations from Genesis 1 helps the Hebraic-Christian thinker consider the authority underlying the study of law, or of anything else.

Reality. There is a God who is separate from His cosmos established from the simple phrase, "God created" (Gen. 1:1). In my classes we have called this "the Creator-creature distinction." Further, our focus has always been upon the nature of reality based upon what is eternal. Either matter is eternal, or God is eternal. If matter is eternal, then evolutionary principles dictate the results of human law which becomes nothing more than raw, judicial power, based on convention, utility, materialism, and endless linguistic constructs which are constantly under construction. However, if God is eternal, the world exists as disclosed by God, ordered in a natural way, laws existing because the law comes from a Lawgiver. The very basis of an originalist position producing authorial intent from the framers of the Constitution comes originally from the God who has given the law.

Meaning. Such a designed universe not only declares the basis for meaning (the universe and its inhabitants made for a purpose) but indicates the value of the thing created. From the start, the eternal, Triune, personal, transcendent Creator of the universe embeds His authority within the created order, granting dignity through purposeful design. "In the beginning, God created the heavens and the earth" (Gen. 1:1) suggests the essential existence of time. Numerous repetitious phrases imply origination. "Beginning" gives the inception of time while the repeated reference to evening and morning (1:5) gives creation a rhythm. Space, separating the waters above from those below (1:7), and matter ("waters" and "dry land"; 1:6, 9) round out the triad, making the physical world possible. Matching Pentateuchal law codes, the Declaration of Independence gives humans meaning with "self-evident" and "inalienable rights."

Order. Precision is built into creation. God conceived and constructed His creation in a certain way. The exclusive nature of the Hebrew God is suggested by repetitious phrases. God provides utility: He gives us all the plants for food, prioritizing what is useful for living life (Gen. 1:29). Structure is a necessary component of everyday life. Rhythm and systematic form are highlighted: "light," "darkness," "waters," "heavens" (1:3–10). Structure, mode, and orderly arrangement of the parts of a whole show that God's world is interrelated—each part working within the whole. The US Constitution with individual articles focused on three branches of government, for instance, resembles the systematic, complementary organization of God's world.

Coherence. Nothing is left out; everything is included, which is the idea behind the Hebrew phrase, "the heavens and the earth." Repetitious phrases in Genesis 1 and 2 substantiate the idea of the structure, mode, and orderly arrangement of the parts making the whole (Gen. 1:3–2:3). The Genesis account teaches the reality of design. The statements "it was so" (1:7) and "the heavens and the earth were finished" (2:1) indicate both unity and diversity in God's creation; there is variety "each according to its kind" and "according to its kind" and "according to their kinds" (1:11–12, 21, 24–25). Law, like all disciplines, depends upon wholeness, the interconnectedness of the harmony of the created order. Coherence gives law codes a sensible nature applied to all of life.

Roles. Repetitious phrases in Genesis 1 and 2 again promote the need to appreciate function, each thing having a purpose (Gen. 1:14 "let them be for"); uniqueness, emphasized with the statement that God separated (1:4, 6, 7, 14, 18), literally assigning each part a place; variety according to their kinds (1:11–12, 21, 24–25); and harmony, each thing interrelated properly with everything else (1:12). God brought together all the different parts of creation into a collection. The collection was then organized and arranged. We call creation a "cosmos"—an ordered world. The US Constitution mandates a clear process for the passage of bills in Article I, Section 7 following an orderly process of governance. The original construction of the universe, from an originalist perspective, necessitates the need for roles.

Evaluation. Genesis 1 gives repetitious phrases conveying assessment. Important highlights are beauty—"And God saw that it was good" (Gen. 1:10, 12, 18, 21, 25)—and appreciation—God saw what He had made (1:4). If there is no original, objective understanding of knowledge or words, evaluation is left up to individual subjectivism where there is no universally accepted aim or goal. Intention must give direction to any kind of justice; otherwise we simply exchange one kind of judicial power for another. Article III in the Constitution gives the judiciary the power to interpret law, one of the three branches of government given the task of evaluation. The framers of the Constitution had a horizontal line of three authorities (executive, legislative, and judicial) as well as two vertical authorities (federal and state, ninth and tenth Amendments to the Bill of Rights), giving layers of accountability and assessment.

The higher law, the natural law, is the background to the American Constitution, a law for the common good. Madison, in Federalist no. 10, provides a necessary backdrop to what he and others hoped would be a "well-constructed union." Madison addresses concerns about "factions," by which he means groups whose opinions oppose each other. Amid his argument, Madison clearly references the grounding problem: "As long as the reason of man continues fallible," he says, further commenting that "the latent causes of action are thus sown in the nature of man, and we see them everywhere brought into . . . civil society." Why is the original intention of God necessary from Scripture and the original intention of the US Constitution necessary in the affairs of the people? Because original sin is in need of original authority.

ORIGINAL SIN IN HUMANITY, NEEDING INTENTIONAL AUTHORITY

"Morality has to come from somewhere!" The class had just read an article about human nature saying we are made of "crooked timber." I applauded the student's point, adding questions to consider what or who might be that source. But other student entries showed me early in the semester what many believe. One student wrote "Original sin is an opinion." Another speculated that our "moral compass" comes from our experiences. According to others, ethics are "ever evolving." Still more—most of the class—conjectured that "morality is found within yourself." Other student thoughts included "morals are pretty much universal," the notion that everyone should aspire to have "good character," and even "I find my answers in Google."

I respond to every journal challenging student ideas, asking questions such as the following. If ethics are changing, how do we know how to act from one day to another? If everyone has their own morality, who is to say that one person's morality is better than others? Is there an umpire or a rule to judge something good or bad? What is the definition of "good," and where do I go to find a standard for "character"? Google may give a definition of "morality," but leaves empty the categories of "right and wrong, good and bad."

Early in the semester we address ethics. I create a five-step pyramid and begin by discussing what everyone desires: *truth.* I place that word in the middle of the five levels, reiterating that *truth* suggests reliability and credibility, asking, "Who do I trust?" The word above truth is *authority*, asking the question, "Who says?!" Above authority I place the word *ethics* where we address definitions for "right and wrong" and "good or bad," as well as the question, "By what standard will we judge?" But under *truth* is *timelessness* and at the bottom of the pyramid, *transcendence.* Standards for ethics should be consistent over time and from a place outside us. Transcendent beginnings force students to consider assumptions that question, "Do our ethics come from humans or God?" Without a transcendent origin, ethics depend on a roll of the dice.

Around a table of collegiate undergraduates, a continuing concern for the concept of ethical origins emerged. Christian students and I text throughout the week: when I will be on campus, prayer requests, helpful essays about their studies, and what they are learning in class.

One student sent me a screen shot, the opening questions for a university classroom discussion. "Where do ethical standards come from? Are they universal or dependent on local norms?" The same student had been sending me texts about a long-standing, long-running interaction about the source of ethics in their discipline, American jurisprudence.

Responding to the text, I asked about the source or origin of "local norms." The reply was immediate; "Good news!" the law student responded, "All truth of morality and origin can be traced back to a human law association! Problem solved!" The young student's tongue-in-cheek response dripped with sarcasm but made the point well. Mentioning that I would be willing to drop by class sometime to offer an alternative explanation for ethical standards, my young friend said, "The prof would be less than thrilled to justify their answer. Accountability is a stubborn thing."

Another text appeared on my phone.

> It just got better. We were discussing ethical situations in case law such as lying to customers about the use of survey data, and the prof used the curious phrase to initiate participation: "There are no right or wrong answers here."

The student continued, "I looked around the room for someone to be as incredulous as I was, but clearly it did not strike anyone else as an ironic phrase."

In a different class, the same law student was reading the textbook basis for "standards." The text claimed that there are three sources for ethical standards: universalism (based on outside, transcendent sources), relativism (based on individual choice), and something called "social responsibility." The last standard in the words of the law professor gets its sources from whichever camp, group, or organization makes the most "instinctive sense."

Later, the future lawyer and I discussed the origin of "responsibility," the need to identify whatever "social" group is being addressed. I asked then, and continue to ask now, two questions about any discussion point. First, what is the source or origin of the subject, idea, or standard? Second, what is the end result, the consequence of any action based on the standard?

Perhaps a third question could be added to the list: What happens if standards based on a transcendent, universal source are removed from cultural influence or social groups? Stated a different way, we could ask: Why are transcendent ethical standards for law so important for any people, culture, time, and place? Ethics can be established and accessed because the Personal Eternal Triune Creator was pleased to leave it there, intending delight and wonder for the discoverer (Job 26; 28:1–11; Prov. 25:2). An originalist view of scholarship may contain the following commitments. First, no dichotomy exists between secular and sacred—the whole world and all of life belong to the Creator (1 Chron. 29:10–16; Ps. 24:1; 50:9–12; 89:11). Second, common grace—natural law found within creation—can be accessed because the Personal Eternal Triune Creator was pleased to leave it there, intending delight and wonder for the discoverer (Job 26; 28:1–11; Prov. 25:2). Third, ways of knowing and interpreting law are premised upon "the fear of the LORD" (Prov. 1:7; 9:10), and are given to human image-bearers (Gen. 1:26; Ps. 8). Fourth, the Christian Scriptures are the central organizing core (2 Tim. 1:14; 2:15; 3:14–17) which both begin the process of evaluation, interpreting law, while giving purpose to the judicial process. Fifth, the originalist scholar (2 Chron. 17:7–9; Prov. 2:1–6; 2 Cor. 10:3–5) bears the responsibility to develop a Christian theological-philosophical grid, a Christian thought process in the pursuit of understanding natural law.

If special revelation is ignored, the original intention of God's law for humanity, then the basis for any law is left up to individuals and groups who may have only their own interests at heart. The only revelation or disclosure desired in a transcendent-less culture is that of the powerful. At least four imperatives for a transcendent source of law exist because of the human condition.

The concept of human and civil rights is directly derived from transcendent authority. If governments grant rights, governments can take them away. If

God grants rights, they should not be taken away. Government's responsibility is to protect human rights. Civil rights protect groups against exclusion from opportunity and access that may be granted to any majority. However, just because law is established does not mean the law will be followed properly by sinful people. The first, second, and eighth Amendments in the Bill of Rights are meant to protect the individual against government coercion.

The importance of accountability in business or government has its roots in a universal requirement. A concept such as duty has no foundation for efficacy without worldwide, common regulations embedded in human nature, a construct of an ethical requirement outside us. Contractual obligations based on "if," as in "If I do this for you, you will do this for me" are acknowledged by the contract clause in Article I, Section 10 of the Constitution. In like manner, the Electoral College (Article II, Section 1) places a limit on pure democratic rule (50% + 1). Today's laws might well be circumvented by other laws erected tomorrow without the original source of law found in the Constitution.

The idea of judicial or legislative law is predicated on an external origin protecting the reputation of a person. "Bills of attainder," for instance, are declared unconstitutional (Article I, Sections 9–10). Such bills defamed a person, automatically casting them as guilty. Similarly, Article I, Sections 9 and 10 forbid "ex post facto" laws where a law is passed after an act which may now be a crime. Personal protection under the law even applies when the law does not exist. The problem with "bills of attainder" or "ex post facto" laws is how people will twist and subvert it to their own ends in order to oppress and subjugate others. The individual person is protected by the law. Such ideas of "life" and "freedom," for instance, must derive their mandate from a divine source. The creation of life and the granting of freedom shift and change if humans are in authority. Justice is impossible if it's left up to just us.

The ordered patterns of biological and physical daily life are embedded in the world, giving the basis for scientific research. Laws that protect humans should be ubiquitous, without regard for ethnic, class, political, or national boundaries. The Bill of Rights is very clear about individual, human protections. The fifth Amendment to the Constitution protects the inviolability of the individual person. A person need not incriminate himself and should not be placed in double jeopardy or be "deprived of life, liberty or property without due process of law." The third and fourth Amendments, in similar fashion, protect a person's home and property, whereas the sixth Amendment protects a defendant who must be able to confront witnesses against him.

Students are right to question the source of ethical standards in their discipline. The underlying question for such a concern is essential: "Why are ethical standards necessary at all?" The answer is obvious to all: humans have a penchant for wrongdoing. Transgression, iniquity, wickedness, and sin are words we know exist because we know ourselves. Sinfulness has permeated every part of our person. The need for originalism in law and theology comes immediately from the original problem of human nature.

Questions of origin set the stage: When did sin begin and why does it matter? What is the nature of humanity such that law is even necessary? While God's image is maintained in the human person (Gen. 1:26; 5:1), it is now distorted through the sinful father's imprint (Gen. 5:3). Humanity is now thoroughly permeated with evil from the intent of their thoughts (Jer. 17:9–10) to the results of their actions (Tit. 1:15–16). The conscience, still the standard of human judgment for those without special revelation (Rom. 2:14–15), is warped, darkened, and hardened by sin (Eph. 4:17–19). Thinking is so futile that anything "spiritual" cannot be fathomed apart from restoration of the Spirit (1 Cor. 2:14).

In so far as redemption from sin is concerned, people are blind (2 Cor. 4:4), lifeless (Rom. 6:23; Eph. 2:1), and helpless (John 6:44; 8:31–36; Eph. 2:3). Humanity cannot save itself (John 3:18; Acts 4:12). Gen. 3:22–23 maintains that immortality—apart from the Personal Eternal Triune Creator—eludes man and is unattainable through the temptation to be like God (3:2–5). So, people are born with the seeds of sin planted deep within the soil of their person (Gen. 5:3; Ps. 51:5; 58:3; Rom. 5:12). There is no way that human beings can do anything to gain God's acceptance or do good apart from the Good God or His wisdom in law (Rom. 3:19–20). As it relates to eternal life, the "good" that people do is considered as putrid trash (Isa. 64:6; Phil. 3:7–9). Christians struggle with sin (Rom. 7:17–25) even though the Father no longer holds our sin against us (Rom. 8:1–2).

Christians should fear God, the One who gave the law (Ex. 20:18–20; Gal. 3:19–26; 1 Tim. 1:8–11), who controls our eternal destiny (Matt. 10:26–28), and who holds the key to true education (Prov. 1:7, 9:10). Eccl. 7:20 places the capstone on the discussion: "Surely there is not a righteous man on earth who does good and never sins." Current cultural teaching suggests that environment, biology, psychology, or a combination of the three may be the reason for human perversions. While these may accentuate human behavior, they are not the root cause of it (Mark 7:20–23). Sin is said to go through a "gestation" process where death is the result (James 1:14–15). While some would contend that true freedom is removal of restraint, Scripture is clear that sin enslaves (Prov. 5:22; Rom. 6:6, 14, 16, 19–21). Self-gratification is the central compulsion of humanity (Eph. 2:3).

Natural aversion to responsibility tries to avoid culpability at every turn (Gen. 3:9–13). Each person sins as if they themselves were Adam (Rom. 5:12). Nothing is hidden from God: Even our thoughts are known (Ps. 139:24–25; Heb. 4:12–13). It is not only the act of rebellion for which all are accountable, but also the desire that spawns the deed which is also under judgment (Matt. 5:21–22, 27–28). Sin results in personal estrangement from God (Is. 59:2), bringing required wrath (Is. 53:6) as well as internal conflict (Is. 48:22), misery (Mic. 7:1), self-loathing (Ezek. 20:43), and restlessness (Is. 57:20–21). Ultimately the sinner hardens themselves (Ps. 95:8) and hates God (Ps. 139:21). Men will venture down every avenue of trespass, but "the Lord will by no means clear the guilty" (Nah. 1:3).

Perhaps it is the Smeagol-Gollum character in *Lord of the Rings* that best captures our nature as humans. The one-and-the-same character is a picture of the internal struggle everyone faces within themselves. We protect life because all people are conceived with worth, value, and dignity. We protect people from other people because all people are also conceived with inherent corruption, disobedience, and sin. Both protections are true at the same time. Every institution is permeated by corruption because all individuals are corrupt. Internal restraint is the best recourse to limit and lessen sin. Necessarily, accountability within community is the best human boundary, a result of transcendent light pushing back the darkness within the human mind and every human neighborhood. Nowhere is the intersection of ethics and human nature seen better than in the American Constitution.

GENERAL GUIDELINES FOR THE APPLICATION OF ORIGINALISM

Untethered from a transcendent source of ethics, people, left to themselves, will look for ways to bypass any structure, any limitation, any boundary. It is necessary to wed the need for transcendent origin of ethics with corrupt human nature by applying universal designs beginning in the Bible's book of Genesis. Christians have a responsibility to analyze and filter all subjects through the lens of Scripture to supply reasons for life's activities and decisions. The following guidelines apply biblical truth to all of life.

The Creation Order

The American Constitution constitutes the mechanism whereby the republic is to be ordered. Levels of governmental oversight as well as specific processes for order are the intent of America's founding document. The very existence of the American Constitution, even the ordered Articles I–VII, arises out of a human need, orchestrated by the Creator who designed creation to operate in a certain manner. Jurisdiction is given to a person or universal law which oversees the planning, development, or activity in earthly relationships. The original ordering of creation in Genesis 1 and 2 sets the premise for gender roles, family relationships, organizational leadership, economics, employee-employer relationships, and the scientific method. The applications are endless.

The Cultural Mandate

God's intention for humanity was to manage and conserve, not use and abuse, the creation as set forth in clear commands in Gen. 1:27–28 and 2:15. Both production from and preservation of earth's resources are possible. The need for both creational care and production for human need is possible with the original intention of God for His creatures. Heaven's mandate for human involvement with creation includes all environmental issues, business principles, creative creations by God's creature in the arts and humanities, agricultural practices, and industrial consumption. Article I, Section 8 of The Constitution, for instance, establishing a "uniform Rule of Naturalization," is one of many American laws that carries mandatory duties. Even with the invasive corruption of human persons, the original intention of God for His world can be carried out by applying Genesis principles in the United States of America.

The Rights of the Individual

The attribution of God's image to every human person from the creation (Gen. 1:27–28; Ps. 8, 139) gives all people worth, value, and dignity. It follows then, based on the original and continuing nature of humanity, that each person should be guaranteed certain inalienable rights, which can only be given by their Creator; so says the Declaration of Independence. Each person has the right to protection if they cannot defend themselves, to liberty, and to fair opportunity through equitable access based on their original rights. A list of applications which may be preserved could include prison reform, political freedom, independence, patriotism, social safety nets, care for minorities by the majority, free speech, free assembly, and the freedom to worship. Any and all human rights begin with the origin of those rights given by God, not men, the prescriptive form of which resides in the Bill of Rights and the first ten Amendments to the US Constitution.

The Responsibilities of the Individual

At the same time humans recognize God's image in man, so they must recognize the image of their first father, Adam, as the progenitor of wrongdoing (Gen. 5:1, 3; Rom. 5:12–17). Everyone is therefore inherently corrupt, permeated by tendencies of transgressions which affect thought, attitude, and action. The original history of human sin necessitates the role of human responsibility. Culpability for disobedience of God's original intentions in Genesis must be both acknowledged and recompensed. The problems of sinfulness have universal examples: reproductive evil (abortion and infanticide), racist evil (sex trafficking and slavery), lying evil (falsehood and propaganda), stealing evil (theft or embezzlement), employment evil (low wages and no rest). Not only do these codes find their origin in Scripture (Ex. 20), but they are also like-mindedly mirrored in the US Constitution: impeachment (Article I, Section 3), financial advantage (i.e., the "emoluments" clause; Article I, Secion 6), the "Progress of Science" clause (Article I, Section 8), extradition (Article IV, Section 2), and the "good Behaviour" of judicial appointees (Article III, Section 1).

The Tension of the Ideal and the Real

The Creator God never compromises His original intention, nor does He lower His original standards for His creation and creatures. He does, however, lower Himself, stooping to our level so as to save us from ourselves through both the Written Word of Revelation, the Bible, and the Living Word of disclosure of Himself, the person of Jesus. So God's standard is not *compromised* but it is *conditioned* because of corrupted human thought and action. God's intention is to limit and lessen the consequences of human behavior against the weakest in a patriarchal society (i.e., divorce laws benefiting women) and an economic society (i.e., work laws benefiting slaves). Laws that demand care for the most vulnerable (i.e., Deut. 20–25) are exemplified in the US Constitution, for instance in the 14th (all persons are fully citizens) and 15th Amendments (all persons have the right to vote). No one can be excluded from participation in the American Republic just as all people were to be afforded protections in the Hebrew Pentateuch. Anything good can be corrupted or used for evil, and no perfection can be presently expected on earth. The intention of God's laws mirrored in human laws maintains original standards with the understanding that the standards have been compromised by sin, at times conditioning laws to deal with the human intention to sin.

Genesis provides the principles necessary to show the basis for a benefit of original, authorial intention for universal law. Care for the individual maintains frameworks for institutions. Institutional regulations hem in proclivities for human nefarious actions in governance. Governing bodies in education or business are corralled by the authority vested in those organizational rules. The original Bill of Rights and the Amendments that followed are carefully controlled by Article V, with restrictions maintaining constitutional law over political interests. Ultimately, the order of originalism gives the possibility of an even playing field, even while living with the continued results of human sin.

CONCLUSION

The signs and placards expressed the same idea over and over: "No Justice, No Peace!" I watched from the sidelines of a street demonstration. The agitation of the crowd was bent toward disruption. If their views of justice could not be enforced, then they would disrupt the peace until their voices were heard. But I wanted to interrupt the march to ask, "What is the basis for your justice?" The protesters would have a better basis for their desired outcome if justice had a righteous standard. Romans 5:1–5 makes clear Heaven's ideal that peace is dependent upon justice which is founded in righteousness. The clear universal need of salvation from sin is met in One Savior, Jesus.

Our speech, communication, and words give us commitments, deliberations, and actions desiring the pursuit of an object, an idea, that can be known, apart from human agreement or assent. So, when injustice becomes the standard for justice apart from righteousness, now the standard is sin rather than righteousness. Evaluation of any thought, word, or deed is judged not on an immutable, timeless, transcendent standard, but on the shifting sands of vox populi. Now the standard is moved from original design to personal depravity. Truth, goodness, and beauty is no longer the ideal. Judgments are no longer based on what is "good" but on what is "bad." Standardless, all that is left is gain, success, and dominance, no matter what happens to others. Removing the *imago Dei* gives no ideals to pursue, no "liberty and justice for all," and no "life, liberty, and the pursuit of happiness."

Removing the Lawgiver from the law leaves only corruption as the standard by which people will judge. Without an "original" law, "temporal" becomes law. Truth is left up to each person. Judicial vigilantism will be practiced by those in power. Every dispute will be decided by human-centered rules without a set standard, save *progress*, by which is usually meant *control.* The outcome is a dictatorship. Definitions of words will shift to suit cultural powers. "Facts" will be the interpretation of those in power who seek to compel allegiance by maintaining a narrative. Challenges to progress will be summarily dismissed as immoral on their face, for lack of compliance or acceptance. No "arguments" will be allowed since to question is an act of violence against the new order. Data and science will only be allowed in the court of jurisprudence if they support the current position. Those who disagree with the spun story will have their thoughts eviscerated with words such as "misinformation," "disinformation," and even "lies." In the end, people must decide to obey or disobey the people who bark the orders.

Why is the discussion even necessary? The simple answer is that humans will rebel, vacate the rules, seek favors for friends, and obliterate any opposition. The corruption of humanity necessitates a transcendent source of authority. Individuals and organizations today focus on what is referred to as "values." The meaning of *values* can be characterized as arbitrary—individual or institutional choice reigns; acceptable—current conditions or cultural dictate is what matters most; and authority—tied to the consumer such that "what sells" is often the basis for *values*. I refer to *values* as a weak word. We need stronger terms that clearly designate our intentions. A better word is "virtue," which describes conformity to a standard or to what is right. In church history scholars such as Augustine and Aquinas subscribed to justice, prudence, temperance, and courage as key *virtues*. Virtue is infused by God with an ultimate good in sight not inflated by human pride.

To thwart humanity's propensity for self-governance without a supernatural origin of law is best noted in historical records. The great revolutions for social good were begun by those who believe in transcendent principles. Antislavery laws promoted by William Wilberforce in England or the Mennonites in America displayed care for humans in need of protection. Civil rights laws were promoted by Frederick Douglass, Booker T. Washington, or Dr. Martin Luther King Jr. Alcoholics Anonymous has its roots in the Oxford Group, born of religious redemptive practices. Anti-sex trade groups such as the Tamar Center in Thailand or The Phoenix Alliance are actively caring for those lives hurt by sexual predators. Florence Nightingale is credited with the inception of the nursing profession. Michael Faraday's discoveries gave the world usable electricity, essential for one of the greatest care products in hospitalization: refrigeration. Dorothy Day's social activism led to the Catholic Worker's Movement, bent on helping those who had trouble helping themselves. The list of dedicated Christians whose influence on the world is for good is endless.

Origins and outcomes are great concerns in my teaching. For instance, I have colleagues in public university that do not believe what I believe. However, we all agree to basic outcomes like practicing justice, equal rights, freedom of speech, and a desire for world peace. Those ideals are all the outcomes, the results of what comes at the end of any teaching. But it is usually the "origin" question where my professor friends and I might disagree. As a Hebraic-Christian thinker, I am most concerned about the source or the cause of everything. To me, everything begins in the Bible's book of Genesis. I think the best explanation for the results we desire comes from the God whose original intention was for the good of His creatures and creation. It is the question I ask of those who may agree with good outcomes but disagree about where those come from. And then there is the question of ethics. How do we know the ethical way to get to the outcomes we desire? Over the years, I have reduced the idea to this mantra: knowing where you've come from, and where you're going to, helps you know how to live now. Nowhere is this more evident than in the contrast between the creational structures taught by the Bible—extending all the way down to the meaning, purpose, and authority of law—and the absence of all such structures in a world in which the final authority over humanity is humanity itself.

NOTES

1. Conversations in this essay (and my former essay in this volume) are true stories from my years of teaching. The quotations include the exact ideas expressed with verbiage allowing for smooth flow of thought.

2. By "natural law" I refer, roughly, to moral standards independent of and prior to any human law or convention. Principles of natural law are the foundation for principles of just human law. They are "natural" as opposed to artificial products of human endeavor. They are not products of "nature" in the sense of the physical world, for in my view both they and the physical world are created by God. Nor are they natural in any sense suggesting that we obey them automatically; the reverse would be nearer the truth. We are sinners, and can go against natural law automatically if we are not conscientious!

Index

About the Authors

Micah Allred studied at Regent University where he earned his BA in Government. He remains a curious student of American politics and policy, moral philosophy, just war theory, and Augustine's political thought. He and his wife live in Minneapolis, MN, and recently welcomed their first child.

Mark J. Boone is assistant professor in the Department of Religion and Philosophy at Hong Kong Baptist University. Mark earned his BA in Biblical Studies and Philosophy from Dallas Baptist University in 2005 and his PhD in Philosophy from Baylor University in 2010. He has previously edited two books, written three books on Augustine, and written various articles on Augustine, religious epistemology, and other areas of philosophy and religion. Mark also manages the educational video channel TeacherOfPhilosophy, available on both YouTube and Rumble.

Mark D. Eckel is president of The Comenius Institute (ComeniusInstitute.o rg) and associate faculty for various institutions, including Indiana University Indianapolis and Capital Seminary & Graduate School, Lancaster, PA. Mark has been teaching for over four decades: junior high through PhD. He is a contributor to books on various subjects, including science fiction, education, and apologetics. He is the author of dozens of peer-reviewed journal and encyclopedia articles, several curricula, and a number of books on subjects such as reflective thinking, faith-learning integration, and film. Mark holds a PhD in Social Science research, a ThM in Old Testament, and a MA in English. Mark writes regularly online at www.MarkEckel.com/.

John Ehrett is an STM candidate at the Institute of Lutheran Theology, where he focuses on political theology and the Continental philosophical tradition, and serves as law/political science editor of the journal *Verba Vitae*. He holds a BA in government (international politics and policy track) from Patrick Henry College, an MAR (concentration in theology) from the Institute of Lutheran Theology, and a JD from Yale Law School. His scholarship has appeared or is forthcoming in the *Yale Law Journal Forum*, *Notre Dame Journal of Law, Ethics and Public Policy*, *Journal of Law and Politics*, *Journal of Classical Theology*, and *Logia: A Journal of Lutheran Theology*, among others.

Nicholas Higgins is chair of the Department of Political Science, Criminal Justice, & Legal Studies at North Greenville University. He earned his BA from Patrick Henry College, his MPol from the University of Dallas, and his PhD in Political Science from the University of North Texas. He has published several peer-reviewed articles on religion, politics, and philosophy in such prestigious journals as the *Journal for the Scientific Study of Religion, Politics and Religion, Journal of American Studies*, and others. He is married with six children and an irenic member of the Orthodox Presbyterian Church.

Jonathan Johnson holds a BA in Studio Arts and a PhD in Religion and Philosophy from Hong Kong Baptist University, focusing on aesthetics with a special focus on ugliness. He has published on Chinese society both in religion (in the book *Citizens of Two Kingdoms*, published by Brill) and technology (in the *South China Morning Post*), but his passions are negative aesthetics and ugliness (in *On the Ugly*, published by Cambridge Scholars), and his paintings have been featured on the cover of collections about ugliness (*Sur la Laideur*, published by Éditions Complicités). Jonathan works with Hong Kong University's Faith and Global Engagement program, and lectures for Hong Kong Baptist University's Department of Religion and Philosophy. Combining interests as an artist, an aesthetician, and a practicing minister, his current projects include research into ugliness and the Problem of Evil, as well as the Chinese sublime.

Menashe C. Roberts completed his undergraduate degree at the University of Nevada, Las Vegas, graduating magna cum laude with a BA in Philosophy. Later he completed an MA in Philosophy at the University of Mississippi. Menashe is currently pursuing a PhD in Philosophy at Saint Louis University. Menashe's interests include philosophy of religion, metaphysics, philosophy of language, and philosophy of mind.

Mark A. Snoeberger has served as professor of systematic theology and apologetics at the Detroit Baptist Theological Seminary in Allen Park, MI, since 2008. Dr. Snoeberger received his MDiv and ThM from DBTS and earned a PhD in historical theology from Baptist Bible Seminary in Clarks Summit, PA. He is an active member of the Evangelical Theological Society, for which he has made numerous presentations. He has also contributed dozens of articles/essays to peer-reviewed books and journals in his field.

Daniel Weissglass is assistant professor of philosophy at Duke Kunshan University. His work is centered in three areas: fundamental concepts of cognitive science, applied ethics of health and technology, and normative legal theory. His work has been published in leading journals in philosophy, health policy, and other disciplines. You can find more about his work at https://danielweissglass.com/.

www.ingramcontent.com/pod-product-compliance
Lightning Source LLC
LaVergne TN
LVHW090012271026
851116LV00002B/27